LINCOLN
Seen and Heard

H. B. Hall, *Diogenes His Lantern Needs No More./An Honest Man Is Found.*
The Search Is O'er. Engraving, published in 1865 by N. P. Beers, New York.
  (Library of Congress)

Harold Holzer

LINCOLN
Seen and Heard

University Press of Kansas

Published by the University Press of Kansas (Lawrence, Kansas 66049), which
was organized by the Kansas Board of Regents and is operated and funded by
Emporia State University, Fort Hays State University, Kansas State University,
Pittsburg State University, the University of Kansas, and Wichita State
University

Library of Congress Cataloging-in-Publication Data

Holzer, Harold.
Lincoln seen and heard / Harold Holzer.
p. cm.
Includes bibliographical references and index.
ISBN 0-7006-1001-4 (alk. paper)
1. Lincoln, Abraham, 1809–1865 — Pictorial works.   2. Lincoln, Abraham,
1809–1865 — Oratory.   3. Lincoln, Abraham, 1809–1865 — Public opinion.
4. Public opinion — United States — History — 19th century.   5. Political
culture — United States — History — 19th century.   6. Prints, American.
7. Prints — 19th century — United States.   I. Title.
E457.6.H66   2000
973.7'092 — dc21

99-043535

British Library Cataloguing in Publication Data is available.

Printed in the United States of America

10 9 8 7 6 5 4 3 2 1

The paper used in this publication meets the minimum requirements of the
American National Standard for Permanence of Paper for Printed Library
Materials z39.48-1984.

For John O'Keefe, with respect and affection.

"The better part of one's life consists of his friendships."
—Abraham Lincoln, 1849

Contents

Acknowledgments

Each of the chapters in this book originated, usually in substantially different form, before a lectern at a Lincoln or Civil War symposium or on the pages of a journal or magazine. The appearance of this collection provides a welcome opportunity to thank the many friends and colleagues who originally invited and edited its contents, as well as those who generously granted permission for their inclusion on these pages.

"The Image of the Great Emancipator in the Graphic Arts" was first presented, in vastly different form, at the New York State Museum Conference on the Emancipation Proclamation in Albany, on February 23, 1985. A revised version was delivered on October 21, 1995, at the Lincoln Home Colloquium in Springfield, Illinois (then published in the Colloquium *Papers*), and later to a Civil War Education Association (CWEA) forum in Leesburg, Virginia, on June 6, 1997. I am grateful to Tim Townsend, historian of the Lincoln Home National Historic Site, for permission to publish the talk here, and to both Tim and Robert Maher of the CWEA for inviting me to deliver the original talks. And I gratefully acknowledge the late Lincoln Home historian George Painter, who originated its annual colloquium and extended many invitations to me to speak there.

"The Image of Lincoln as Commander in Chief" was presented at the Lincoln Memorial University centennial seminar at Harrogate, Tennessee, on April 11, 1997, and later as the Frank and Virginia Williams Lecture at Louisiana State University at Shreveport on February 14, 1998. I thank LSU political science professor William Pederson for inviting me to Shreveport and particularly extend my gratitude to LMU historian Charles Hubbard for consenting to the publication of the paper here, even as he prepares a separate collection of papers from those proceedings. An abbreviated version of the paper also appeared as "Abraham Lincoln's Image Problem" in the February 1997 issue of *American History Magazine*.

"Prints of the Lincoln Assassination" has been delivered at several venues: at Ford's Theatre National Historic Site on April 14, 1995, the 130th anniversary of Lincoln's murder there; at the Lincoln Fellowship of Wisconsin, on April 14, 1996, and, thanks to the Reverend Lee Moorehead's kind invitation, at his annual Lincoln seminar in Springfield on July 11, 1997. My appreciation goes to Michael Maione of Ford's Theatre for first asking me to prepare this paper, and to Steven K.

Rogstad and Daniel E. Pearson of the Lincoln Fellowship of Wisconsin for the invitation to Racine to deliver it in revised form and for arranging for its subsequent publication as a *Bulletin* of that organization.

"The Mirror Image of Civil War Memory" was the seventeenth annual R. Gerald McMurtry Lecture at the Lincoln Museum in Fort Wayne, Indiana, delivered on September 21, 1996, and published by the museum as a monograph the following year. I am most grateful to Director Joan Flinspach and historian Gerald Prokopowicz for inviting me to deliver the paper and for consenting to its republication in this book. It was particularly meaningful for me to participate in a lecture series named for a man who did so much to encourage my work in the Lincoln field in the 1970s.

"With Malice Toward One" is perhaps the most thoroughly revised paper in this collection. It began as a lecture, "The Anti-Lincoln Image," delivered at an Ottawa, Illinois, Lincoln-Douglas debate anniversary symposium on August 20, 1994, and then at the Lincoln Home Symposium on October 22, 1994, which later published it in the Symposium *Papers*. When I was asked by Tim Townsend to deliver a new paper on Lincoln caricature at the Lincoln Home Symposium three years later on October 25, 1997, I completely rethought the subject and presented it as "Ridicule Without Much Malice." In its present form, it represents my current thinking on this difficult topic, for in many ways caricature presents not only the most engaging but also the most mysterious and challenging aspect of Lincoln iconography.

"Lincoln in Confederate Cartoons," under a slightly different title, appeared in somewhat altered and, I must confess, rather simplistic form in the *Illinois Historical Journal* 80 (spring 1987). I thank Mary Ellen McElligott, the journal's editor in those days, for commissioning the original piece and greatly improving it at the time with her useful suggestions. But after twelve years, not surprisingly, the essay needed to be thoroughly rethought and rewritten for this book.

Mary Ellen McElligott also commissioned and first edited "How Lincoln Coped with Presidential Gifts," which appeared in the *Illinois Historical Journal* 77 (autumn 1984). This, I will say, is the chapter in which I made the fewest revisions for its republication.

"Lincoln and the Legacy of Impromptu Oratory" was presented at the Huntington Library in San Marino, California, on October 15, 1993, as part of the symposium, "The Last Best Hope of Earth." The paper later appeared in the book, *"We Cannot Escape History": Lincoln and the Last Best Hope of Earth,* edited by James M. McPherson (Urbana: University of Illinois Press, 1995). I am grateful to John Rhodehamel and the organizers of that superb Huntington meeting for inviting my participation.

V. Chapman-Smith, director of the New York State Archives in Albany (I serve on the Archives Trust Board), asked me to present "The Poetry and Prose of the Emancipation Proclamation" at the New York State Museum on November 16, 1998. I will always be grateful to V. and the several hundred people who chose to attend the lecture that night, even if it meant missing the last episode of *Seinfeld.*

Finally, "The Gettysburg Myth Revisited" traces its roots to several articles I published on the occasion of the 125th anniversary of Lincoln's greatest speech: " 'A Few Appropriate Remarks': The Gettysburg Address," in *American History Illustrated* (November 1988); "Lincoln's Inspired Address at Gettysburg Was First Thought to Be a Failure," in *MD Magazine* (November 1988); and " 'Thrilling Words' or 'Silly Remarks': What the Press Said About the Gettysburg Address," in the *Lincoln Herald* (winter 1988). Eight years later, my good friend Frank J. Williams invited me to prepare a new paper on the subject for delivery at the first annual Lincoln Forum symposium at Gettysburg on November 17, 1996, and I have since given versions of the talk at the Lincoln Group of New York (February 12, 1997) and the Lincoln seminar in Springfield (July 11, 1997). In its current form, it appears as it was edited by John Y. Simon and William Pederson for inclusion in a book of the first Lincoln Forum papers.

I am indebted to all the editors, symposium organizers, museum officials, Lincoln Group officials, and others named here, but particularly to Michael Briggs at the University Press of Kansas for issuing the irresistible invitation to gather these papers for publication as a single volume.

Writing these lines on my twenty-eighth wedding anniversary reminds me anew how grateful I am as well to my wife Edith for her patience and encouragement through more years than we can believe. And my love and thanks go, too, to our daughters Remy and Meg, who shared their childhood, and now share their visits, with Mr. Lincoln.

Finally, I could not end these acknowledgments or begin the book that follows without affectionately thanking my longtime friends and colleagues, Gabor S. Boritt of Gettysburg College and Mark E. Neely Jr. of Pennsylvania State University, with whom I have enjoyed many happy, productive, and rewarding years researching and writing about the prints of Abraham Lincoln.

Rye, New York
February 27, 1999

Introduction

WHENEVER I am asked what first inspired my interest in Abraham Lincoln — and I get the question often — I worry that my answer is far too mundane to live up to the inspiring standards of scholars like Stefan Lorant, who was introduced to Lincoln while languishing in one of Hitler's prewar prisons.

The truth is, I simply picked Lincoln's name from a hat in which my fifth grade teacher had stuffed slips of paper bearing the names of historical figures from the recent and distant past. Our assignment was to select a name at random, then compose a brief biography of the person we had chosen. At this serendipitous, life-altering moment, I happened to dig into the pile and come up with the paper bearing the name of Lincoln. (My best friend, next in line, picked Genghis Khan, and I have often thought that there but for the luck of the draw I might have gone.)

Instead, the next stop was the school library of the Louis Pasteur Junior High School in Little Neck, Queens (the easternmost tip of New York City), where fate happily intervened again. The very first reference book I pulled from the shelves that day was Richard N. Current's engrossing work, *The Lincoln Nobody Knows*. Within minutes I was not only assigned to Lincoln, I was transfixed by him. And forty years later, I am still laboring under his irresistible spell.

But the course that directed me to my special area of interest, the political culture of the Lincoln era, specifically Lincoln iconography — the image of Lincoln in the popular arts — was influenced by an altogether different muse. For this direction I have to acknowledge a debt of thanks to a rather unlikely inspiration: Richard M. Nixon.

It was 1973, and I had recently purchased at a Manhattan auction for thirty or forty dollars a faded old hand-colored print of Lincoln and his family sitting around a table on what appeared to be the White House lawn. I brought it home to our apartment on the Upper West Side, where my wife of two years, Edith, and I hung it in our dining alcove. True, it looked rather bizarre. Lincoln seemed so uncharacteristically muscular in the picture it appeared as if his torso had been pumped full of air. Mary Lincoln was drawn with a full figure but a pin-sized head. And though the eldest of the Lincolns' three sons was clad appropriately in a Civil War uniform, and another was shown leaning affectionately close to his father,

Lincoln Seen and Heard

the youngest was dressed in what seemed to be a costume from an earlier era, sporting long, wavy hair, and beating a drum. Most laughably, a disproportionately large American flag seemed to be flying right behind the small table around which the family gathered.

Why was the picture so grotesque? Who had created it? (Its original owner had clipped off its caption to fit it into its glittering gold-gesso frame.) What was this image supposed to convey to period viewers? Why had anyone purchased such a primitive piece, much less saved it? I certainly had no clues at the time, but the picture remained on display above our own family table while we pondered. Little did we know then that we had done with it precisely what families of Lincoln's own era had done when such pictures first appeared: purchased it, placed it in our home, assigned it a place of honor, and through its presence acknowledged an affection for Lincoln, along with a tacit endorsement of the myth that he had secured comfort from his own family circle while the Civil War raged.

That is where President Nixon, of all people, comes in. It was later that same year, around the time the Watergate story was peaking. *LIFE Magazine* published a picture spread showing the beleaguered president relaxing comfortably in a White House sitting room. He was seated on a plush easy chair, his feet resting on a matching ottoman, but dressed stiffly in a full suit with the jacket buttoned—a typical Nixon photograph. Yet something else in the scene quickly caught my eye.

There, above Nixon's face, hanging on the White House wall, was a picture of the Lincoln family—not just any picture of the Lincolns, but the very same picture my wife and I had been displaying in our own home. Well, not exactly the same. I examined it carefully, then took a magnifying glass to look closer still. The composition closely resembled ours, but there were subtle discrepancies: Lincoln had a different face, for one thing, and instead of a flagpole emerging so awkwardly from behind the table, a fountain spouted in its stead in the White House version.

Intrigued, I clipped the picture and dashed off a letter to the curator of the White House, then another to my friend and early mentor, the late R. Gerald McMurtry, director of the Lincoln National Life Foundation in Fort Wayne, Indiana. I received no definitive answers, and by then I had more questions. So I launched my own research into the Lincoln family image, and when I had collected and analyzed all the data, I put together an article that Dr. McMurtry ultimately published in the *Lincoln Herald,* the quarterly of Lincoln studies published then, as now, by Lincoln Memorial University. It was my first piece on Lincoln iconography, and though it may not have registered very strongly with many readers, it threw open new windows for its author.

What I had discovered, thanks to President Nixon's choice of decoration, was that a lithographer named Anton Hohenstein of Philadelphia had created the print and then revised it, issuing a new edition to correct its all-too-evident faults. I found that Hohenstein had followed such a course with other print projects, working constantly to refine his lithographic stones until he got the designs right — which he seldom quite did. More important, I learned that it was not at all unusual for printmakers to publish second and even third states of original works, sometimes changing not only the design but also the identity of the subjects portrayed (in order to reuse outdated plates and stones of onetime celebrities). I began acquiring more Lincoln prints, studying examples in public collections, and cataloging them. I learned to piece together supportable assumptions about public response to Lincoln's policies by studying and analyzing printmaking trends. And I began for the first time to see prints not just as illustrations of the Lincoln story but as crucial elements in reflecting, and perhaps influencing, the development of Lincoln's image in his own lifetime and in public memory as well.

In the twenty-five years since, I have learned a great deal more about Lincoln prints and have written about them in articles and books and delivered papers at symposia and colloquia across the country. And the subject still intrigues me. Barely a week goes by when I do not uncover a new piece of information that helps me to better understand the evolution of Lincoln's nineteenth-century image in the graphic arts. Barely a month goes by when I do not see a print that I have never seen before, enabling me to make a historical connection that had never before been evident.

The early pursuit of Lincoln pictures in turn led me to explorations of other aspects of Lincoln's public image: his citizen correspondence; his changing style of, and belief in, public oratory; the press response he evoked. Each discipline led to new symposium papers and new journal articles and, eventually, to books.

But not until 1998 did Michael Briggs, editor in chief of the University Press of Kansas, invite me to collect some of my essays and lectures for an illustrated collection. This book is the result. I confess that when I first accepted his offer, I believed I could simply resubmit work that I had crafted years earlier. I soon learned otherwise. For one thing, technology has changed so much that publishers no longer accept manuscript copy; floppy disks are now required, and more than two-thirds of my work had to be reformatted.

It was a lucky thing. Modern technological demands compelled me to look closely at my earlier work, and I have used the opportunity to revise and rewrite extensively. The following chapters were published or delivered previously, but in rather different form. All of them have, I think, benefited from new and extensive editorial attention. My hope is that they might continue to illuminate the subjects of Lincoln iconography and nineteenth-century American political culture — and help us to see Abraham Lincoln, to paraphrase his favorite poet, Robert Burns, as others saw him.

Lincoln remains very much on view in today's White House. On a May 1998 visit to the Lincoln bedroom (once Lincoln's office and cabinet room, in the days before there was an Oval Office), President Clinton proudly pointed out to my wife and me a copy of the Alexander H. Ritchie engraving of the first reading of the Emancipation Proclamation, illustrated in this book on page 10. But now it is half-obscured by a giant-screen television, a sad if powerful reminder that moving images have replaced the static images that once evoked such an emotional response from the people who purchased, displayed, and preserved them. It is surely useful to recall the culture that first nourished such simple but cherished imagery, because in helping to establish the powerful Lincoln myth, it set a standard against which, for better or for worse, all future presidents would be measured.

I hope that the subject of Lincoln iconography might prove as valuable to Lincoln students of the new millennium as it remains to me, four decades after I magically selected the right slip of paper from a hat and a quarter century after noticing what the Holzers and the Nixons had in common.

Part One

Father, Martyr, and Myth

1

"Prized in Every Liberty-Loving Household": The Image of the Great Emancipator in the Graphic Arts

As MOST Lincoln students know, July 22, 1862, was the historic day on which Abraham Lincoln first read to his cabinet the initial draft of his Emancipation Proclamation. Historians have long reported that the proclamation was tabled that day when Secretary of State William H. Seward cautioned that it might seem an act of desperation in the absence of Union battlefield success. But far less known is what occurred in the same White House chamber exactly two years later.

On July 22, 1864, Lincoln found himself presiding over yet another cabinet meeting. Once again, the subject of the Emancipation Proclamation arose. This time, Lincoln adjourned the meeting and led the cabinet secretaries into the state dining room of the White House. There, set up for their inspection, was Francis B. Carpenter's newly completed painting of that momentous event of two years before: *The First Reading of the Emancipation Proclamation Before the Cabinet.* Carpenter had spent six months working in this very room creating the huge, fifteen-by-nine-foot canvas showing the ministers, neatly divided by political philosophy, with progressives on the left and conservatives on the right, reacting to the president's thunderbolt announcement.[1]

Now, in 1864, a few grumbles were heard from the ministers portrayed in the painting—more than had greeted the proclamation itself in 1862. Salmon P. Chase, for one, reportedly did not like the prominence that the artist gave to Seward. But Carpenter remembered that Lincoln had reassured him that there was "little to find fault with. The portraiture is the main thing, and that seems to me absolutely perfect." Added Lincoln: "It is as good as it can be made." He would not, Lincoln told the artist, change a single accessory.[2]

With Lincoln's approval, the private viewing for the cabinet was followed by a two-day, free public exhibition in the East Room. Carpenter recalled a White House "thronged" with thousands of appreciative visitors.[3]

Father, Martyr, and Myth

One of those in attendance was the incisive journalist Noah Brooks. And while he admitted in his subsequent report that the painting had "excite[d] considerable attention," he also found fault with it, noting a "rawness, lack of finish, and commonplaceness, such as might be expected in the work of a young artist who has grappled with a subject so difficult."[4] Inspecting it closely, Brooks saw little more than "a group of men, wearing the somber-hued garments of American gentlemen," and added, "No amount of accidental lights, warm coloring, and dramatic pose can invest Seward, Blair, and the 'Marie Antoinette' of the Navy Department [the bewigged Gideon Welles] with the supernal glories which gleam on the canvas of painters who had for their subjects kings and emperors in gorgeous robes."[5]

Brooks appeared far more impressed by the news, as he reported, that the picture "will soon be popular and familiar with all people through the medium of engravings." And this gave him hope. "The artist has anticipated an inevitable demand (and perhaps abler hands)," he wrote, predicting, "The chief faults which are now noticeable will be remedied in the engraving, and when this large, life-size painting is reduced to a fine, clear engraving of the size of the Signing of the Declaration of Independence, there will be furnished a picture which will be prized in every liberty-loving household as a work of art . . . a perpetual remembrance of the noblest event in American history."[6]

Brooks proved correct, at least for a time. And in his prediction he perceptively evoked the potential power of all popular prints, not only to mask the flaws of original art but also to commemorate, to inspire, and to testify in visual terms to the political convictions of their patrons. Prints achieved broad distribution in an age in which art museums were still virtually unheard of; both The Metropolitan Museum of Art in New York and the Museum of Fine Arts in Boston were not founded until 1870, five years after the Civil War ended. Prints could bring art to the masses and bring the masses to art. The medium of photography was in its infancy: camera portraits were still rigidly posed and lacked spontaneity, and they offered no more timely coverage of newsworthy events than did prints. There was no official White House photographer on the presidential payroll to record Lincoln's movements. And years would pass before photographs could even be reproduced in newspapers; technologically speaking, an eon would come and go before pictures could move, fill movie screens, dominate the American home through television, or dazzle home computer screens on the Internet. Lincoln's was an era in which pictures were still considered rare and precious. And well-crafted, widely distributed prints, Noah Brooks understood, could provide the kind of "perpetual remembrances" that historical milestones deserved.

Yet even Brooks did not realize at the time that the engraving of the Carpenter painting (Fig. 1.1), when issued two years later, would also solidify an iconographical metamorphosis that helped transform Lincoln into a modern Moses in the popular consciousness. That metamorphosis was illustrated, and very likely influenced, by the proliferation of popular prints. Eventually such prints made the Great Emancipator seem even more important than his great act. But it took longer to reach that point in the chronology of Lincoln image-making than most students of the Civil War era may realize.

To be sure, the proclamation sparked immediate public interest. Yet it took American printmakers a surprisingly long time to find an appropriate and profitable way to portray and market the document and its author. And the modern verb "market" is here employed for a purpose: today's viewers must keep in mind that the engravers and lithographers of the mid-nineteenth century were businessmen first and artists second. Their goal was to find timely, potentially appealing subjects whose illustration would sell widely and enduringly.

Printmakers had been instrumental in introducing Lincoln to the American people in 1860. Nominated unexpectedly to the presidency by the Republicans that May, he was portrayed in the graphic arts by late spring in portraits manufactured in Chicago, New York, and Boston, among other places — usually respectfully, but sometimes comically, since with celebrity came, inevitably, caricature. By the time of his election, the engravers and lithographers had transformed Lincoln's into perhaps the best-known face in America.

Later, printmakers helped refine Lincoln's image when, as president-elect, he assumed a more statesmanlike appearance with the addition of whiskers. And four years thereafter, printmakers responded with unprecedented speed, taking just a few days — a major feat in that comparatively primitive era — to publish depictions of Lincoln's assassination and death.[7]

But such promptness was conspicuously absent when it came to the most momentous act of Lincoln's presidency, the Emancipation Proclamation. True, Noah Brooks witnessed an overnight "grand rush" for copies of the text of the document when it was first announced publicly in September 1862. But words were one thing; pictures quite another. The fact is, the document may well have seemed too controversial at first to suggest pictorial interpretation that would appeal to large numbers of the print-buying public. Notwithstanding the widely

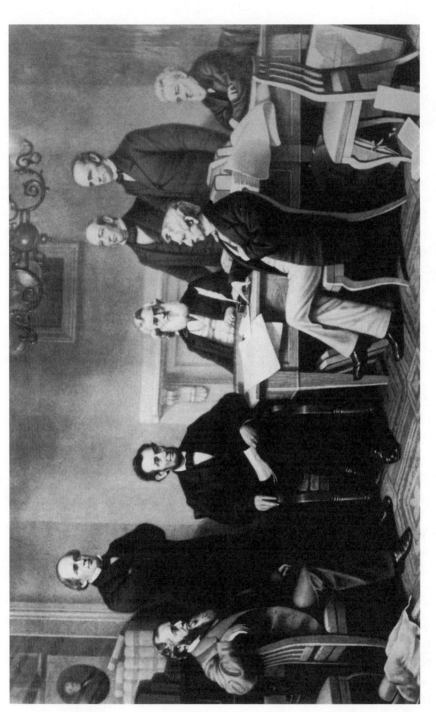

Fig. 1.1 Alexander Hay Ritchie, after a painting by Francis Bicknell Carpenter, *The First Reading of the Emancipation Proclamation Before the Cabinet*. Engraving, published by Derby & Miller, New York, 1866. *(Library of Congress)*

held twentieth-century judgment of Lincoln as a beloved Great Emancipator, not to mention the late-century assaults on his reputation as a liberator, his emancipation order in its time was bitterly controversial and widely condemned not only in the Confederacy but also in the Union. The Democratic *Chicago Times,* for example, quickly attacked it as a "monstrous usurpation, a criminal wrong, and an act of national suicide." The president himself lamented six days after announcing the proclamation that "stocks have declined, and troops come forward more slowly than ever," admitting, "This, looked soberly in the face, is not very satisfactory." The political atmosphere most likely seemed far too charged at first to suggest heroic Moses imagery for mass audiences.[8]

Moreover, at its most basic level, the proclamation promised to change the status of black people, and from what we know, whites did not then display pictures of blacks in their homes. Since the proclamation logically suggested the vivid unshackling of African Americans, white printmakers might have had difficulty determining how to portray such an event in graphics that whites would hang in family parlors. Black people themselves were not yet potential customers for prints. That sea change in the marketplace arrived much later.

Further, the preliminary proclamation's immediate effect on the South was negligible. It took the January 1 proclamation, and then the steady march south of Union armies, to make Lincoln's promise come true. So, perhaps, as far as printmakers were concerned, the proclamation's bold words really seemed at first, as Seward had feared back on July 22, like a "last shriek on the retreat."[9]

Then there were the words themselves. They were hardly the stuff to inspire great art (a matter examined in detail in chapter 9). Massachusetts senator Charles Sumner, for one, had hoped that Lincoln would include "some sentiment of justice and humanity." But in the end, as the *New York Times* reported, Lincoln determined not to "place the Proclamation upon high moral grounds."[10]

These factors most likely conspired to inhibit the immediate production of emancipation prints, widespread interest notwithstanding. It was controversial, and except for caricature, printmakers usually steered clear of controversial subjects. Its effect was still unknown. It called for portrayals of black people. And its language did not easily suggest graphic interpretation, much less inspiration. Mid-nineteenth-century American audiences purchased prints and displayed them in their homes to attest visually to their patriotism, loyalty, and political beliefs. The absence of prints celebrating the emancipation in the year it took effect strongly suggests that Lincoln's policy was not warmly or universally greeted by a sizable portion of Northerners, for had the reverse been the case, a supply of

Father, Martyr, and Myth

prints would surely have been produced to meet public demand. The absence of such graphic tributes in 1862 and 1863 suggests how the medium of popular prints (even in cases in which they are not produced) can testify to public opinion during the Civil War.

Yet a handful of publishers did immediately make the proclamation a staple of their lists, at least in text form. Charles Eberstadt, in his 1950 bibliography of emancipation printings, has noted that separately printed emancipation texts in pamphlet and sheet form began appearing as early as 1862. "Framed and displayed in thousands of homes and prominent places," Eberstadt claims, "emancipation became a watchword of almost hysterical power and incalculable effect . . . an ever-present reminder of the war's true justification . . . important as a propaganda and morale factor." [11]

Eberstadt was wrong, at least in terms of immediate hysteria. Otherwise, publishers would have created pictures as well as reprints of the text, and this they did not do until later. Lincoln's words alone, even if some buyers did hang them on their walls, could not conceivably have excited the passions Eberstadt ascribes to them.

The iconography of the Emancipation Proclamation was not truly born until two years after the document was first issued—in 1864, to be specific, the year of the wartime presidential election. The timing was no coincidence. For years, historians have wondered why that milestone political campaign seemed to inspire so few banners and broadsides, compared with the flood of graphics that had been generated four years earlier. Observers have largely attributed the disparity to the fact that Lincoln was far better known in 1864 and thus required fewer pictorial introductions.

The truth is, the 1864 race did inspire its share of campaign prints, but they have been masquerading ever since in both history and iconography as emancipation pictures. This they certainly were. But significantly, they were used both to praise and to assail Lincoln in the year of his reelection, and they merit at least equal recognition as election images. They were clearly inspired more by the campaign than by the proclamation of the previous January.

Lincoln personally helped advance two such projects himself. This supposedly modest and self-deprecating president welcomed to the White House two different artists-in-residence to work on paintings celebrating emancipation. Although there is no direct evidence to suggest that Lincoln fully understood the image-building potential of these efforts, it remains remarkable that he proved so willing to sit still for these painters in the midst of his grueling wartime schedule. On no other subject — not his roles as commander in chief, orator, or political leader — did Lincoln ever prove as willing to see his image immortalized, whatever the demands on his time and attention.

The first artist to appear on the scene to pursue this ambition was Edward Dalton Marchant of Philadelphia, who arrived in Washington in 1863 to paint a Lincoln portrait for Independence Hall. "He will need little of your time," promised the introductory letter from newspaperman John W. Forney that Marchant carried with him to the White House. "There is no likeness of you at Independence Hall. It should be there; and as Mr. Marchant is a most distinguished Artist, and is commanded by the most powerful influences, I trust you will give him a favorable reception." Lincoln must have loved the thought of his portrait hanging beside those of the heroes of the Revolution. He not only agreed to sit, but he also ordered the painter's son placed on leave from the Union army to work with his father on the canvas.[12]

"My studio was for several months in the White House," Marchant later recollected, "where I was in daily communication with the remarkable man whose features I sought to portray." Marchant described Lincoln as "the most difficult subject who ever taxed" his skills as an artist, a complaint heard from a number of painters who encountered problems in capturing Lincoln's elastic features as he moved about his office or worked on his correspondence (the president often agreed to pose for artists but seldom consented to sit still for them).[13]

The painter aspired to make an "intellectual portrait" of the emancipator, but as he conceded:

Our worthy, noble and heroic President has little of the grace of the Apollo, or the Antinous [Emperor Hadrian's famously handsome page in ancient Rome, inspiration for many works of art], so desirable for pictorial purposes, as all the world knows. But if the man can be found, who, on seeing Mr. Lincoln when his feelings are stirred by emotion, or touched with some grand moving theme, or remarkable event will say he cannot see intense feeling, great intellectual power, and the boldest decision of character, beaming from his salient but manly features, I must say that I shall be sorry for all three of us. And all this a painter must get or he gets nothing of Mr. Lincoln.[14]

Ultimately, Marchant was compelled to refer to a two-year-old photograph of the president. Using this image as a model, he created a neoclassical work depicting Lincoln literally emancipating the slaves, that is, signing the document with a quill, which symbolically breaks the shackles on a liberty statue looming over his

right shoulder. Marchant thus achieved more than mere portraiture. By imposing emblematic pillars of state in the background of the scene to suggest national
durability in time of crisis, he presented Lincoln as a national hero fitting perfectly
into his unique place in history.[15]

But as was the case later with the Carpenter canvas, the second by an artist-
in-residence, the reputation of Marchant's painting was secured by its engraved
adaptation (Fig. 1.2). After a brief exhibition at Independence Hall, the original
found a permanent home in Philadelphia's Union League Club, one of the political
organizations created to support the Republican party in 1864 (a most appropriate home for the canvas considering that it was the 1864 campaign that evidently
inspired the Marchant print adaptation). Fewer Philadelphians enjoyed the opportunity to see it than its artist and subject undoubtedly hoped. But the unique
white-tie Lincoln was duly engraved and enjoyed wide circulation as a result. Far
more than the original canvas, it achieved artist Marchant's goal: "to symbolize,
on canvas, the great, crowning act of our distinguished President."[16]

Significantly, the engraving by John Sartain did not appear until 1864—the
year of the presidential election campaign, for which it served as an ideal campaign print. And it must have proven popular. Marchant himself reported, "The
demand for it on my publisher has been of late, and for some time, fully up to
a thousand a day; and the press which prints it is never idle during any of the
twenty-four hours, except those which include the Sabbath; and I fear, at times,
even that has been entrenched on, despite my positive injunction against it." Further proof of its popularity came when the Sartain engraving was pirated for a
cheap lithographic version (Fig. 1.3) and then recopyrighted and reissued by artist Marchant himself. In all its incarnations, the image marked a sea change in
artistic appreciation of Lincoln's greatest presidential act. But it had not occurred,
significantly, until politics, focused rancorously on race issues that campaign season, made emancipation at last a safe subject for the printmaking industry and
pro-Republican audiences.[17]

The 1864 campaign season was briefer than the image-filled campaign of
1860—Lincoln did not even have a formal rival until George B. McClellan was
nominated on August 31—but in the nine weeks between then and election day,
campaign prints rolled off the presses, many of which featured emancipation
themes.

First came more elaborate reprints of the text of the final Emancipation Proclamation, many decoratively illustrated. Martin & Judson of Milwaukee, for example, issued a broadside featuring slave and freedom scenes surrounding a flag-

Fig. 1.2 John Sartain, after a painting by Edward Dalton Marchant, *Abraham Lincoln,/ 16th President of the United States* (with facsimile signature: *Abraham Lincoln*). Engraving, published by Bradley & Company, Philadelphia, 1864.
   (The Lincoln Museum)

Fig. 1.3 Printmaker unknown, after the Sartain engraving of Marchant's painting, (*Abraham Lincoln Signing the Emancipation Proclamation*). Lithograph, ca. 1864. (*The Lincoln Museum*)

festooned portrait of the emancipator, much of it pirated from an 1863 Thomas Nast woodcut from *Harper's Weekly.*

Chicago's Edward Mendel, who had been one of the first to portray Lincoln in lithograph in 1860, issued a so-called "facsimile" of the proclamation featuring the text of the document in a replica of Lincoln's handwriting, along with a copy of a current Lincoln photograph. And L. Haugg of Philadelphia published a printed version (Fig. 1.4) featuring an elaborately decorated border festooned with symbols of war and power, log cabins and brick mansions to represent American opportunity, and a bald eagle squatting on an American flag—above all of which loomed a small, severe-looking portrait of Lincoln.

Other publishers, like W. H. Pratt and E. C. Smith, among others, contributed "calligraphic" portraits, in which a likeness of Lincoln's face was created by highlighting certain words of the proclamation in bold ink to form his features in outline against the background of his text (Fig. 1.5). More ambitious artists eventually began exploring the forces they supposed influenced Lincoln in writing it.

One was David Gilmour Blythe, an expressionist painter from Pittsburgh who in 1863 produced a symbol-laden canvas showing an informally clad Lincoln (wearing a linen shirt and bedroom slippers, as if to emphasize his status as a man of the people), wrestling with reference books as he sits in a crammed office composing his historic document. This scene, too, was issued as a print in time for the election campaign the following year, with printmakers Ehrgott, Forbriger & Co. of Cincinnati retaining most of the dizzying array of artistic symbols from the original. Prominent among them were American flag drapes; a bust of Andrew Jackson on the windowsill, near a companion bust of James Buchanan strung rudely by the neck from a bookcase; the scales of justice; a Lincolnian rail-splitter's maul; and even a Masonic emblem, attributable not to Lincoln but to artist Blythe's affiliation with Freemasonry. Surviving copies are extremely rare, suggesting that in its day it did not please audiences, for whom it might have proven simply too arcane and complex. But its delayed appearance, a year after the original Blythe painting was completed, does provide further evidence that the vogue for Great Emancipator images did not begin until Lincoln ran for reelection in 1864.

Somewhat easier to comprehend, but on the opposite side politically, was the work of Baltimore Copperhead artist Adalbert Johann Volck, whose etching of Lincoln writing the proclamation suggested dark influences ranging from that of Satan himself (who holds an inkstand in which Lincoln dips his pen), to alcoholic inebriation (suggested by a decanter and drinking glasses on Lincoln's

Fig. 1.4 L. Haugg, *The Emancipation Proclamation.* Lithograph, published by
F. W. Thomas for the *Philadelphia Free Press,* ca. 1864.

(*Library of Congress*)

Fig. 1.5 E. C. Smith, *Proclamation of Emancipation./Abraham Lincoln.*
Calligraphic lithograph, ca. 1865.
 (The Lincoln Museum)

table). And just as Blythe had exhumed an all-but-forgotten Lincolnian symbol of earlier years, the tools of the self-made railsplitter, Volck revived a more pejorative emblem to remind viewers of another side of Lincoln's character, his alleged cowardice. For as Mark E. Neely Jr., has noticed, the prop that can be seen stretched over the head of a baboon perched near the window in Volck's composition is a Scotch cap, the same kind of headgear, the viewer is invited to assume, that Lincoln allegedly wore to disguise himself to thwart assassination threats while passing through Baltimore en route to his inauguration in 1861.[18]

As personified by Volck, an explosive combination of political passion and race prejudice was inspiring a series of vitriolic, anti-emancipation campaign prints. In the resulting anti-Lincoln images, the president was portrayed not as an emancipator liberating a race but as a closet integrationist plotting to impose "miscegenation" — the period word for race-mixing — on complacent white America. In one prototypical effort, *Miscegenation/Or the Millennium of Abolitionism* (see Fig. 5.9, p. 123), published by Bromley & Company of New York, Lincoln tells a mixed-race couple in a friendly gesture designed to inflame fears of black equality: "I shall be proud to number among my friends any member of the . . . family." Another print, *The Miscegenation Ball,* allegedly inspired by a shocking, true incident at Lincoln campaign headquarters in New York City, depicted "leaders of the Black Republican Party" demonstrating "their faith" by dancing with blacks in public.

And then there was *Behind the Scenes* (Fig. 1.6), which showed an acting troupe presenting—what else?—*Othello,* with Lincoln depicted not only as the architect of a scandalous biracial national future but as a black man himself, performing a provocative scene before a wastebasket cluttered with the discarded touchstones of American democracy, including the Constitution itself.

Muted counterpoint to the vitriol came in the seemingly endless supply of emancipation calligraphy, those floridly written tributes that invited reverence for the uninspiring text of the document by suggesting quite literally that it reflected the very essence of Lincoln himself. Perhaps the best explanation for the popularity of this odd genre was that the process of accenting certain words of the proclamation made the resulting text even more difficult to read and focused attention instead on the reassuring image of Lincoln himself and the interesting artistic conceit by which his portrait was created. Lincoln was no stranger to these artistic contrivances. He said of one example: "It is what I call ingenious nonsense."[19]

The man to whom he offered that opinion was Francis Bicknell Carpenter,

Fig. 1.6 "CAL" (initials of printmaker), *Behind the Scenes*. Lithograph, probably published in New York, 1864. (*Library of Congress*)

who by the time he elicited the comment had all but moved into the White House to create the painting that became the definitive artistic representation of Lincoln's Emancipation Proclamation. Carpenter's goal was to portray, as he expressed it, "how a man may be exalted to a dignity and glory almost divine" by giving "freedom to a race." Unlike Marchant, Carpenter determined to do so in realistic style, free of what he called "imaginary curtain or column, gorgeous furniture, or allegorical statue." If he were to fail — as Noah Brooks later claimed he did — Carpenter was content, he said, to do so "in the cause of truth." [20]

The artist had a canny sense of public taste. Unfortunately, he lacked an ability to paint that matched his ambition and that sense of public taste. Considering that he suffered from this rather daunting problem, he did remarkably well. Carpenter worked diligently. He launched his emancipation project by commissioning photographs, both in nearby galleries and in the White House itself. From these he then sketched out the models he proposed to fit into his group portrait. He made separate model heads of each person in Lincoln's cabinet, along with a haunting study of the president himself, all of which have survived as a group because, years later, the painter donated them to the Union League Club of New York in lieu of cash payment for membership. Then Carpenter meticulously sketched details of Lincoln's cabinet room and recorded precise measurements of its accessories.

Finally, he sketched out the whole scene, locating Seward, at the center, offering his crucial yet somehow ironic suggestion that announcement of the proclamation be postponed until Lincoln could back it up with a Union battlefield victory. This is the emphasis that so irked Chase when he first saw the result at the White House. Why portray Seward speaking, and Lincoln listening, instead of the other way around? One reason may have been that Carpenter hailed from an upstate New York village located not far from Seward's home base of Auburn. He was originally a Seward man politically, and he remained subtly faithful to these roots in the most famous of all Lincoln paintings. Perhaps this is why Carpenter briefly considered, then rejected, the idea of depicting Lincoln standing at the cabinet table, looming over his ministers. Carpenter's surviving sketchbooks show that the artist experimented with such designs but ultimately chose to portray the president seated.[21]

As a result, the final painting proved a masterpiece of understatement, although it showed that Carpenter the realist succumbed to one symbolic impulse, portraying the administration's radicals on the left and conservatives on the right. The result was "perfectly satisfactory to me," Lincoln told the artist. Even the notoriously critical Mary Lincoln liked it, slyly nicknaming it, to the president's delight, "The Happy Family." The *New York Times* declared, "It is, by all odds, next to Trumbull's Picture of the 'Declaration of Independence' . . . the best work of this class that has been painted in America." [22]

Unfortunately, Carpenter was an incurable revisionist, and notwithstanding such praise he repeatedly took his brush to the picture over the coming months, drastically altering its appearance for the worse until it assumed the almost petrified look that characterizes it today. After sending it on a national tour, Carpenter campaigned for nearly fifteen years to have Congress purchase the painting. Finally it was bought by a patron who donated it to the Capitol, but today it is relegated to a stairway on the Senate side of the building. Carpenter had long hoped to see the picture hung in the Capitol Rotunda—only this aspiration can explain the immense scale he chose for it, roughly the same dimensions as the great paintings rimming that exalted gallery during the Civil War era.[23]

But Carpenter was, if not the most gifted artist of the Civil War era, certainly the greatest marketer ever to portray Lincoln. He quickly contracted with New York publisher Derby & Miller to bring out a popular print of the picture and then painted a small model of his unretouched canvas from which engraver Alexander Hay Ritchie worked on the plate. By the time the project came to fruition two years later, it had been so well publicized that its success was ensured.[24]

Lincoln himself signed on as the first subscriber to the print, although he did not live to receive his copy. Other prominent Northerners subscribed, too, and the sales book they autographed was undoubtedly used in turn to entice hundreds more customers to order expensive fifty-dollar proof copies during the next two years of production. A period advertisement called attention not only to the forthcoming print but also to the subscription book. As the *Pittsburgh Chronicle* marveled: "The order-book for copies of the engraving of Carpenter's picture of the 'Cabinet Council considering the Emancipation Proclamation' contains some very valuable and interesting autographs," among which were not only "the distinguished men whose portraits are on the canvas" but "many more of equal note." The marketing was, in short, irresistible.

Audiences followed the progress of engraving breathlessly. When a fire struck a room in which the plate-in-progress was being stored, the *New York Times* rushed out a report reassuring readers that the plate had escaped the blaze unharmed. Such was the degree of public interest.[25]

The final engraving proved, just as Noah Brooks had predicted, a vast improvement over the original. It also became an immediate and overwhelming success, boosted immeasurably by the appearance of Carpenter's memoirs as well as by detailed, page-one advertisements in both the *New York Times* and in Carpenter's own best-selling book, notices that featured glowing reviews of the print by the men portrayed in it — endorsements Carpenter had cleverly solicited himself.

Predictably, the design was promptly stolen by print pirates, another certain sign of its popularity. Emboldened by the loosely enforced copyright laws of the time, yet somehow conscience-struck to add some touch of originality, printmaker Edward Herline rearranged the original placement of the liberal and conservative members of the cabinet, ironically obscuring Carpenter's one and only attempt at artistic symbolism. And printmaker Thomas Kelly of New York shuffled the deck yet again and inserted General Grant for another thinly disguised Carpenter piracy.

But no copy succeeded as did Carpenter's original. Its publisher later claimed that 30,000 impressions had been printed, eventually wearing out the steel plate. Ultimately, the print set longevity records that defied changes in artistic taste and publishing technology. New editions appeared into the next generation, including one version copyrighted by Carpenter himself in 1895 (Fig. 1.7), which included a facsimile of the emancipation text, not very much unlike the primitive calligraphy prints introduced thirty years earlier (and destined to remain in circulation in subsequent reissues until at least 1910). Despite Carpenter's deficiencies of craft, his print had more than lived up to its advance description as a "splendid steel engraving." [26]

Carpenter deserves much credit for fixing Lincoln's image as the Great Emancipator, but the artist was denied the full recognition he coveted because other picturemakers were able to capitalize on the vogue for emancipation images more quickly. The print medium always depended on timeliness; those who arrived on the market first sold most. By the time the painstakingly slow Ritchie engraving was completed, Lincoln had died, unleashing a torrent of portraits, among which was a landslide of overt Great Emancipator images. Carpenter reigned supreme, but not alone. There was plenty of competition after April 1865.

It was almost as if a national catharsis had been required before the printmakers could be liberated to celebrate emancipation uninhibitedly. It also helped that in 1865, printmakers were searching frantically for original ways in which to memorialize Lincoln. In other words, it took a burgeoning demand for all Lincoln images to inspire the body of Great Emancipator images that by all rights should have poured off the presses in 1862 and 1863. The news-conscious team of Currier & Ives, inexplicably silent and late on emancipation in 1863 and 1864—

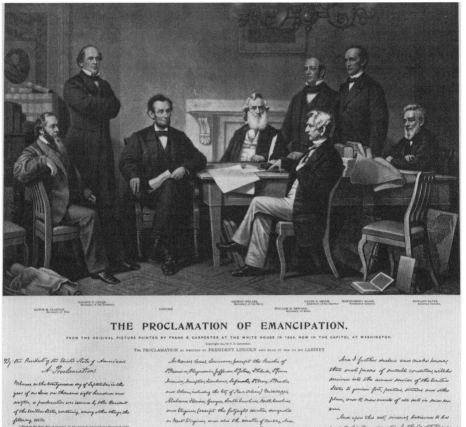

Fig. 1.7 Francis Bicknell Carpenter, *The Proclamation of Emancipation,/From the Original Picture Painted by Frank B. Carpenter at the White House in 1864, Now in the Capitol at Washington.* Photo-engraving, New York, 1895.
(*Prints Division, New York Public Library, Astor, Lenox, and Tilden Foundations*)

years in which they typically responded to news of a Civil War battle by producing a print within weeks — did not issue their lithograph of Lincoln signing the
document until 1865. The sluggish response to emancipation by these, the most
news-conscious of all American printmakers, offers the most convincing evidence
that for many publishers, the document remained too controversial to cover until
Lincoln's martyrdom made it safe.

Finally, Lincoln the Christ figure, who died for his nation's sins on Good
Friday, was also memorialized as a modern Moses. The burst of graphic activity
seemed finally to sustain Lincoln's own belief, which he expressed in signing the
document on January 1, 1863, that "if my name ever goes down in history it will be
for this act." Ironically, several of the prints that offered wholly imaginary scenes
of Lincoln affixing his name to the proclamation also highlight the fact that the
Great Emancipator did not in life provide a signing ceremony worthy of the day
of jubilee.[27]

But by then, even if Lincoln had not, like today's media-obsessed presidents,
staged a "photo opportunity" worthy of his greatest act, Currier & Ives performed
the task retrospectively. They created an example of what David Brion Davis has
called an "Emancipation Moment": a ritualized, symbolic scene designed "to emphasize the . . . moral obligation of the emancipated slaves as well as their dependence on the culture of their liberators." Such works of art were typically con-
cocted by white people to provide the reassurance of eternal gratitude by blacks.
Currier & Ives's variation on this theme was entitled *Freedom to the Slaves.* Trans-
ferring the moment of liberation to a wholly invented and idealized outdoor setting, Lincoln is shown raising his arm to the skies to invoke heavenly guidance as
the chains shackling a representative slave family are forever broken. And since his
own prose was not sufficient to suggest that he had acted in concert with God, the
caption to the print included the relevant lines from Leviticus: "Proclaim Liberty
throughout the land unto all the inhabitants thereof."[28]

It would be misleading, however, to suggest that such thoughts of noblesse
oblige had occurred to Currier & Ives when they created this print. In fact, they
did not create it at all. They copied it from an original by a little-known lithographer, J. Waeschle, who had probably issued it in 1864, the year of the presidential
campaign, the only event besides the assassination itself to inspire emancipation
graphics. In the end, just as all politics is said to be local, all printmaking is surely
commercial, and not even the famous firm of Currier & Ives was above copying
the work of their competitors.

Currier & Ives's interest in "borrowing" this scene the following year may also have signaled the first stirrings of a new market for prints among freedmen. It was not long thereafter that Frederick Douglass wrote to one printmaker: "Heretofore, colored Americans have thought little of adorning their parlors with pictures. . . . Pictures come not with slavery and oppression and destitution, but with liberty, fair play, leisure, and refinement. These conditions are now possible to colored American citizens, and I think the walls of their homes will soon begin to bear evidence of their altered relations to the people about them." [29]

If ex-slaves actually did begin purchasing prints around this time, they surely preferred the Emancipation Moment graphic by an unknown printmaker, titled simply *Emancipation,* which offered standard symbolism (with Lincoln treading on the Christian symbol of evil, the serpent, and on the classical symbol of bondage, the chain and shackle) but also boasted genuinely revolutionary political imagery. Here Lincoln offers "freedom to all, both black and white." The suggestion of equal access to education is punctuated by depictions of a downtrodden white as well as a black family, both responding to Lincoln as their savior. The remarkable aspect here is the print's bold universality: this Lincoln emancipates not only slaves but the starving whites of the ravaged South, as if to give meaning to his own 1862 pledge that "in *giving* freedom to the *slave* we *assure* freedom to the *free.*" It is unique in the iconography of emancipation. [30]

African Americans might also have favored the 1864 election-year print, *Reading the Emancipation Proclamation,* in which a Union soldier reads aloud to members of a slave family the words of the long-awaited announcement of freedom. The image of Lincoln does not even appear in the body of the print, but merely as a remarque, or incidental, portrait in the margins. The image convincingly reminds viewers that the president's document alone had not liberated the slaves; Union troops, and the slaves themselves, had been called upon to make the promise of the proclamation a reality.

The message of self-emancipation was conveyed with equal effectiveness and propagandistic bluntness in *Freedom to the Slave,* a recruitment broadside issued in 1863 specifically for African-American audiences, suggesting through such symbols as broken shackles, discarded farm implements, and stray bullets and shells that the progression from slavery to education could be achieved by fighting in the ranks. Similarly, Currier & Ives's famous lithographed depiction of the Fifty-fourth Massachusetts Colored Infantry storming and dying at Fort Wagner may not officially rank as an emancipation print, but it did take emancipation to

Father, Martyr, and Myth

the next logical step: the need for former slaves to fight for their own freedom in order to secure the blessings promised in Lincoln's executive order.

By 1865, however, most emancipation prints had begun emphasizing the emancipator, not his two-year-old words or the beneficiaries of the order. Even calligraphy changed. Lincoln's face no longer emerged in relief from the text; in a typical updating of the genre, the words peeked out from around a finished portrait of Lincoln, drawn in the classical hand-on-hip pose of patriotism. Its printmaker added allegorical scenes representing the inhumanity of slavery and draped the words of the title so they resembled fasces, the classical emblems of power.

So intent were the printmakers on celebrating emancipation, and so starved were they for models, that they also rather brazenly updated older prints, re-designing them with an emancipation focus. The most ludicrous such adaptation was surely the print whose roots could be traced to an outdated engraving of the godfather of secession, John C. Calhoun, depicted standing beside papers repre-senting states' rights. Adapting the now-familiar Mathew Brady "five-dollar bill" photograph (Fig. 1.8) as a model, a print pirate simply burnished out Calhoun and placed Lincoln's head atop the old nullifier's flowing robes (Fig. 1.9), relabeled the now-inappropriate Calhoun documents as "Constitution," "Union," and, of course, "Proclamation of Freedom." No doubt, neither Calhoun nor Lincoln would have appreciated this particular transformation. But Lincoln would cer-tainly have been pleased with the prints that showed him standing arm-in-arm with George Washington, presiding together in a special afterlife reserved for national heroes, particularly those, like J. C. McCurdy's *The Father and the Saviour of Our Country* (Fig. 1.10), that showed Lincoln clutching the Constitution and the Emancipation Proclamation.

Unfortunately, there is no evidence to indicate what Lincoln really thought of any of his portrayals as emancipator, beyond his demonstrated willingness to pose for artists so focusing their works. Until recently, in fact, it was believed that Lincoln had never even seen an Emancipation Proclamation print, only the "in-genious nonsense" of calligraphy.

But a recently unearthed advertising brochure (Fig. 1.11) for an allegorical calligraphic print by Max Rosenthal of Philadelphia suggests that Lincoln person-ally accepted a copy on March 6, 1865, just two days after his reinauguration and six weeks before his death. The presentation ceremony was evidently recorded by an artist on the scene and then used to illustrate a sales sheet. Predicted its publisher: "The print will be in the house of every lover of his country. One finer

Fig. 1.8 Mathew B. Brady Studio, photograph of Lincoln taken in Washington, February 9, 1864.
   (The Lincoln Museum)

Fig. 1.9 William Pate, after an engraving of John C. Calhoun in Evert A. Duyckinck's
National Portrait Gallery of Eminent Americans, Abraham Lincoln. Engraving,
New York, 1865.

(Library of Congress)

Fig. 1.10 J. C. McCurdy & Company, *The Father and the Saviour of Our Country.*
Lithograph, Philadelphia, 1865.
  (The Lincoln Museum)

PROCLAMATION OF EMANCIPATION.

THE SECOND

DECLARATION

OF

INDEPENDENCE!

Presentation to A. Lincoln, March 6, 1865, by L. Franklin Smith.—See Descriptive Pamphlet.

BY PRESIDENT LINCOLN.

JANUARY 1st, 1863.

In presenting to the public, the Liberty-loving people of the United States, this elegant historical memorial, we feel that no comment is needed upon its great and noble subject, the undying parchment that sealed to Fame the name of our beloved Martyr-President, that made Abraham Lincoln the great liberator of a race, that made 1863 a great era in the history of the Republic, and wiped away the great stain that for eighty years had darkened its glorious annals. It is undying and immortal, beloved and revered, and further comment is unnecessary.

A suitable copy or memento of this great document should be and will be in the house of every lover of his country. One finer or better adapted to the demands of the public than this, we hesitate not to say, has not yet been produced. In beauty of design, artistic finish, and yet within the means of all, it is unsurpassed.

SUN, LIBERTY, EAGLE, NATIONAL BANNERS.

GEORGE WASHINGTON,
Benjamin Franklin,   Thomas Jefferson.
Chief Justice Story,   John Quincy Adams,
John Wesley,   William Penn.
Lucretia Mott,   . L. Maria Child.

ABRAHAM LINCOLN,
William H. Seward,   Horace Greely,
Salmon P. Chase,   Charles Sumner,
James H. Lane,   Cassius M. Clay,
John S C. Abbott,   Wm. H. Burleigh.

JOHN C. FREMONT,
Wendell Phillips,   Owen Lovejoy,
Rev. Nathan Brown,   H. Ward Beecher,
Benjamin F. Butler,   Gerrit Smith,

Ten Vignettes,
Representing the Curse of Slavery and Blessings of Liberty.

Fury, Satan, Calhoun and Jeff Davis.
Plantation Scene.
Slave, Auction, Separation.
Branding Slaves, C. S. on forehead. Barbarism.
Goddess of Liberty, Upas Tree, Slave, Hounds.
Purity, Dove, Olive Branch.
School.
Happy Family, Restoration.
Church, House, Plowing, Civilization.
Justice, Man, Railroad, Steamboat, Ship.

The Proclamation is on fine plate paper, 20 by 26 inches, appropriately and beautifully colored, 32 portraits; in all, over 120 figures, with descriptive pamphlets sent to any address by mail; postage paid on receipt of $2.00.

The Greatest Novelty of the Age! The Proclamation of Emancipation Illustrated!!

Card Photograph containing 721 words, 10 vignettes, 38 Portraits, and over 124 figures, should adorn every loyal lady's Album. *Price 20 Cents.*

LITHOGRAPHED BY ROSENTHAL, AND PUBLISHED BY L. FRANKLIN SMITH,

No. 327 Walnut Street, P. O. Box 2423 Philadelphia, Pa.

Fig. 1.11 L. Franklin Smith, advertising poster, *Proclamation of Emancipation./ The Second Declaration of Independence!/By President Lincoln. January 1st, 1863.* Woodcut engraving, Philadelphia, 1865.

(*Library of Congress*)

and better adapted to the demands of the public than this . . . has not yet been produced. In beauty of design, artistic finish, and yet within the means of all, it is unsurpassed."[31]

To the printmaker's credit, it is difficult to contradict the hyperbolic estimate, at least of the quantity, if not the quality, of its portraiture. Rosenthal's print featured no fewer than 120 symbolic figures, including Satan, Fury, and Jefferson Davis, along with 32 portraits, including that of emancipator Lincoln. In truth, it was merely a transitional effort — typical of the preassassination prints that gave more attention to the words of the proclamation than to their author or their impact.

A month after the president received a copy, Lincoln's image was dramatically altered. He became the acknowledged martyr of liberty and finally emerged fully in prints as the Great Emancipator, no longer half-obscured among calligraphy or cameo portraiture but larger than life, larger even than the document he had promulgated, a figure catapulted from history to myth in a process that not only sanitized but sanctified his once-controversial proclamation.

In assessing the power and endurance of the Great Emancipator image that emerged during the racially tinged 1864 presidential election campaign, flowered fully after Lincoln's assassination and martyrdom, and lasted at least until 1895, the date that Carpenter reissued his landmark engraving of his singular emancipation painting, one might look again to the words of the advertising brochure for the Max Rosenthal print given to Lincoln in 1865. What was said about that print might well be said about the Great Emancipator image itself: "It is undying and immortal, blessed and revered, and further comment is unnecessary." So strong was that image, however surprisingly long it took to introduce it, that further comment did prove unnecessary — for about 100 years. Lincoln's image as Great Emancipator has more recently been subjected to serious question. But printmakers helped make that image so indelible that even the most relentless revision has failed fully to erase it.[32]

"That Attractive Rainbow":
The Image of Lincoln as Commander in Chief

O F ALL THE MEN in and about Washington," the *Chicago Tribune* proclaimed during one of the bleakest hours of the Union war effort, "the best fitted to take command of the army" was Abraham Lincoln, who was later depicted by both the *New York Illustrated News* (Fig 2.1) and *London Punch* as a Roman warrior vanquishing Jefferson Davis.[1]

According to the *Tribune,* the reasons were abundant. Lincoln understood more about strategy than any of his advisers, "civil or military." If only his instructions to his generals had been followed, the rebel army would long ago have been "cut to pieces and destroyed, and the war virtually ended." He even knew the terrain — "every path, road, defile, mountain, stream and wood." The *Tribune* therefore urged "that Old Abe take the reins into his own hands." As "President, General-in-Chief, and Secretary of War in one," he would surely "lead our armies to victory."[2]

But few Northerners, civil or military, joined the bandwagon. Heard far more often than endorsements of the *Tribune*'s call to arms were charges that the president had already assumed far too much power: nothing short of "despotism" and "absolutism" in the words of the *New York Daily News*.[3]

Union men had other reasons to doubt Lincoln's ability to lead troops, even after formally trained commanders such as Ambrose P. Burnside and Joseph Hooker failed miserably on the battlefield. By the time the *Tribune* issued its call, Northern civilians had for three long years been inundated with popular prints — pictures made to be displayed in family homes — that suggested in the strongest graphic terms that Abraham Lincoln was in fact the quintessential civilian.

Emphasis on such an image was understandable. Amid charges of dictatorship fueled by Lincoln's extraordinary executive actions — suspending habeas corpus, introducing the nation's first military draft (one cartoonist portrayed him as an insatiable warrior in an armored skirt, swallowing new enlistees whole),

Fig. 2.1 Thomas Nast, *The President's Inaugural/This is the way the South receives it (War)*. Wood engraving published in the *New York Illustrated News,* March 23, 1861. (*Illinois State Historical Library*)

and proclaiming emancipation for slaves in the rebel states — many Northerners needed reassurance that Lincoln was not assuming vast and unprecedented new powers. During the Civil War, Lincoln prints provided just such reassurance. They portrayed the president not as a soldier but as a statesman.

The man whom many newspapers labeled a tyrant seemed in scores of period pictures the model of civilian restraint — at least, for a while. Eventually, he was portrayed as a commander in chief, but it took at least two years for such tributes to begin in earnest. They might well have appeared sooner, but for the fact that Lincoln suffered from a stubborn image problem that he brought on himself during the journey to his inauguration: the image of a coward. Printmakers did not routinely issue commander in chief prints depicting Lincoln until three major events occurred that were momentous enough to correct his early image of cowardice:

> First, Lincoln issued the Emancipation Proclamation.
> Second, he sought reelection in 1864 as the war candidate against a peace Democrat.
> Third, he was assassinated, becoming, in a sense, the last casualty of the rebellion.

Popular prints of the period vividly recall the evolution of the military aspect of Lincoln's image. It is important to remember that the images were produced by commercial publishers, not political artists-for-hire. They are not mere illustrations, though they often turn up as such today in magazines and books. In their time, proudly displayed by their owners, they truly reflected public sentiment about Abraham Lincoln. And, in a way, they may have reflected as well Abraham Lincoln's own sentiments about himself. For as president, he occasionally entertained the idea of taking to the field. Throughout his adult life, in fact, he seemed to harbor deep ambivalence about the allure of military distinction.

In 1832, while still a young man living in New Salem, Lincoln enlisted to fight in the Black Hawk War and, to his "surprize," was promptly elected captain of his company by his fellow volunteers. "No success before or after," he admitted, ever gave him "so much satisfaction."[4] But Lincoln harbored no illusions about his subsequent war service, the only time he spent in uniform. He never saw any Indians, he confessed, "but I had a good many bloody struggles with the musquetoes [sic]." In a more reflective moment, Lincoln worried profoundly about the hypnotic allure of military glory, "that attractive rainbow, that rises in showers of blood — that serpent's eye, that charms to destroy." Later, as congressman, he opposed the Mexican War and paid a heavy political price: he was out of elective office for years.[5]

When he sought a comeback by running for the Senate in 1858, his opponent, Stephen A. Douglas, reminded voters that Lincoln had "distinguished himself" in the House of Representatives "by taking the side of the common enemy, in time of war, against his own country." Lincoln lost the Senate race but two years later won the Republican nomination for president. In a sense, he was thus exonerated for his early opposition to American military glory, at least by party leaders casting votes at the Republican National Convention of 1860. To ordinary American voters outside Illinois, however, he remained virtually unknown. Print portraits introduced him to America that year and provided biographical context as well.[6]

Many printmakers responded by stressing Lincolnian attributes that were physical, though decidedly civilian. In prints showing him as a railsplitter and flatboatman, Lincoln was portrayed as an American success story who escaped frontier poverty by sweat and strength. Even in caricature that mocked him, reminders of his strenuous life were much in evidence. He might be depicted as a baseball player, swinging with a railsplitter's maul, as a tight-rope walker making his way across troubled waters, or as a gymnast desperate for a boost to avoid being split in two by his own log rails. And when the race was reduced in graphic terms to a boxing match, there could be little doubt that the legendary wrestling champion was destined to prevail.[7]

But even the prize-fighting metaphor was pugilistic, not military. Perhaps that is why even after the election, at least for one printmaker, it did not seem quite enough that Lincoln rose from log cabin to White House. The engraver added a bit of family glory by noting that Lincoln's father had been killed by Indians. The only problem was that the story was not true. Other image-makers thought that Lincoln's rugged appearance suggested Jacksonian determination. Who could be more military than Old Hickory? But one artist who tried to portray him as a second Jackson earned only laughter. Lincoln was elected in spite of such portraiture.[8]

Thus he took the oath of office bearing neither military credentials nor a military image. Perhaps recalling Lincoln's first inaugural address, artist Thomas Nast was so confused by the president's vow to hold federal property in the South on the one hand and his conciliatory "we must not be enemies ... but friends" plea on the other that he could not decide whether Lincoln was a man of peace or a man of war. So Nast portrayed him as both, one panel of his cartoon *(War)* showing a fierce, armor-clad Lincoln standing over his beaten Confederate counterpart, bloodied sword in hand, and the other (*Peace,* Fig. 2.2) depicting him smiling benignly, wearing a flowing dress and daintily holding aloft the scales of justice. Less than six weeks after his inauguration, Fort Sumter was attacked, and Lincoln was suddenly commander in chief of a nation at war. Unfortunately, his preinaugural entrance into Washington had not been calculated to inspire confidence.[9] Warned that an assassination plot awaited him in hostile Baltimore, Lincoln agreed to rush through the city by night, wearing an uncharacteristic soft hat and overcoat to avoid recognition. Thus attired, he was reported to have admitted, "I was not the same man." He arrived in Washington safely, but with his image about to be badly tarnished.[10]

Northern artists quickly exaggerated Lincoln's Baltimore disguise into a comic Scottish cap and military cape and bombarded the illustrated weeklies with lampoons showing Lincoln cowering in fear before wholly imaginary assailants (see Fig. 5.6, p. 117). When, months later, a Richmond-based printmaker portrayed Lincoln fleeing comically from the first, feeble Confederate cannon, he showed him still dressed in the absurd Scotch cap and flowing cape. The Baltimore image did not easily go away.[11]

At first, printmakers mustered only tepid responses to the onslaught of "coward" pictures. One such image showed Lincoln not as soldier but sportsman (see Fig. 5.8, p. 122), recoiling from his poorly aimed rifle shot as his target, a bird labeled "C.S.A.," thumbs his nose at the hapless hunter. Evidently, not even a gun-toting Lincoln was to be taken seriously.

Ironically, the one print that might have had an ameliorating impact on Lincoln's prevailing postinaugural image failed to have much impact, for an altogether different reason: it was never completed or distributed. On May 24, 1861, a lithographer, Carl Anton, copyrighted a sketch (Fig. 2.3) of Lincoln holding off a bayonet-wielding Jefferson Davis with one of his signature log rails. But just a few weeks after Anton registered this optimistic design, the Union suffered a humiliating defeat at the first battle of the war, and the picture may suddenly have seemed overly optimistic. Perhaps that is why it survives today only in preliminary form, its caption written hastily in ink; no finished copy has ever been found. It was apparently never formally published because its creator determined that the public would not accept it.

Astoundingly, Lincoln ultimately overcame the humiliating early images, eventually earning praise for military leadership. According to T. Harry Williams, Lincoln grew into a better strategist "than any of his generals" and "did more

Fig. 2.2 Thomas Nast, *The President's Inaugural/This is the way the North receives it (Peace)*. Wood engraving published in the *New York Illustrated News*, March 23, 1861. *(Illinois State Historical Library)*

Fig. 2.3 Carl Anton, *I am glad I am out of the scrape! Now or never. This is the way we serve all traitors. I am ready!* Proof of an unfinished lithograph, Cincinnati, 1861.
(*Library of Congress*)

than Grant or any general to win the war for the Union." He became "in actuality as well as in title the commander in chief." But as David Herbert Donald has maintained, the sixteenth president came to office both "inexperienced" and "insecure" as an administrator, a military tyro who might be reading a war primer like Henry Halleck's *Elements of Military Art and Science* at the very same time he was issuing orders to professional soldiers. His own attorney general early on concluded of Lincoln, "He has not the power to command," and Gen. George B. McClellan dismissed him as "an idiot" and "nothing more than a well-meaning baboon."[12]

Lincoln proved Bates, McClellan, and his many other critics wrong, but it took time—in life as well as in art. At the beginning of the Civil War, Lincoln still understandably seemed to most image-makers to be facing the battle of his life against his Confederate presidential counterpart, the almost wholly military Jefferson Davis.

Like Lincoln, Davis had fought in the Black Hawk War, but there the prepresidential résumés sharply diverged. Davis went to West Point, and when Lincoln was fighting against the Mexican War, Davis was fighting in it. And Davis had served before the rebellion as the nation's secretary of war. Even Northern image-makers immediately understood the differences between America's two Civil War presidents.

In New York, for example, before secession made it impossible to export such pictures to Southern audiences, one lithographer issued a print not only showing Davis beside Generals Robert E. Lee, Joseph E. Johnston, "Stonewall" Jackson, and others, but like them, garbed in full military uniform. Later, inspired by rumors — false, as it turned out — that Davis appeared at Bull Run in uniform to rally his troops there to victory, a Richmond lithographer issued a best-selling portrait of Davis on horseback, riding dramatically onto the battlefield to lead the army.[13]

Lincoln could not hope to compete with such powerful martial imagery, even if it was undeserved. The best that prints could do was to show him in early councils of war. One example, modeled after a drawing by Christian Schussele (Fig. 2.4) managed to make "Old Fuss and Feathers," Winfield Scott, look younger — but did little to make the seated Lincoln seem very commanding. Another, equally unconvincing, print added George B. McClellan, John C. Frémont, Robert Anderson, and others to the conference table, generals who in life were no more likely to gather together in the same room than Lincoln and Davis.

Even though such pictures suggested harmony in pursuing strategy, they could hardly promote the notion that Lincoln, in his familiar swallowtail coat, white shirt, and tie, was anything but the nation's representative civilian magistrate. "Black coats are at a discount in the presence of the blue," Lincoln admitted, "and I recognize the merit of the discount." But trading black for blue was something Lincoln could not do.[14]

Attempts to crown Lincoln with allegorical glory seemed equally ill-advised. David Gilmour Blythe's painting, *Lincoln Crushing the Dragon of Secession,* for example, depicted a president wearing neither uniform nor formal mufti but appearing in homespun clothing suggestive of his prairie days. Not surprisingly, the canvas was never copied for a popular print. Another symbolic effort, *The Outbreak of Rebellion,* faced different problems. The lithograph somehow suggested

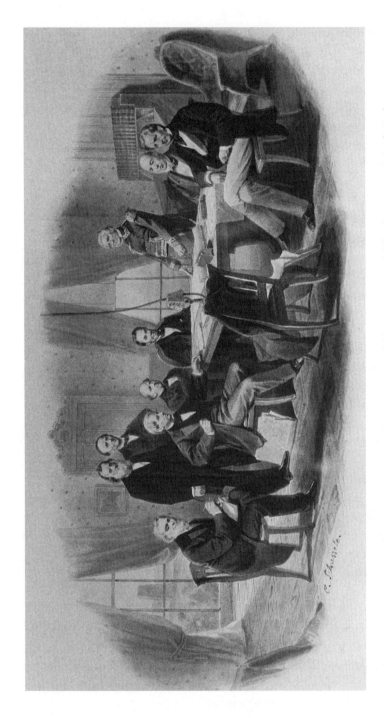

Fig. 2.4 Christian Schussele, *Lincoln and His Cabinet with General Winfield Scott*, 1861, model for the 1861 engraving by Robert Whitechurch, *President Lincoln and his Cabinet, with Lt. Genl. Scott,/In the Council Chamber at the White House.* (*Courtesy Harold Holzer*)

that Lincoln spent the early days of the war fighting money-mad Northern capitalists, not Southern secessionists.[15]

Lincoln could hardly live up to such grandiose imagery. Instead, he made every effort to show support for his soldiers — doffing his hat to regiments as they marched past the White House or traveling to the front to review troops in person, often to "thunderous applause."[16]

Not everyone appreciated such appearances. One critic was emboldened to inform the president bluntly that "soldiers write home to their friends . . . with reference to their disappointment in your bearing and manners when reviewing them." Explained the angry author, "They say when you are on horseback, and platoons of men marching by you, that you lean about and turn your head to talk with people behind you, when . . . you should sit erect & talk to nobody and look straight at the saluting soldiers — that you ought to assume some dignity for the occasion even though your breeding has not been military." The president's bad form, the outspoken correspondent added, "dont require half so much sacrifice on your part to rectify as it does of the men to go from their homes for the hardship they undertake. . . . For God's sake consult . . . some military man, as to what you ought to do on these occasions in military presence."[17]

Much to Lincoln's benefit, such occasions, however undignified they looked to some observers, were usually sketched sympathetically by the "special artists" covering the war for the widely read illustrated newspapers. Alfred R. Waud, for one, drew Lincoln reviewing a New Jersey brigade at the White House in 1861. Arthur Lumley sketched Lincoln together with General McClellan, reviewing General Edwin Vose Sumner's II Corps after the Battle of Antietam (Fig. 2.5). And when Lincoln visited Hooker's army on April 9, 1863, Waud was there once again to provide a drawing for the picture press. Such confirmation of Lincoln's presence among his troops could doubtless be comforting during the darker days of the Union war effort, not only to the troops he visited but also to those on the home front who saw the pictorial reports.[18]

On another such occasion, for example, photographer Alexander Gardner was on hand to record Lincoln's visit to McClellan after the Battle of Antietam. Gardner posed the tall president and his diminutive field commander face-to-face in several famous poses. In revealing the contrast in height between general and president, Gardner provided a perhaps unintended, but powerful, reminder of the dominance of civilian authority. To suggest the rough life on campaign, he also photographed Lincoln and McClellan meeting inside a tent. Modern viewers who have seen the uncropped original photos know that directly behind these

Fig. 2.5 A. Lumley, *President Lincoln and General McClellan Reviewing General Sumner's Corps after the Battle of Antietam*, published in *Frank Leslie's Illustrated Newspaper*, September 30, 1862.

(Library of Congress)

tents stood a large house. The two men could easily have met in more comfortable surroundings, but not without sacrificing an irresistible photo opportunity.[19]

Understandably, however, neither newspaper woodcuts nor photographs exerted the same emotional impact on American audiences as popular prints designed for permanent display in that most sacred of all domestic settings, the wall above the family hearth. And these still, stubbornly, failed to acknowledge Lincoln's growing military authority.

Ironically, Lincoln's image seemed least military around the time he probably most yearned to fulfill the *Chicago Tribune*'s wish that he take personal command. In May 1862, he cruised to Hampton Roads, Virginia, and for a time actually assumed direct control of a Union action against Norfolk. Secretary of the Treasury Salmon P. Chase, no great admirer, was moved to admit in his diary, "I think it quite certain that if he had not come down, [Norfolk] would still have been in possession of the enemy." But no artist was on hand to record Lincoln's triumph. A drawing by Charles Reinhart (Fig. 2.6) showing Lincoln plotting tactics on board ship with Secretary of War Edwin M. Stanton, Secretary Chase, and Gen. Egbert Viele was not made until years later, for a Lincoln biography written by his onetime private secretary.[20]

Once tested in action at Norfolk, Lincoln became less tolerant about "procrastination on the part of commanders." Even military successes did not ease Lincoln's frustration. "After every small victory," he complained, "I am crowded by men of every rank from a colonel down to a corporal, each one claiming the honor to themselves . . . and of course demanding a promotion." Once, after learning that Confederate raiders had seized a Union general and twelve mules, Lincoln is reported to have remarked, with uncharacteristic sarcasm, "How unfortunate; I can fill his place with one of my generals in five minutes, but those mules cost us two hundred dollars apiece."[21]

He remained a divided man. Part of him believed, as he told Hooker, that "you do not mix politics with your profession." But he knew all too well that "defeat and failure in the field make *everything* seem wrong." So part of him still yearned to take up arms. "How willingly would I exchange places," he confessed, "with the soldier who sleeps on the ground in the Army of the Potomac." When that army failed to follow its victory at Gettysburg with the pursuit he believed could have ended the war, Lincoln exploded, "If *I* had gone up there I could have whipped them myself." He confided to one contemporary that soon he "must take these army matters into his own hands."[22]

Prints of the day still did not pave the way for such a transfiguration. Even

Fig. 2.6 Charles Stanley Reinhart, *General Egbert Viele, Lincoln, Secretary of the Treasury Salmon P. Chase, and Secretary of War Edwin M. Stanton at Norfolk,* model for the woodcut, *A Council in the Cabin of the "Miami,"* published in *Scribner's Monthly Magazine,* October 1878.

(*Courtesy Harold Holzer*)

an image praising the government for resisting threats of British intervention assigned the credit to only a representative Uncle Sam. Offering promise to Lincoln's iconographical future, however, was the change in that old symbol. For years, depictions of the Uncle Sam character had made that figure look like the father of his country. Then he suddenly began to resemble Father Abraham (Fig. 2.7).

Fig. 2.7 E. Stauch, *Uncle Sam Protecting His Property Against the Encroachments of His Cousin John.* Lithograph, Philadelphia, 1861.
(Library of Congress)

Lincoln's only subsequent exposure to combat did not come until summer 1864, when Jubal Early's troops threatened Washington. Lincoln rode out to the scene of the action at Fort Stevens. Climbing onto a parapet, his tall stovepipe hat an easy target for enemy sharpshooters, he exposed himself to enemy fire. Legend holds that for this display of bravery, a young officer, Oliver Wendell Holmes Jr., bellowed, "Get down you fool!"[23]

Like an echo, the image-makers still refused to portray Lincoln rising up in military glory. Few of his contemporaries ever knew that Lincoln had displayed personal courage at Fort Stevens or that during one inspiring review of his army, he rode six miles on horseback within 300 perilous yards of Confederate entrenchments, in full view of Rebel pickets. Urged to move his procession elsewhere, Lincoln responded, "Oh, no . . . the commander in chief . . . must not show any cowardice in front of his soldiers," adding softly, "however he may feel." [24]

The closest his earliest image-makers had come to creating an equestrian portrait of Lincoln was an 1860 campaign print by Currier & Ives, lampooning him as an organ-grinder's monkey, riding a hobby horse. In the more sophisticated, but equally unflattering, wartime equestrian view by Adalbert Volck, a gifted pro-Confederate Baltimore artist, the best that could be said of Lincoln as president was that he was a modern version of the hapless Don Quixote, tilting at distant windmills alongside his latter-day Sancho Panza, the controversial Gen. Benjamin F. Butler. [25]

Some of the pictorial indifference to Lincoln's military leadership finally ended on January 1, 1863, the day Lincoln unleashed the most powerful weapon of the entire war: the Emancipation Proclamation. Rejecting recommendations that he place the order "upon high moral grounds," Lincoln crafted the document "as a war measure from the Commander-in-Chief." [26]

Printmakers immediately embraced a similar approach. They sold their pictures primarily to the same white Americans to whom Lincoln framed the proclamation as a military, not a moral, instrument. Thus, it was in their interest as well to portray emancipation as a war measure rather than as an abolitionist decree, in order to make their pictorial commemorations more attractive to mainstream white buyers. Of all the familiar images of Lincoln personally liberating grateful slaves — most known to modern Americans from illustrations in history books — not one was issued while the war still raged. They were, rather, products of the period following Lincoln's assassination, when his life's work was reinterpreted in the warm glow of universal reverence. [27]

Another event occurred that election year, and it became factor number two in the metamorphosis of Lincoln's military image: the nomination of George B. McClellan as his opponent for president, a former field commander incongruously running for commander in chief on a peace platform. Suddenly, printmakers found it inviting to portray McClellan, not Lincoln, as a coward, lampooning the general for allegedly watching the disastrous Battle of Malvern Hill from the safety of a distant gunboat, or suggesting that as president he might collaborate with Jefferson Davis to return free blacks, even military veterans, to slavery. [28]

In this highly charged atmosphere it became just as natural for image-makers to present Lincoln, convincingly armed with a bayonet, personally repelling the threat to liberty that McClellan, and by complicity, Jefferson Davis himself, posed to America's future. Such prints did not totally acknowledge Lincoln as a military leader, but they moved his image closer in that direction than ever before. As a politician, he now seemed undeniably commanding. And it was a general, ironically, who made him seem so. As a French printmaker neatly put it in a telling graphic commentary on the results of the 1864 contest, Lincoln's reelection proved a military bombshell: the "rudest projectile" yet hurled by the Union against the Confederacy.[29]

Yet only after Lincoln fell victim to an assassin's bullet (the third and final factor to influence his military image) did a significant number of American graphic artists finally, fully recognize his seldom-acknowledged role as commander in chief. Prints commonly began showing him, together with Grant, as *Columbia's Noblest Sons,* or beside the most famous of all general-presidents, George Washington, as "founder" and "preserver" of the Union.[30]

At last, for example, Currier & Ives belatedly issued its very first council of war print, showing the president conferring, implicitly on military strategy, with Generals William T. Sherman, Philip H. Sheridan, and Ulysses S. Grant. True, even when the setting for such scenes was moved outdoors, which New York printmakers Jones & Clark did for their 1865 lithograph, *Lincoln and His Generals,* the mufti-clad president still did not seem altogether military. But at least he was now made to seem retrospectively the very center of attention, as Admirals David D. Porter and David G. Farragut, together with Generals Sherman, Grant, Sheridan, and George H. Thomas face him in rapt attention. In this celebratory marketplace for Lincoln pictures, even an instantly recognizable tribute, *The First Reading of the Emancipation Proclamation,* one of the best-selling Lincoln prints of all time, could be believably pirated and modified by a rival engraver, with the resulting composite purporting to show as a convincing scene the late president and his cabinet in council with Grant to plan the end of the war.[31]

Perhaps the clearest signal of the posthumous improvement in Lincoln's military image came not from a print that was published but from one that was never issued—recalling printmaker Carl Anton's similarly abandoned effort four years earlier. Anton had believed that audiences would not accept an image of Lincoln making war. Much had changed. In 1865, it seemed unlikely that audiences would accept an image of Lincoln making peace.

On February 2, 1865, Lincoln had gone to Hampton Roads, for a secret peace conference with Confederate Vice President Alexander Stephens. The meeting failed, but that did not prevent engraver J. C. Buttre from sensing its historical importance. He began work on a print he tentatively called *Lincoln & Stephens in Hampton Roads.* Had it been polished and issued to the public, it might have become one of the most realistic of all group portraits of Lincoln, showing him presiding over a genuine "council of peace" in an effort to end the war. It was not to be. By the time Buttre finished work on the print, the peace initiative had collapsed, Grant had overpowered Lee, and Lincoln was dead. Suddenly, it no longer seemed appropriate to portray the martyr as anything less than tough, resolute, and at least somewhat military—an integral part of the action as the war drew to a close. Buttre never finished his proof print, and only one copy of the rough first impression has ever been found. Martyrdom effectively inoculated Lincoln against charges, verbal or visual, that he was a timid warrior.[32]

Instead, it was the wholly imaginary outdoor war council that seemed realistic enough to inspire at least one photographer to copy Jones & Clark's print of Lincoln and his generals, retitle it *Lincoln and His Generals in Council Before Richmond,* and issue the result as a carte-de-visite that suggested Lincoln had personally devised the strategy that led to the capture of the Confederate capital.

Actually, Lincoln was quite close to the scene of that Union triumph. On March 23, 1865, he took the steamer *River Queen* to visit Grant's headquarters at City Point. He stayed for more than two weeks, his longest and last trip to the front. One of its most famous moments came on March 27, when Grant, Sherman, and Porter boarded the ship for a final strategy meeting. It was by all accounts a war council, at which Lincoln pressed his commanders to fight on to a speedy victory. As Lincoln maintained, the "great lesson of peace" came from "teaching . . . all the folly of being the beginners of a war."[33]

But when painter G. P. A. Healy decided to immortalize the scene three years later, he entitled his canvas *The Peacemakers,* going so far as to insert a symbolic rainbow bursting forth outside the ship's windows. The shift in focus in what otherwise might have been the most potent of all commander-in-chief images of Lincoln was quite likely attributable to the artist's friendship with Sherman. It was Sherman who advised Healy on the composition, convinced Grant to pose, and persuaded Porter to furnish details about the boat. Perhaps in return for his help, Healy's painting showed Sherman doing the talking, as the others, including Lincoln, look on in deep thought. Whatever its shortcomings, the result inspired a chromolithograph designed for home display. But the relative scarcity of surviving copies strongly suggests that in its day it was not popular. By the time

Fig. 2.8 F. Hartwitch after Gustave Bartsch, *Lincoln in City Point*. Lithograph, printed by J. Hesse, published by Oswald Seehagan, Berlin, ca. 1865.

(*Harold Holzer*)

it was issued, American audiences probably preferred images that did not stress Lincoln's efforts at conciliation.[34]

A German, not an American, lithographer may have come closest to satisfying postassassination public taste with a highly romanticized picture of commander Lincoln, looking positively warlike on horseback, riding triumphantly into City Point (Fig. 2.8). The problem was that Lincoln surely never did so in real life. City Point was a bustling Union supply center, not a bombed-out ruin, as this image suggested. Wounded soldiers did not crowd its streets, and ex-slaves did not celebrate Lincoln's arrival there. Apparently, the distant European printmaker simply mistook City Point for Richmond. In so doing, he had ironically created the kind of heroic equestrian picture with which Lincoln was never honored in life. But he altogether missed the opportunity to suggest accurately the quiet entrance that Lincoln ultimately made into conquered Richmond on April 4.[35]

Dennis Malone Carter painted that event in 1866, portraying Lincoln in a grand carriage being greeted by black and white residents alike. The president indeed took such a ride in the occupied capital, but he was not greeted with equal enthusiasm by residents of both races. In fact, the white people aware of his visit responded, in the words of an eyewitness, with only "sullen, glazed stares . . . as if it was a disgusting sight."[36]

Far more moving—in its utter simplicity—was the moment, a few hours before this carriage tour, when Lincoln first stepped unannounced from a small boat onto the shores of the city. For a time, he walked in eerie silence. Then, a black woman suddenly recognized Lincoln. Within minutes Lincoln was surrounded by a crush of African-American well-wishers. With shouts of "glory, glory, glory," the newly liberated slaves joyously heralded the arrival of the Great Emancipator, in a scene beautifully captured by engraver Benjamin B. Russell. "Such wild, indescribable joy I never witnessed," wrote a newspaperman on the scene. "It was the great deliverer, meeting the delivered." Tears came to Lincoln's eyes as he made his way through the crowd, looking for all the world not like a commander in chief, but "a private citizen."[37]

One eyewitness quickly grasped the meaning of this, Lincoln's last and greatest military moment: "He came not as a conqueror, not with bitterness in his heart, but with kindness. He came as a friend, to alleviate sorrow and suffering—to rebuild what had been destroyed." The man of war had finally won enough battles to become a man of peace. And blessed indeed—in popular prints and in history alike—are conquering heroes who become peacemakers.[38]

3

Dying to Be Seen:
Prints of the Lincoln Assassination

How shall the nation most completely show its sorrow at Mr. Lincoln's death?" That was the question the nation's most famous historian, George Bancroft, asked the 2,000 people who crowded into Union Square in New York City for a memorial tribute to the fallen president on April 25, 1865, just ten days after Lincoln had died in Washington. "How," Bancroft wondered, "shall [the nation] best honor his memory?" On the very next day, New Yorkers had an answer, from only a few miles south in lower Manhattan.[1]

That morning, agents of the Nassau Street print publishing firm headed by Nathaniel Currier and James Merritt Ives arrived at the government copyright office for the Southern District of New York to register a hastily drawn but wrenching lithograph (Fig. 3.1) of the assassination of the martyred president. By the standards of the mid-nineteenth century, Currier & Ives's artistic response to that national tragedy had been breathtakingly swift. And the result provided American print-buying audiences with precisely the kind of remembrance they could display and cherish to testify to their sorrow.[2]

To be sure, this was not the primary kind of recollection Bancroft had in mind. In his Union Square speech, he had urged New Yorkers to celebrate Lincoln's life rather than dwell on his death. But then, just as now, New Yorkers had their own ideas. And within days after the print's publication, they so demonstrated by making it one of the great best-sellers in the history of the graphic arts in America. No precise statistics exist to support that claim; Currier & Ives's own records did not survive. But judging from the number of copies extant, it was popular indeed.

But why? When Ronald Reagan was shot a century and a quarter later, it is doubtful whether many Americans clipped the widely published photographs of the attack and displayed them on their living room walls. Yet Currier & Ives's print, along with countless variations on the theme, decorated American parlors

Fig. 3.1 Currier & Ives, *The Assassination of President Lincoln./At Ford's Theatre Washington D.C. April 14th 1865.* Lithograph, New York, 1865. (*The Lincoln Museum*)

throughout the North for months and years after Lincoln lost his life at Ford's Theatre, displayed in the manner of crucifixion scenes as domestic shrines to history's newest Good Friday martyr.

To appreciate the popularity and power of the visual arts in the 1860s requires that we comprehend how rare and precious such images were in Lincoln's time. By contrast, within minutes after the attack on President Reagan, the videotape of the gunshot, the frightened expression in the intended victim's eyes, the collapse of Press Secretary James Brady on the street, the horde of security officers pouncing on the shooter—all these scenes were played on television, over and over again, for days thereafter.

But in nineteenth-century America, pictures were nowhere near as ubiquitous as they have since become. They could not be beamed into private homes via television or the Internet; they had to be obtained from picture-sellers and physically carried or delivered to homes for display. They were not only rarer, but the heroes they portrayed were generally held in higher regard than today's leaders. To purchase a print of a national hero was to express patriotism, testify to political loyalties, and practice what has been called the "civil religion" of politics at home by hanging political icons above the family hearth beside—sometimes in place of—the religious icons of old. And that became true particularly of the pictures that illustrated, occasionally imagined, Lincoln's transfiguration into national sainthood.

By the time of his murder, Lincoln had been a subject for the engravers and lithographers for a total of five years, portrayed, successively, as Honest Old Abe the Railsplitter candidate and as the bearded president and commander in chief. Some of the portraits idealized him, and others derided him. In an era in which Americans, in Richard P. McCormick's words, "eagerly assumed the identity of partisans . . . perhaps for much the same reason that their descendants were to become Dodger fans," Lincoln was the most popular, but also the most controversial, "player" on the scene. Yet it is instructive to remember that after issuing a torrent of images aimed at introducing a virtually unknown candidate to a curious public, engravers and lithographers had significantly reduced their focus on Lincoln as the years passed.[3]

The moment he fell at Ford's Theatre, however, Lincoln was transformed in public memory from sectional political celebrity to national secular god. With preachers eulogizing him on the Easter Sunday after his death as another Jesus, dying for the nation's sins, and as an American Moses, sacrificing his life just as he led his people to the promised land, Northern printmakers cemented Lincoln's

Father, Martyr, and Myth

new mythical image onto the public consciousness. That process began in a sense the day Currier & Ives registered their print of the murder scene.

As a work of graphic art, the lithograph had much to recommend it. Primarily, though it may appear strange so to praise a picture that did not appear for a full eleven days after the event it portrayed, the print had genuine news value. According to the copyright registries for all the major publishing centers of America, this lithograph of April 26 constituted the very first published separate-sheet print to show the shooting at Ford's. It was through prints like this one, in the age before news photography, newsreels, cinema, television, and the World Wide Web, that America finally got to "see" what was arguably the most important single event of the entire century.

Of course, the image was also somewhat flawed. For example, as transcendent a symbol as it was, there is no proof that the American flag was being grasped by Lincoln at the moment John Wilkes Booth fired the pistol shot that killed him. If he was, no one in the audience noticed. Contrary to Currier & Ives's portrayal, the victim was also facing in the other direction, peering into the audience when struck from behind, at least so the trajectory of Booth's bullet suggested. And it is difficult to believe that even as alert a guest as Maj. Henry Rathbone was already on his feet reaching for the assassin just as the shot was fired, as Currier & Ives's print asked American audiences to believe. But here is the display print America first saw: a president clutching the emblem of his beloved Union as he becomes the final casualty of the war to preserve it. Compared to the rival interpretations that were soon pouring off presses in New York, Philadelphia, and other publishing centers, however, it was virtually photographic in its accuracy.[4]

By 1865 standards, even subsequently issued assassination prints may be said to have been rushed to the public in the heat of intense competition for audience favor. (Typically, publishers consumed approximately three weeks preparing engraved and lithographic depictions of great events.) But in addition to relying on the patience of their patrons, print publishers had the additional good fortune to be serving an audience that had absolutely no idea what Ford's Theatre looked like, or how the tragic events in the president's box had truly unfolded on Good Friday. The first woodcuts, in *Harper's Weekly* and *Frank Leslie's Illustrated Newspaper,* had skirted the issue by showing the murder from behind.[5]

Errors thus also marred, but did not inhibit circulation of, a print by an unidentified lithographer, *The Martyr of Liberty.* Here, Lincoln was mistakenly placed in the center of the theater box, looking as if he were about to plunge over the railing and into the orchestra seats below. Yet this print was redeemed by the clever inclusion of four lines from Lincoln's favorite play, Shakespeare's *Macbeth*. "This Lincoln," the verse began,

> Hath borne his faculties so meek; has been
> So clear in his great office that his virtue
> Shall plead, trumpet-tongued, against
> The deep damnation of his taking off.[6]

On the one hand, the lines were entirely fitting, neatly expressing national sorrow. But Shakespeare originally had Macbeth pronounce the speech to justify murdering King Duncan because of his "vaulting ambition." Used now as a caption for a Lincoln assassination print, it seemed almost to invite justification for Booth's act. It may be difficult to imagine a public aware of and sensitive to the double meaning of this caption, but nineteenth-century print buyers were arguably more sophisticated about literature than they were about graphics, quite the reverse of the television addicts of the late twentieth century, and they may not have missed the point.

On the other side of the spectrum, there was room enough in the frenzied market for other assassination depictions, such as H. H. Lloyd's engraving, *Assassination of President Lincoln* (Fig. 3.2), which drew its inspiration, doubtless without the permission of Currier & Ives, from their New York competitors' April 26 lithograph. The Lloyd print featured an accurate likeness of Booth but presented Rathbone in much the same irrational pose and Lincoln clutching the American flag (here, interestingly, presented more accurately as bunting, not wall drapery). Unfortunately, Lloyd's Lincoln figure looks impossibly muscular, and the head, modeled after the Brady photograph that also inspired the portrait on the five-dollar bill, appears far too small for its pumped-up physique. On the other hand, a print of the same title by an unknown lithographer (Fig. 3.3) compressed the presidential box into an inexplicably tiny space, piling all the eyewitnesses together, and mysteriously adding a fifth occupant to the box (along with President and Mrs. Lincoln, Major Rathbone and his fiancée, Clara Harris).

Through such graphics, however absurd, Americans were able to see the great tragic event of their age. But where the Lincoln image was concerned, the graphics represented only a beginning or, to be more accurate, the second coming of an industry that was at the time dormant: the production and dissemination of the Lincoln image. Lincoln was no stranger to American popular prints, but he had not been one of the industry's major characters for some months.

Engravers and lithographers helped introduce Lincoln to the public when he

Fig. 3.2 H. H. Lloyd, *Assassination of President Lincoln,/At Ford's Theatre Apl. 14th 1865./ "Treason and Murder Work Together."* Engraving, New York, 1865. *(Library of Congress)*

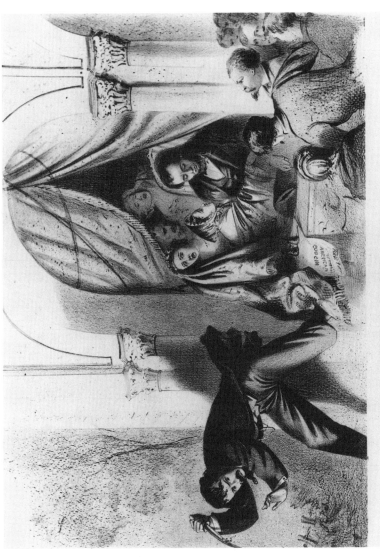

ASSASSINATION OF PRESIDENT LINCOLN.
AT FORD'S THEATRE WASHINGTON DC APRIL 14 1865.

Fig. 3.3 Printmaker unknown, *Assassination of President Lincoln./At Ford's Theatre Washington D.C. April 14th 1865*. Lithograph, 1865. *(The Lincoln Museum)*

Father, Martyr, and Myth

emerged from the 1860 Republican National Convention as its surprise nominee. A few months later, they were among the first artists in any medium to portray the president-elect with his new whiskers. Later, in the election of 1864, he had dominated a flood of caricature, both supportive and critical, issued during that campaign. Helping trace his transformation from prairie politician to bearded statesman, prints helped illustrate, and perhaps influence, that evolution. In the process, picture publishers undoubtedly made a handsome profit from the enterprise. But by and large, printmakers had stopped portraying Lincoln after November 1864; no new portraits were necessary, undoubtedly because no new public demand had been expressed. Lincoln was well known and well depicted. Neither his Second Inaugural in March 1865 nor Lee's surrender to Grant the following month inspired new prints of the president.

But nothing Lincoln ever did in his life quite so excited the public or inspired, and profited, the artists as did his death. The shot that killed Lincoln may have snuffed out a great life, but it simultaneously breathed unprecedented vitality into the printmaking industry, igniting a major national demand for what passed at the time for "overnight" pictures of the slain president, prominently among whose subjects was the slaying itself. The assassination clearly influenced printmakers to make Lincoln a far more frequently portrayed, and more exalted, subject than he had been when he was living; and the renewed focus apparently pleased American audiences enormously, or they would not have welcomed the cruder assassination portrayals along with the better ones.

Though many postassassination Lincoln prints revealed poor research, limited imagination, constricting dependence on outmoded photographs as source models, and even occasional outright fakery, they achieved considerable popularity. Some were also graced with a timeless quality that makes it easy to forget that they, too, were part of the direct news response to Lincoln's murder. Prints inspired by the assassination were not limited to the murder itself, and in calculating its true impact on Lincoln iconography, modern audiences should be sensitive to the larger body of work.

The first category of assassination prints was, of course, the depiction of the murder itself. The second might be called cause-and-effect prints. It is difficult to imagine that Americans would have wanted to purchase pictures of the assassin. But there was sufficient public curiosity about him to make the yearning for pictorial accompaniment seem acceptable. After all, a carte-de-visite photograph of John Wilkes Booth was owned by a family that had more reason than any other to shun it: the Lincolns themselves.[7]

Prints could do what straightforward photographs could not; attempt to explain why a well-known actor had suddenly resorted to murder. One such lithograph, by an anonymous artist of 1865, claimed, for example, that the "theory" behind the murder originated with George W. Bickley, the first leader of the secret, proslavery, anti-Union organization known as the Knights of the Golden Circle. Some Northerners seemed eager to believe that the mysterious group had inspired Booth into "practice," the "effect" being the martyrdom of Lincoln. Another print actually suggested that there was a kind of "magic bullet" involved in Lincoln's murder, bringing to mind to modern observers the Kennedy assassination a century later. The print proposed that the projectile, animated by a serpent's fire, enclosed the form and face of John Wilkes Booth. Was it convincing? Surely not, but it apparently found an audience, so intense was public demand for a visual analysis of the act that had deprived the nation of its leader. In the wise words framing the top of the print, "Death is not death; 'tis but the ennoblement of mortal man."

At least it seemed a more plausible explanation than that advanced by Philadelphia lithographer J. L. Magee (Fig. 3.4), who suggested in his 1865 lithograph that it was Satan himself who tempted a pensive Booth to Lincoln's murder. Here the grotesque figure of Satan is contrasted sharply to that of the matinee-idol assassin, as Lincoln himself is glimpsed in the background apparently enjoying the play whose conclusion the viewer knows he will never see. The implication is that only the darkest influences could have inflamed Booth to such villainy.

Public curiosity about the events of that Easter weekend was apparently insatiable, and it also embraced a third type of print response to the assassination: the deathbed print. Americans had learned that after Booth fled, Lincoln was carried gingerly across the street into the back bedroom of a boardinghouse, where he lingered for nearly nine hours before breathing his last on the morning of April 15. That is what Americans read. Beyond these raw and sketchy details, however, particulars could be imagined, and that is precisely what printmakers did.

Again it was Currier & Ives who, if they did not set the standard, certainly set the pace, first with a lithograph copyrighted on April 26, 1865, the same day as their assassination print. Like most of the portrayals that soon followed it on the marketplace, this one showed Lincoln without a trace of pain or discomfort. There was no sign of blood in these prints, and certainly no trace of the black pallor that had discolored his eye by the morning of his death. His surgeons were usually depicted stoically by his bedside, but not at work—as they really were— periodically removing blood clots from his wound so bits of brain could ooze

Fig. 3.4 J. L. Magee, *Satan Tempting Booth to the Murder of the President.* Lithograph, Philadelphia, 1865.

(The Lincoln Museum)

forth and permit his breathing. Nor was Lincoln's widow customarily depicted in the hysterical frenzy that in reality overtook her that night; instead, she was presented as a calm, resolute woman moving almost gracefully through the event, gowned as if for an inaugural ball.

Like its companion print of the murder, however, the Currier & Ives scene was not free of errors, such as the insertion of little Tad Lincoln crying on his mother's lap as she sits at the president's bedside. Tad, in reality, was never brought to the deathbed that night, even though Mary Lincoln more than once cried out that she was sure her husband would awaken if he could only hear the little boy's voice. What is perhaps more surprising is how many details Currier & Ives did get right: the small size of the death chamber, the cluster of shocked witnesses, and particularly, the print-within-the-print on the wall behind the deathbed. Printmakers subsequently proved unaware, or unwilling to accept, the modest size of the room and the onlookers it could contain, but most seemed to know that the print, *The Village Blacksmith,* had occupied a place in the Petersen House bedroom and took care to draw it into their Lincoln scenes.

Currier & Ives was not only first and fairly accurate but also unsatisfied. Within days they had second thoughts about one major omission from their April 26 print. The new chief executive, Andrew Johnson, was not portrayed in that picture, but the firm reconsidered its artistic decision and in a burst of artistic license removed Gen. Henry W. Halleck from a second version and transformed him into Johnson. In truth, Johnson's visits to the scene had been brief and perfunctory, and Mrs. Lincoln so despised him that it was beyond comprehension that the two could have occupied the same room at the same time, as this second Currier & Ives print suggested. But with Johnson so included, a print of the last moments of President Lincoln could simultaneously become a print of the first moments of President Johnson and thus represent not only national tragedy but peaceful succession and national continuity in the face of unprecedented crisis. Perhaps that is why the third and final interpretation of Lincoln's death by Currier & Ives was the most politically correct, with Johnson advancing even closer to the bedside and Mary banished to the doorway, weeping alone while her husband expires inside — much the way, ironically, that it really happened.

More expensive, lavish, and skillfully marketed deathbed scenes followed later. One of the most impressively produced and advertised, even if it was not the most historically precise, was the engraving by Alexander Hay Ritchie, the same printmaker who had undertaken the task of mass-producing the adaptation of Francis B. Carpenter's painting of the first reading of the Emancipation Proclamation, a print destined to become the best-selling Lincoln print ever.

Ritchie consumed two years producing the painting *The Death of President Lincoln*, which he engraved himself. Although he claimed that he personally visited the Petersen House to make sketches, and there he surely came face-to-face with the almost claustrophobic reality of the death chamber, his work depicted no fewer than twenty-six recognizable onlookers in the tiny room. In Ritchie's imagination, the death chamber took on the proportions of a royal chamber, and within it, Lincoln's final moments, the trappings of the death of a king. At the same time, Ritchie was scrupulous enough to exclude both Vice President Johnson and Mrs. Lincoln.

"There is much variety of pose throughout the composition," a specially produced sales brochure promised. "Every mind is absorbed by one idea, and we read it on every face." Here, the advertisement suggested, was a subject of irresistibly "deep national interest." Ritchie's print was not only ambitious in conception and large in size (nearly two by three feet) but also expensive: twenty dollars for plain proofs and thirty dollars for signed proofs, hefty sums in post–Civil War America. But its promoters argued that it was a bargain for such a priceless "record of the passing history of the nation." [8]

Those portrayed in the scene agreed. The Reverend Phineas Gurley, who had spent three hours beside the deathbed, declared, "It renews to my eye and heart with surprising vividness, the scenes and impressions of that sadly memorable morning." Ritchie's picture was, he said, "a work of surpassing merit." Former Secretary of the Navy Gideon Welles agreed, calling it "artistic and strikingly impressive of the scene on that memorable and sad occasion." And Quartermaster General Montgomery Meigs, another visitor to the death chamber that night, volunteered his hope "that the engraving may well have a place in thousands of American homes." [9]

But judging by its rarity today, Meigs's hope — and that of engraver Ritchie — went unfulfilled. Perhaps its large size and even larger cost ruined the print's chances for success. Perhaps it simply arrived on the market too late to win the kind of following the less accurate, more laughable, but more timely interpretations had excited. But we know that only a few years ago, a cache of mint-condition signed artist's proofs was unearthed at the John Hay Library at Brown University, unseen and apparently unsold for more than a century. Perhaps they had been given when first published to former presidential secretary John Hay, whose papers later entered the library that bears his name. If so, he had no more luck distributing them than did Ritchie.

But another, even grander deathbed print production was yet to come, that of artist Alonzo Chappel, who exaggerated the size of the claustrophobic Petersen House bedroom to contain a staggering forty-seven mourners, all of whom actually visited the death scene during the night but never gathered there together.

Widely exhibited and lavishly praised when the original painting was completed, Chappel's work boasted perhaps the most realistic portraiture of any of the deathbed scenes ever attempted by artists in any medium, a success achieved through an ingenious and audacious research effort: Chappel convinced the principals he intended to portray to pose for photographs assuming the precise poses that he desired them to strike in his design. Even Lincoln's son, Robert, notoriously private and protective of the sanctity of the late president's memory, agreed to do so — posing with head bowed and handkerchief clutched in his right hand.[10]

Chappel planned that his canvas be quickly adapted into a popular print. A key was designed (Fig. 3.5) and an order book circulated to subscribers, promising that "a First Class, Steel Engraving, from this beautiful painting is about to be published" in thirty-one by seventeen-inch size. Artists' proofs were to cost $100, india proofs $60, plain proofs $60, and plain prints $15, prices that made even the Ritchie print seem a bargain. The surviving original subscription book reveals no shortage of customers, including Robert Lincoln and Ulysses S. Grant, who each ordered the most expensive proof available.[11]

"No expense has been spared to produce a work worthy of the scene it represents," a period circular declared, "and the high encomiums given it by eminent judges is the best proof of the result. The print would be "engraved in the finest style of line and stipple . . . believing that nothing short of a *genuine work of art* will meet the approval, and secure the patronage of the American people."

Again, the celebrities portrayed were generous with their praise. "The majority of the portraits could hardly be improved," declared Gen. O. O. Howard. And Surgeon General Joseph K. Barnes echoed the belief that "those in attendance" had been painted "truthfully."

A *Washington Sunday Herald* writer declared, "Portraits so minutely like I have never seen, even from the brush of [Charles Loring] Elliot. . . . The greatness of the picture lies in its correct transcription of an actual scene and perfect portraiture of American men. It is just such a work as, above all others, should be American property, for if ever there was a *National* picture, this is one."[12]

1 Pres. LINCOLN.	13 Gov. OGLESBY.	25 Gen. TODD.	37 Col. PELOUSE.
2 Mrs. LINCOLN.	14 Speaker COLFAX.	26 ROBᵗ LINCOLN	38 Maj. HAY.
3 Vice Pres. JOHNSON.	15 Dr. STONE.	27 Rev. Dr. GURLEY.	39 Gen. MEIGS.
4 Maj. RATHBONE.	16 Surg. Gen. BARNES.	28 Assᵗ Secᵞ FIELD.	40 Maj. ROCKWELL.
5 Mr. ARNOLD, M.C.	17 Mrs. Sen. DIXON.	29 Adjᵗ Gen. HAYNIE.	41 Ex. Gov. FARWELL.
6 P.M. Gen. DENNISON.	18 Dr. TODD.	30 Maj. FRENCH.	42 Judge CARTTER.
7 Secᵞ WELLES.	19 Assᵗ Surg. LEALE.	31 Gen. AUGER.	43 Mr. ROLLINS, M.C.
8 Attᵞ Gen. SPEED.	20 Assᵗ Surg. TAFT.	32 Col. VINCENT.	44 Gen. MARSTON, M.C
9 Dʳ HALL	21 Assᵗ Secᵞ OTTO.	33 Gen. HALLECK.	45 Mrs. KINNEY.
10 Dr. LEIBERMANN	22 Gen. FARNSWORTH. M.C	34 Secᵞ STANTON.	46 Miss KINNEY.
11 Secᵞ USHER.	23 Sen. SUMNER.	35 Col. RUTHERFORD.	47 Miss HARRIS.
12 Secᵞ McCULLOCH.	24 Surg. CRANE.	36 Assᵗ Secᵞ ECKERT.	

Fig. 3.5 M. David, *Key to the Last Day of Lincoln* [by Alonzo Chappel]. Lithograph, reissued from an 1866 original, 1908.
  (The Lincoln Museum)

Enthusiasm notwithstanding, there is no evidence that a print of Chappel's "national picture" painting was ever produced in the nineteenth century. By the time New York print publisher John B. Bachelder was ready to adapt and publicize the effort, the American marketplace for Lincoln deathbed prints had been oversaturated, and it seems likely that the project collapsed.[13]

By then, the assassination had inspired other tangential, but highly popular, print genres as well, pictures that hitherto have not been considered as part of the postassassination Lincoln print boom, although they were clearly inspired by the murder itself. They should be so categorized: prints of the Lincoln family (none of which, significantly, appeared before the assassination); Great Emancipator prints (discussed in chapter 1 but unpublished until the murder created a public appetite for such portrayals); depictions of the president's funerals in such cities as New York, Columbus, and Cincinnati; and martyr portraits that framed his image with dedicatory captions that identified the depictions as "sacred to the memory" of the late president (Fig. 3.6). One typical martyr portrait overtly identified Lincoln as "the best beloved of the nation" and included such symbols as the slain dragon of rebellion sprawled in the foreground, a grateful liberated slave in the background, and the representative figure of the entire nation, Columbia herself, overcome with emotion at the gravesite.

The first such postassassination tribute portrait may have appeared as early as a week after Lincoln's death. On that anniversary, Moore, Wlstach & Baldwin advertised in Cincinnati a timely new Lincoln print priced at fifty cents. Their notice declared, "We will publish on Saturday Morning, April 22d, in tint, on Plate Paper, 11 by 14 inches, the most recent, accurate and perfectly engraved Portrait of President Lincoln in the market. Himself, family and friends pronounced it the finest likeness that had been produced." But no copy of such a print has come to light. The same issue of the local newspaper also offered an advertisement from Middleton, Strobridge & Company, heralding their "just published . . . new and beautiful portrait of our late President, in fine Plate Paper, 19 by 24, in black and tint, with gold border," and priced at one dollar each. And this print most likely did appear that weekend. Elijah Middleton had been working on his Lincoln lithograph since 1864 and had even elicited a comment on a preliminary proof from the president himself.[14]

But a print did not have to be lined with "black tint" and "gold border," dominated by tombstones or eulogistic calligraphy to qualify as a martyr portrait. Postassassination portraits demonstrated, merely in the heroic manner in which a previously partisan subject was depicted, that the martyred Lincoln had entered a new realm among picturemakers and their audiences: that of myth.

The April 29, 1865 issue of *Harper's Weekly* had been the first national publication to feature advertisements for pictorial products inspired by the assassination, and for the next twelve weeks, its pages were filled with offerings for medals, mourning badges, and of course, prints. By July 22, the advertisements for murder and mourning images had ceased. After only three months, the vogue for assassination, deathbed, and funeral prints had quickly come (by the sluggish standards of 1865) and even more quickly gone. A. H. Ritchie's large deathbed failure and John B. Bachelder's inability to publish an engraving of Alonzo Chappel's painting strongly suggest that national interest in murder and deathbed pictures had abated by the end of that year.

Fig. 3.6 Printmaker unknown, *Sacred to the Memory of the Just Merciful and Most Liberator* [sic] *Abraham Lincoln/16th President of the United States/Who died by/ Assassination on the 15th day of April 1865 in the 56th year of his age/During four years of the most determined civil war.* Lithograph, ca. 1865.

(*The Lincoln Museum*)

But Americans were still eager to see Lincoln, and so he remained a phenomenon of American iconography for months and years to come: in scenes showing him together with George Washington; holding center stage within the bosom of a presumably happy, loving family; celebrated as a liberator; and portrayed in hundreds of flattering portraits that flooded the country for the remainder of the decade. This output, too, seldom judged as publishers' responses to the Lincoln assassination, deserves to be so categorized. Only then can we properly appreciate the breadth and duration of public interest in the martyred president.

"The event has passed into history now," declared the advertising brochure for A. H. Ritchie's ambitious deathbed print, "and like other great historical occurrences, it has formed an inspiring theme for the orator, the poet, and the painter, alike." Not to mention the printmaker. John Wilkes Booth may have snuffed out the life of the greatest of Americans, but in the pictures his act inspired, Abraham Lincoln was truly born again.[15]

Part Two

Controversy and Public Memory

The Mirror Image of Civil War Memory: Abraham Lincoln and Jefferson Davis in Popular Prints

THE CIVIL WAR, as the title to a long-forgotten wartime print portrait reminds us (Fig. 4.1), was above all a "trial by battle." But the very existence of such an image, showing the commanders in chief of the Union and the Confederacy confronting each other with swords—an image that reduced the entire conflict to a personal fight between two representative heads of state—reminds us that the Civil War was a war of art, too.

No other war had ever been so well illustrated. From the outset, gifted military and marine painters depicted its battles and leaders. Illustrated news weeklies sent "special artists" to the front to make sketches that could quickly be copied and published in the press. And for the first time, photographers, too, covered the war, sending home horrifying records, if not of the battles themselves, at least of their grisly aftermath. But no other medium produced so many depictions of the Civil War and its leaders, in so many variations, for so many tastes, as did that of popular prints.

Prints reached a wide public, achieved relative immediacy, and earned permanent display in one of the most sacred settings in American culture: the parlor wall of the family home. As early as 1811, a Russian visitor to the United States marveled, "Every American considers it his sacred duty to have a likeness of Washington in his home, just as we have images of God's saints." [1] By war's end, the New York lithographers Currier & Ives could confidently boast, "Pictures have become a necessity, and the price at which they can be retailed is so low, that everybody can afford to buy them." [2] By the dawn of the Civil War era, the walls of thousands of American homes bore witness to the beliefs of those who lived within.

Of course, we do not decorate our houses with politicians' faces today (John F. Kennedy and Martin Luther King Jr. were perhaps the last public figures whose pictures were hung in family homes). In our own era, which boasts nothing short

IS CO|TTON
KI|NG?

For one or both of us the time is come,
If Slavery is fit to live,let Freedom fall.

TRIAL BY BATTLE.

Oh, ho, if that's the case come on, Old Link
And down with him who first cries __ Hold !
Let's have a drink.

Fig. 4.1 E. B. & E. C. Kellogg, *Trial by Battle*. Lithograph, Hartford, Connecticut, ca. 1861.

(The Lincoln Museum)

of image bombardment from the likes of C-Span, CNN, and *People Magazine,* the only formal portraits that adorn our walls, aside from family pictures, tend to depict rock stars, actors, ballplayers, and *Sports Illustrated* swimsuit models. Mercifully, these are usually relegated to teenagers' bedrooms, not living rooms.

It is understandably hard for modern Americans to appreciate an era in which images were rare and prized, and in which political beliefs were so boldly and publicly illustrated at home. But such was the degree of reverence audiences held for both pictures and politicians at the precise moment when two men, born eight months and less than 100 miles apart, each took oaths of office declaring themselves American presidents. The inaugurations of Abraham Lincoln in the North and Jefferson Davis in the South launched not only a war between the states but a war between presidential images that was to last as long as the guns fired and beyond, into the quest for national memory.

The lithograph *Trial by Battle* might be described as an early skirmish from that war of images. To be sure, it is a pro-Union print, the work of E. B. & E. C. Kellogg of Hartford, Connecticut. The setting, discernible from the Capitol dome in the background, is Washington. Lincoln is shown backed by a rather absurd-looking American eagle dressed in a Revolutionary War uniform and gripping an American flag. Davis is being jeered by an African American who thumbs his nose while trampling on a Confederate flag. The only dissent comes from the clichéd caricature of a disloyal Irishman, a stock figure often found in wartime prints attacking Democrats. But his lack of solidarity for the Union is attributed to the whiskey that rests on the barrel beside him.

What makes this lithograph unique is that it depicts Lincoln and Davis doing direct battle against one another—brandishing swords in the manner of ancient gladiators. It was the first and the last separate-sheet display print ever to so portray them. (The only other known example, a Cincinnati lithograph showing Lincoln brandishing a large log rail to fight off a sword-wielding Davis, survives only in the rough draft submitted to the Library of Congress for copyright registry [see Fig. 2.3, p. 40]). Perhaps because Davis seemed to many observers Lincoln's superior in dignity, many Northern printmakers grew reluctant to compare them directly. If one looks closely, the print hints at how different their images were. Lincoln has been given an advantage. In his left hand he holds a second weapon: an ax. The printmaker surely did not intend to suggest that Honest Abe was fighting unfairly, clutching two weapons to Davis's one. He was merely arming the character with one of the familiar symbolic props that had been employed in earlier campaign prints to help introduce him to the public: the tools of the railsplitter who had risen inspiringly from frontier obscurity to national fame.

Such accoutrements remained staples of Lincoln imagery for years and set him distinctly apart from his more rigidly formal Confederate counterpart, whom one biographer called "the aristocratic type of Southern politician."[3] Endearing frontier symbols identified Lincoln as a man of, by, and for the people. Yet, surprisingly, they did not give him an automatic image advantage over Davis—at least not at first. Only after Lincoln was credited with liberating the slaves, rewarded with reelection, and transformed into a national martyr would his image fully overcome the challenge from his Confederate counterpart. There were always more prints of Lincoln than of Davis in circulation, if only because Union printmakers continued churning out graphics long after Confederate presses were stilled. But volume alone does not guarantee predominance. Otherwise the Union side would have won the war between images—not to mention the war between the states—within months.

Controversy and Public Memory

Trial by Battle in a sense ushered in a long war of mirror presidential images between America's two Civil War presidents. Just as Lincoln declares in the caption to this print, "For one or both of us the time is come." For a surprisingly long time, at least in the graphic arts, the time was decidedly ripe for both.

Perhaps nothing helped more to elevate the early Davis image than the fact that he was virtually anointed president of the Confederacy. He neither fought for nomination at a party convention, nor competed for votes in a national election. Some scholars have suggested that it was precisely Davis's lack of experience in campaigning among the people that made him an insensitive leader once installed in the presidency.[4]

But standing above the fray helped Davis seem more dignified. He did not seek office; it sought him. Thus he had conducted an 1852 race for senator by remaining in Washington, "drinking champagne," in the words of his rival, while his challenger traveled 3,200 miles and gave 115 speeches. (Davis lost and had to wait five more years to return to the Senate.) To the prospect of assuming the Confederate presidency in 1861 he could say, with credible Washingtonian modesty, "I had no desire to be . . . President. When the suggestion was made to me, I expressed a decided objection . . . against being placed in that position." It was not lost on many that like George Washington himself, in true Cincinnatus fashion, Davis had to be summoned to duty.[5]

Lincoln was granted no such coronation. In his own race for the U.S. Senate from Illinois in 1858, he had conducted the most public campaign in his state's history. A dark horse for the Republican presidential nomination two years later, he had come from behind to defeat the favorites on the third ballot. He did not campaign directly for the presidency in 1860, but no one doubted that the taste was in his mouth a little. And unlike Davis, who was virtually unopposed and certainly unelected, Lincoln faced three rivals in the campaign of 1860.

Thus, Lincoln's earliest images introduced him as a figure of contention. Sensing an audience among those who opposed as well as those who favored him, the same printmakers who published idealized portraits also issued critical lampoons. A typical campaign caricature by Currier & Ives might dress him in a homespun shirt and arm him with a log rail to remind viewers of his humble origins and to imply that if Lincoln could rise, so could any ordinary American. But the same print would also burden him with unpopular viewpoints, in one example suggesting that he so favored black equality that he regarded a well-known Barnum attraction of the day, the half-human African "What Is It," as "a worthy successor to carry out the policy which I shall inaugurate."

Of course, many early prints introduced Lincoln more flatteringly. It was no accident that a print identifying him with the idolized Washington elicited rare praise from Lincoln. As an artist of the day put it, Washington's image seemed "grand and imposing . . . calculated for public buildings." Aspiring presidents yearned to identify themselves with their illustrious predecessor, perhaps imagining grand public displays of their own image in the future. Lincoln and Davis were no exceptions, and in a way, their four-year-long competition for image supremacy became, above all, a symbolic struggle in pictures to claim a direct connection to George Washington.[6]

It was a struggle, as the modern viewer should also remember, that neither had the power to control; such was the nature of nineteenth-century commercial printmaking. Had Lincoln and Davis themselves, or their political friends, enjoyed the ability to craft pictures of their own design, or had it been common at the time for political parties to commission the images they wanted, as they do routinely today, our archives now would be littered with early pictures showing Lincoln and Davis beside Washington. But in mid-nineteenth-century America, prints were created by independent, bipartisan publishers, not politicians. They echoed, sometimes anticipated, public taste and demand. And they truly reflected the ebb and flow of popular opinion toward their subjects and perhaps influenced it as well.

Lincoln thus "arrived" in prints as a figure of controversy. Just as often as he was depicted in straightforward portraiture in 1860, he was also seen in critical caricatures. Once elected, however, Lincoln outsmarted the image-makers by discarding completely his image as frontier railsplitter, growing the famous beard that transformed Honest Old Abe into Father Abraham.

So firmly was his prepresidential image etched onto the public consciousness that citizens at first barely recognized the "new" bearded Lincoln. En route to his inauguration, he stopped at Albany, New York, but elicited only a "faint" cheer when he stepped from his train. Journalist Henry Villard realized that "Lincoln . . . adorned with huge whiskers, looked so unlike the hale, smooth shaven, red-cheeked individual who is represented upon the popular prints . . . that . . . the people did not recognize him." Ironically, the date was February 18, 1861 — the same day that Jefferson Davis was inaugurated provisional president of the Confederate States of America.[7]

Davis had proceeded to his inauguration—a ceremony depicted later in a print aptly titled *The Starting Point of the Great War Between the States*—much as Lincoln had: giving impromptu speeches. "On my way," Davis later recalled, in typically dry language, "brief addresses were made at various places, at which there were temporary stoppages of the train, in response to calls from the crowds assembled at each point." [8]

Lincoln had much the same experience, but in his wonderful description — he always expressed himself much more vividly than Davis — when not too "tuckered out," he would speak wherever "the iron horse stops to water himself." On one such occasion, in Thorntown, Indiana, he began a long, funny story only to have the train lurch out of town before "the laugh came in," as the press put it. So the villagers obligingly followed Lincoln's train to the next town, where they got to hear the end of the joke. Such folksy displays alarmed Charles Francis Adams, for one, who lamented that Lincoln's inaugural-journey rhetoric had put "to flight all notions of greatness." [9]

But the worst was yet to come. Convinced by bodyguards that an assassination plot awaited him in hostile Baltimore, Lincoln put aside what he called "fear of ridicule" and agreed to rush through the city in secret. He had a brand-new top hat, but he set it aside. Instead, he admitted, "I put on an old overcoat that I had with me [and] a soft wool hat the likes of which I had never worn . . . in my life." Changing trains in the dead of night, he sped south, as he put it, "without being recognized by strangers, for I was not the same man." Only later did Lincoln come to regret "stealing into the capital like a thief in the night," although to one visitor he stubbornly insisted: "It ain't best to run a risk of any consequence for look's sake." [10]

Lincoln paid an enormous price for his caution. The *Charleston Mercury* scoffed, "Everybody here is disgusted at this cowardly and undignified entry." [11] And the disgust only increased when the *Illustrated London News* suggested that Lincoln had fled Baltimore wearing a military cape and a Scottish tam for a hat.

Within weeks, picture weeklies were filled with caricatures like *The Flight of Abraham,* showing the president-elect sneaking into Washington (see Fig. 5.6, p. 117). Never had an American president begun his administration shackled with so humiliating a public image. And although the artist Thomas Nast dutifully sketched the March 4, 1861, ceremonies in Washington for adaptation in the *New York Illustrated News,* it comes as little surprise that Lincoln's swearing-in, unlike Davis's, did not inspire a single separate-sheet display print for the American home. Such was the sorry state of Lincoln's image on assuming the presidency.

Almost mercifully, Lincoln was soon thereafter eclipsed in the realm of Union image-making, with the emergence of such new heroes as Maj. Robert Anderson of Fort Sumter, and early martyrs such as Col. Ephraim Elmer Ellsworth, the first

Union officer killed in the war. Public curiosity about new wartime celebrities ran so high in the North that New York lithographers Jones & Clark issued a series of prints depicting Confederate leaders—among them, a handsome portrait of Jefferson Davis himself. No similar picture was ever published in the Confederacy to introduce Lincoln to Southerners. But the Jones & Clark lithograph turned out to be the first as well as the only Union-made print portrait of Jefferson Davis. No printmaker thereafter dared to invite public wrath in the North by sympathetically portraying the leader of the South.

Perhaps the most effective images of Lincoln early in the war were group portraits that reminded viewers that he was heir to a tradition that harked back to Washington himself—the American presidency. As Noble Cunningham has put it, "Popular prints offering portraits of all the presidents in a grand design not only celebrated the presidency but also subordinated individual presidents to the institution of the presidency." Cunningham stressed that such attitudes allowed Americans to criticize individual presidents "without threatening the presidency" itself. But in Lincoln's case, prints placing him among his predecessors allowed him to be associated usefully with presidential tradition at a time when the presidency and the Union itself were both under siege.[12]

Davis, however, fared at least as well as Lincoln in early images stressing the connection to George Washington. In the total absence of a similar presidential tradition in the new Confederacy, Davis became, just like Washington, the first president of a new nation. He quickly emerged in Confederate iconography as Washington's only true heir: the father of his own new country. Hoyer & Ludwig of Richmond responded with a handsome portrait pointedly titled *Jefferson Davis/ First President of the Confederate States of America,* and A. Blackmar & Brothers of New Orleans contributed an illustrated cover for sheet music called *Our First President Quickstep.* For Southerners, such images could not help but neatly illustrate what the Richmond *Enquirer* reported in 1861: "The confidence manifested in our President . . . shows that the mantle of Washington falls gracefully upon his shoulders. Never were a people more enraptured with their Chief Magistrate than ours with President Davis."[13]

Davis enjoyed yet another similarity to Washington with which Lincoln could not hope to compete: military tradition. "By preference," Davis always insisted, "I was a soldier." In his postwar autobiography he went further, explaining that he did not feel "well suited to the office" of president, because "I thought myself better adapted to command in the field; Mississippi had given me the position which I preferred to any other—the highest rank in her army." Writing to a delegate to the Montgomery convention in 1861, Davis admitted he had little confidence in his "capacity" to serve as president. "I think," he hastened to add, "I could perform the functions of genl." Indeed, Davis seems to have accepted the presidency believing it was only "temporary," insisting, "I expected soon to be with the army of Mississippi." Impressed by his "military bearing" and "martial aspect," Richmond matrons like Constance Carey were convinced that Davis felt "quite out of place in the office of President . . . in the midst of such a war. His own inclination was to be with the army." [14]

Like Davis, Lincoln had seen his first — and in Lincoln's case, his only — military service in the Black Hawk War. But there the similarity ended. Davis attended West Point and achieved glory at Monterey and Buena Vista in a war with Mexico that young Congressman Lincoln opposed. As president, Lincoln eventually assumed active management of the Union war effort. But though he was depicted in councils of war, neither printmakers nor print audiences ever mistook him for a military president. "War council" prints of the president together with his uniformed generals took care to present Lincoln as a civilian magistrate, not a commander in chief. He was shown conferring with generals and admirals, but even when depicted sitting on a rock in an outdoor setting meant to suggest a battlefield, Lincoln was always pictured garbed in his trademark frock coat, white shirt, and black tie. He seemed to be inquiring, but not necessarily commanding.

From the onset of his presidency, Davis was viewed differently by printmakers in both the South and the North, in pictures that inevitably reinforced his connection to George Washington. When, for example, lithographer C. P. May of New York portrayed *The Officers of the C[onfederate]. S[tates]. Army & Navy*, Davis's picture was placed squarely among the bust portraits of the men in uniform. No attempt was made, certainly not in the title of the print, to separate him from his military subordinates. He was one of them.

This status was even more blatantly exploited in *Jefferson Davis and His Generals* (Fig. 4.2), in which the commander in chief was shown not only with his military commanders but also in full uniform — a first among command equals. And even after printmakers learned quite a few things about the Confederate high command — that Lee and Jackson had grown beards, for example, and more important, that Davis had never donned a uniform to lead them — they updated the image only peripherally by giving beards to Lee and Jackson and changing the color of the uniforms from Union blue to Confederate gray. But Davis remained front and center, fully garbed for military action.

The man and his iconographical hour truly met at Bull Run. In late July 1861,

Fig. 4.2 Printmaker unknown, *Jefferson Davis and His Generals*. Lithograph, published by Goupil & Company, Paris, and Michael Knoedler, New York, ca. 1861.

(*Library of Congress*)

Controversy and Public Memory

word began to spread through the Confederate capital that Davis had left Richmond for the vicinity of Manassas, where the two armies stood face-to-face. "I always thought he would avail himself of his prerogative as commander in chief, and direct in person the most important operations in the field," Confederate war clerk John B. Jones wrote in his diary. "I . . . believe he will gain great glory in this first mighty conflict." [15]

Three days later the Confederate president's wife burst into her friend Mary Chesnut's room and breathlessly reported, "A great battle had been fought — Jeff Davis led the centre, Joe Johnston the right wing, Beauregard the left wing of the army." Davis, Mrs. Chesnut later confided in her diary, seemed "greedy for military fame." But she was in the minority. One Southern newspaper referred to Davis as "our noble warrior President." [16]

When Mrs. Chesnut published her diary years later, that critical line was expunged. By then the myth of Davis's dramatic appearance at Manassas had been punctuated by the widely disseminated Hoyer & Ludwig print, *President Jefferson Davis. Arriving in the Field of Battle at Bull's Run.* It gave the indelible impression that the commander in chief was personally responsible for the Confederacy's first great military success.

In truth, Davis had arrived near to the scene of the action by train, not on horseback, and was told at first that his army had suffered a major defeat. He saw only the smoke and dust of distant fighting, but after commandeering a horse and riding out closer to the field of action, which by then had shifted farther away, he learned that Union forces, not Confederate, had been routed. The battle was all but over. There is certainly no evidence that Davis wore a uniform that day, as the print suggested, nor any reason to believe that his arrival played any part in rallying dispirited troops.

When he returned to Richmond, however, Davis merely "alluded to his own appearance on the field . . . in a delicate manner," according to war clerk Jones. In other words, he probably did little to deny reports that he had led the army. Although Davis eventually did correct the myth of his appearance at Bull Run in his autobiography, the book did not appear for twenty years. This may explain why the loyal clerk Jones worked himself into "a passion" when he first read in the local press "a dispatch from . . . Manassas stating that the President did not arrive upon the field until the victory was won; and therefore did not participate in the battle at all. From the President's own dispatch . . . we had conceived the idea that he . . . had directed the principal operations in the field." Jones's first instinct was not to doubt Davis but to express the hope that "another paper ought to be established in Richmond, that would do justice to the President." [17]

Only later did Jones learn "that the abused correspondent had been pretty nearly correct in his statement. The battle had been won, and the enemy were flying from the field before the President appeared." But he quickly added, "The people were well pleased with their President." Davis eventually told the full truth about Bull Run, but he clung tenaciously to the military image he had cultivated. As the anti-Davis *Richmond Whig* complained in March 1864: "The President never for a moment relinquished his rights as Commander-in-Chief . . . and among those rights that to which he clings with death-like tenacity is well-known to be the supreme and exclusive control of military operations." Such insistence on full control may ultimately have hampered the Confederate war effort. One diarist complained bitterly that Davis, a onetime secretary of war, spent far too much time on details and was much too rigid and authoritarian. But such details were irrelevant to the forging of his martial image at a time when the Confederacy was under attack. Besides, as yet another diarist confided, "I have long ago . . . expressed my conviction that the President is not endowed with military genius, *but who would have done better?*" [18]

In terms of ability to inspire troops with equestrian grace, real or imagined, Abraham Lincoln was no match for Jefferson Davis. A few weeks before Bull Run, Mary Chesnut conceded of Davis: "His worse [*sic*] enemy will concede that he is a consummate rider, graceful and easy in the saddle." Around the very same time, a New Yorker wrote directly to Lincoln to complain, "Soldiers write home to their friends in this town with reference to their disappointment in your bearing and manners when reviewing them." The critic insisted, "You ought to assume some dignity . . . even though your breeding has not been military." [19]

If Lincoln subsequently learned to inspire his soldiers in review, no pictorial evidence survives. The only important contemporary print to show him on horseback was as outlandish in its way as the print of Davis at Bull Run. Entitled *Mr. Lincoln, Residence and House,* it purported to show him returning home from his 1860 presidential campaign. But the truth was, Lincoln had never left his home to campaign. Nor had he grown his famous beard, shown in the print in defiance of chronology, until after the votes were counted.

Even the supposedly pro-Lincoln print by Charles Magnus, *After a Little While* (Fig. 4.3), did not quite make Lincoln look comfortable in the saddle, although it depicted a tiny figure of Davis below, slumping visibly as he glimpses

Fig. 4.3 Charles Magnus & Company, *After a Little While*. Lithograph, New York, ca. 1861.

(*Author's collection*)

Fig. 4.4 Printmaker unknown, *The Fate of the Rail Splitter.* Woodcut, Richmond, 1861. *(Author's collection)*

preparations for the execution of a "Southern Fanatic" from a gallows labeled "higher law." This is a difficult image to parse. While it cautions against the radicalism of both Southern secessionists and Northern abolitionists, the print warns against Union overconfidence as well. Its very title suggested the need for patience.

In their way, such prints were critical of both Davis and Lincoln, but they offered mild rebuke indeed compared to what other printmakers produced at the time. Few American leaders were ever as relentlessly lampooned as the two presidents of Civil War America. Not surprisingly, the most hostile anti-Davis graphics came from the North and the most hostile anti-Lincoln work from the South (see chap. 6).

To one Confederate printmaker, Lincoln deserved nothing less than execution for his satanic crimes against the South. In the crude but venomous picture, *The Fate of the Rail Splitter* (Fig. 4.4), Lincoln is shown about to be hanged, presumably for treason, from a scaffold constructed of Lincolnian log rails. (Ham-

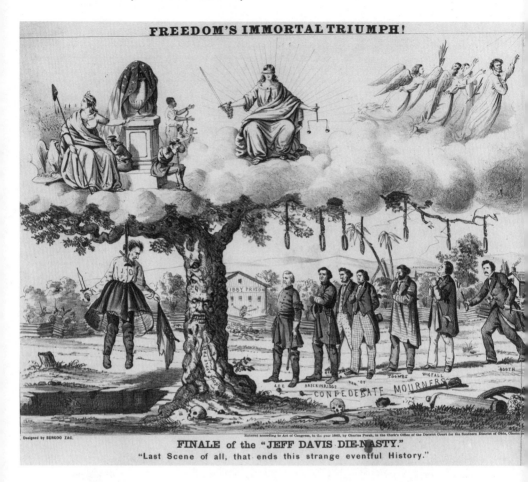

Fig. 4.5 Burgoo Zac., *Freedom's Immortal Triumph!/Finale of the "Jeff Davis Die-Nasty."/ "Last Scene of all, that ends this strange eventful History."* Lithograph, published by Charles Porah, Cincinnati, 1865.

(*Library of Congress*)

pered by the feeblest portraiture, its artist also apparently believed Lincoln was still clean-shaven, an indication, perhaps, of how few Northern-made prints found their way south once the war began.) But Northern pictorial venom could be equally overt: more than a few such prints showed Davis, too, at the gallows (Fig. 4.5). In one variation on the theme, a sniveling Davis was shown going to his death wrapped in the Confederate flag, lamenting, "O dear! O dear! I don't really want to secede this way." Traitors were seldom shown dying bravely.

Davis also appeared prominently in Benjamin H. Day Jr.'s print, *The Emblem of the Free,* which showed the devil — this time decidedly *not* Lincoln — placing a crown on the sleeping Confederate president's head. Here the Washington image was employed against Davis. The ghost of the first president looks on in despair, pointing to the goddess of liberty at center and to the Revolutionary War veterans huddled in the cold at left, to remind Davis and viewers alike of the sacrifice that had been required to create the Union. In the words of the song that accompanied the picture, "The Traitor's Dream," Davis is warned that he has in fact sullied Washington's heritage:

> The shade of WASHINGTON
> Condemns you from above;
> His calm, majestic brow
> Denotes his country's love;
> E'en Royalty could not,
> With all its tinsel glare,
> Induce him to betray
> Our nation's banner fair. . . .
>
> Beneath those brilliant stripes
> Your fathers fought and bled;
> Resplendently they shone
> Above each warrior's head.
> Then, traitor, pause! beware!
> A felon's death will be
> Yours if you dare destroy
> That Emblem of the Free!

A similar assault awaited Davis in *The Soldier's Song — Unionism vs. Copperheadism,* promoted by Ohio printmakers Smith & Swinney as "a token of disapprobation and contempt of Home Traitors." The Confederate president was not mentioned by name in the vilifying poem that accompanied this picture, but he was portrayed as the mother of all Copperheads: a huge snake topped by Davis's head, coiled around a symbolic Southern palmetto tree and staring into the barrel of a Union cannon.

Yet another clever print (Fig. 4.6) confronted Davis's military image with deft comic flair and a talent for what might be called trompe l'oeil caricature. The trick print revealed one image right side up, and another upside down. Looked at one way, it was called *War,* with "Jeff. Rampant," according to the subtitle in one variant, an excessively armored tin soldier ready for battle:

Jeff. Davis going to War.

AN
Jeff. returning from War

Fig. 4.6 E. Rogers, *Jeff. Davis going to war* (right side up)./ *Jeff. returning from War An*
[*Ass*] (upside down). Lithograph, Philadelphia, 1861.
  (Library of Congress)

> With lion heart and frantic mien,
> The warrior seeks the battle scene.
> To risk his precious blood and fight
> For glory and his vaunted right.

Upside down, however, the viewer saw "Jeff. Subdued," a downcast army mule, of whom it was said, perhaps to fight charges of cowardice against Lincoln with similar slanders against Davis,

> When he hears the cannon roar,
> And views the dying in his gore,
> His courage fails and then, alas!
> He homeward travels like an ass.

Thus, by the end of 1861, America's two Civil War presidents had developed startlingly different images. Davis had evolved into a warrior-president—a traitor in the North to be sure, but the second coming of Washington in the South. And Lincoln had progressed in prints from railsplitter to coward and later to the statesman-heir to the Washington tradition though no Washington himself. Both had been exalted in flattering pictures and assaulted in abusive ones. But there was a significant difference. Davis regularly received pictorial abuse at the hands of Northern printmakers and Lincoln from Southern printmakers. Yet while Lincoln was also routinely maligned in prints published in his own section—as in the cartoon attacking him for allegedly responding to horrifying casualty reports with another funny story—Davis completely escaped pictorial criticism at home. It was not that he was above criticism there, at least of the written and verbal kind. But Davis was fortunate in that his image began to be tarnished most just as the Confederate printmaking industry proved able to illustrate it least.

What might have become a "great cannon game," in the words of the title of a cartoon published in *London Punch* in 1863 (showing Lincoln and Davis fighting it out in a game of billiards)—that is, an epic struggle for image predominance between two concurrently serving American presidents—instead became a landslide victory for one, when printmaking itself all but ceased to exist in the country of the other. If Davis's side was "overmatched" in "the cannon game," it became even more outdistanced in the picture game. Paper, ink, and artists were even scarcer in the Confederacy than bullets and uniforms. Demand for Davis's image may well have persisted; supply did not. And in Northern-made prints, Lincoln soon seemed the dominant combatant. In the Currier & Ives cartoon, *Caving In, or a Rebel "Deeply Humiliated"* (Fig. 4.7), in J. Tingley's series, *Cham-*

CAVING IN, OR A REBEL "DEEPLY HUMILIATED".

Published by Currier & Ives, 152 Nassau St. N.Y.

Fig. 4.7 Benjamin Day, *Caving In, or a Rebel "Deeply Humiliated."* Lithograph, published by Currier & Ives, New York, ca. 1861–1862.
(Library of Congress)

pion Prize Envelopes, subtitled *Lincoln and Davis in 5 Rounds* (Fig. 4.8), and in the unusual cruciform fold-out woodcut, *Prize Fight Between Abraham and Jeff,* the Union president was seen pummeling his Confederate counterpart in the metaphorical arena of the boxing ring. In prints, at least, Lincoln was emerging as the undisputed champion even as the outcome of the war itself remained in doubt.[20]

Dwindling Confederate manpower required that all able-bodied Southern men serve in the military, and printmakers were not exempted. Those few who remained in civilian life were assigned to the production of Confederate stamps and currency, which soon boasted the only new images of Davis in circulation. As shortages in engravers and lithographers compounded the chronic shortages of paper and ink, the once-robust *Confederate Illustrated News* began advertising desperately for printmakers. None stepped forward, and the illustrated weekly, along with separate-sheet printmaking anywhere in the Confederacy, died out.[21]

The resulting chasm in image-making power was apparent in early 1863,[22] when, coincidentally, artists arrived in the two American capitals to paint portraits of each president at midstream. James Robertson produced a reassuring, almost defiant painting of Davis. And Edward D. Marchant composed a dignified, white-tie likeness of Lincoln signing the Emancipation Proclamation. Because Southern printmaking had almost ceased to exist, however, Robertson's inspiring likeness went virtually unseen. But in the publishing hub of Philadelphia, Marchant's picture was engraved by John Sartain; and, judging from the number of surviving copies in various sizes, not to mention the later authorized editions and pirated copies it inspired, it became a best-seller.[23]

As the document Lincoln holds in his hand suggests, publishing power was not the only factor to tilt the balance of image dominance toward him; there was also the exercise of presidential power, specifically the Emancipation Proclamation. With a single stroke of his pen, Lincoln expanded the parameters of his place in both history and iconography. In prints, he was no longer just an embattled wartime president but a modern Moses. Whatever hope Davis still harbored of maintaining his tenuous link to George Washington began to fade. Southern printmaking was all but extinct while Northern printmakers came to see the "second Declaration of Independence" and Lincoln in much the same way, sometimes in much the same designs, in which they saw the first Declaration of Independence and Washington.

Lincoln distanced himself further from the nonelected Confederate president by seeking reelection in the midst of Civil War. Predictably, his candidacy unleashed another torrent of image-making, much of it like the caricatures, portraits, and posters that had proliferated four years earlier. Again, a substantial portion was critical, like *The Grave of the Union*, showing Lincoln presiding over the mass burial of the Constitution, Union, habeas corpus, free speech, and free press. Such prints typically featured stock characters who found their way into most anti-Lincoln imagery of the period: the controversial Horace Greeley, Henry Ward Beecher, and William H. Seward, to name a few.

Similarly, caricature critical of Lincoln's Democratic challenger, George B.

Fig. 4.8 J. H. Tingley, *Champion Prize Envelope—Lincoln & Davis in 5 Rounds. 2nd Round*. Woodcut cartoon, one of a series of five envelopes, published by T. S. Pierce, New York, 1861.

(*Author's collection*)

McClellan, began featuring its own recurring cast of principals, the suggestion of their rise under a McClellan presidency designed to frighten the voting public. What set this body of images apart was that some of it featured a sworn enemy of the Union: Jefferson Davis himself. Ironically, it was in this genre that Davis finally found his way into campaign graphics — not as a candidate but as an issue: the living symbol of peace at any price. It was arguably the most remarkable development in Davis image-making, although few people in the South ever saw the results.[24]

Davis is depicted as one of the supporters holding aloft the Democratic party's rickety peace platform, which barely supports its ironically military candidate for president, whom Davis champions as "my last hope." In a variation on the theme, McClellan is shown kneeling to Davis, dressed for Louis Prang's print, *Democracy,* as an evil Southern planter, slave whip in hand, knife in belt, the hopelessness of his inhumane cause betrayed by his tattered trousers. McClellan, clutching an olive branch, whimpers, "We should like to have Union and Peace, dear Mr. Davis, but if such is not your pleasure then please state your terms for a friendly separation."

According to one print by Currier & Ives (Fig. 4.9), the contrast between candidates was stark. Under McClellan, the Union would surrender and hand over to the knife-wielding Davis the representative free black soldier who had already fought for his country. "[I] am glad to hear," Davis says provocatively, "that you are willing to be governed once more by your Southern masters." Illustrating the Republican plan, a triumphant Lincoln holds a beaten Davis at bayonet point, declaring, "Your unconditional submission to the Government and laws is all that I demand . . . the great & magnanimous Nation that I represent have no desire for revenge." Davis can only admit his "madness and folly" and submit.

Not that Currier & Ives was exclusively pro-Lincoln. Reaffirming commercialism as the principal impetus for its Civil War printmaking, the New York firm also published a print, *The True Issue or "Thats Whats the Matter* [*sic*]," showing Lincoln and Davis pulling apart a symbolic national map from opposite ends while a uniformed George McClellan tries heroically to bring them (and the country) together. The print suggested that both Lincoln and Davis would destroy the Union rather than compromise on secession or abolition. Here McClellan is portrayed as the only reasonable man, trying desperately to hold the fractured country, and their improvident leaders, together. One imagines that if commerce had continued to flourish between sections during the war, printmakers like Currier & Ives would have willingly provided flattering portraits of Davis to his image-

Controversy and Public Memory

Fig. 4.9 Currier & Ives, *"Your Plan and Mine."* Lithograph, New York, 1864.
(Library of Congress)

deprived admirers in the Confederacy. Nothing doomed the Davis image in the South more than its isolation from the printmaking centers of the North.

Lincoln won the 1864 race for image dominance just as he won the election for popular and electoral votes. As emancipator and second-term president of a country whose image-makers churned out prints in New York, Boston, Philadelphia, Chicago, and Cincinnati, he became the nation's principal icon. The best that could be said of the Davis image was that it had faded from view—that is, it was no longer produced in once-thriving Confederate publishing centers, no longer produced in the North, rarely produced in Europe, and even more rarely imported through the blockade when foreign-made prints were produced. The most telling evidence of the utter collapse of Confederate printmaking, and with it the Davis image, was the complete absence of prints celebrating one of the president's finest moments: his personal intervention to quell the Richmond bread riots of January

1863. Not a single print was ever issued to commemorate his dramatic plea that day to end lawlessness on the streets of the Confederate capital.

When Jefferson Davis finally did return to prominence in popular prints, it was not as a symbol of Southern rights, or of a Washington, a commander, or a peacemaker. Instead, in the greatest irony of all Civil War iconography, he was portrayed leaving office exactly as Lincoln had been portrayed entering office: in disguise. The fate that awaited him proved even worse than that which had greeted Lincoln after Baltimore. At least the disguise that image-makers had invented for Lincoln in 1861 was male, not female.

The exact details of the event that inspired this final burst of Davis prints have been in dispute almost from the moment it was first reported in May 1865. One point is certain: while Lincoln lived he did nothing to discourage Davis from fleeing Richmond. "He ought to clear out . . . escape the country," he told one associate. And to his private secretary, Lincoln confided, "I hope he will mount a fleet horse, reach the shores of the Gulf of Mexico, and drive so far into its waters that we shall never see him again." Obligingly, Davis escaped Richmond ahead of Union invading forces. On May 10, federal cavalry caught up with the fugitive in Irwinsville, Georgia.[25]

But Davis did not stand and fight. In the dark, as he was preparing to flee his tent, he admitted in his autobiography, "My wife thoughtfully threw over my head and shoulders a shawl." Davis got only fifteen or twenty yards before he was seized, and to his captors, the first, last, and only president of the Confederacy looked to be in women's disguise. Days later, the *New York Herald* reported on Davis's "ignominious surrender" wearing his wife's raglan.[26]

Within weeks, the disguise somehow transformed itself in the popular mind — exactly as Lincoln's soft hat had metamorphosed into a Scottish tam — through the graphic arts. On June 3, 1865, *Frank Leslie's Illustrated Newspaper* crossed the dividing line between fact and fiction by portraying Davis fleeing in a dress and bonnet.

Soon, separate-sheet prints were flooding the North, portraying Davis in hoopskirts, featuring titles like "Jeff's last shift" and "The Chas-ed Old Lady of the Confederacy." In a matter of months, Davis's lifelong, aristocratic reputation was wrecked and replaced by the image, in diarist George Templeton Strong's words, of an emasculated coward "in the cumbrous disguise of hooped skirts," a coward in drag.[27]

Worse humiliation came from printmaker J. L. Magee of New York, whose view of "Hoop Skirts & Southern Chivalry" was wickedly promoted as "the only

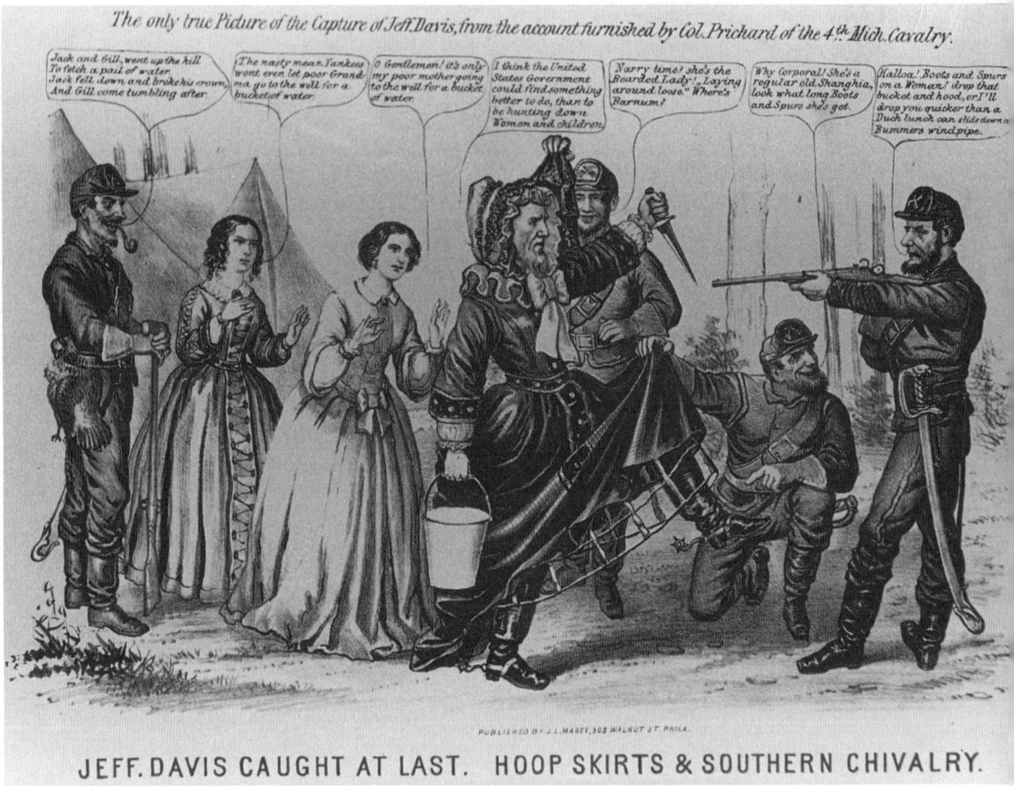

Fig. 4.10 J. L. Magee, *Jeff. Davis Caught at Last. Hoop Skirts & Southern Chivalry.*
Lithograph, Philadelphia, 1865.
(Library of Congress)

true Picture of the Capture." "She's the bearded lady," declares the soldier who lifts up her shawl, while the one who looks under her hoopskirts reports, "Look what long boots and spurs she's got." Four years earlier, a print had introduced Lincoln by suggesting his affinity for a Barnum character, the "What is It." Now one of the taunting soldiers unmasking the half-man, half-woman cries, "Where's Barnum?" Davis himself was the sideshow attraction. And it was perhaps no coincidence that all three captors—especially the general who holds his rifle on Davis from the far right—bore an uncanny resemblance to Abraham Lincoln (Fig. 4.10).

Such pictures, featuring Lincolnesque characters unmasking a disgraced Davis, could also satisfy those who believed that the Confederate president had masterminded the plot to murder Lincoln only a few weeks earlier. "Evidence is in the hands of our government," one preacher told his flock from the pulpit, "which will prove him to have been an accomplice . . . in this plot of damnable guilt." The allegations were repeated in churches throughout the North. And prints of Davis's capture that portrayed him clutching a knife were meant to suggest not that he had put up a brave fight to prevent capture but that he had been Booth's coconspirator in the murder of Lincoln.[28]

The cartoon-character Davis could call his new image a "blessing in disguise" in a second Currier & Ives interpretation of "the capture of an unprotected female." But the real Davis insisted in his autobiography that the entire story was a "lie." In her own memoirs, Varina Davis was a bit more elusive. She vehemently denied the story of the female disguise, of course, but with a jab at Lincoln and his own negative image, she admitted that to conceal her husband, "I would have availed myself of a Scotch cap and cloak." An outraged Richard S. Trapier, an Episcopalian minister from Virginia, may have understood the meaning of the new images better than most of his contemporaries. To Trapier it was nothing less than pictorial revenge for the glut of pictures that had mocked Lincoln before his inauguration. As he put it:

> Look here — taken [in] woman's clothes . . . rubbish — stuff and nonsense. If Jeff Davis has not the pluck of a true man, then there is no courage left on earth. . . . Something, you see, was due to the manner of Lincoln and the Scotch cap that he hid his ugly face with in that express car when he was rushed through Baltimore in the night. It is that escapade of their man Lincoln that set them on making up the waterproof cloak story of Jeff Davis.[29]

But the damage was done. And at the very time such prints were proliferating through the North — and undoubtedly filtering into the South as well, once surrender and peace reopened commerce between the sections — Abraham Lincoln was transfigured into national sainthood.

Lincoln was finally, retrospectively, portrayed as the conquering hero of the Civil War, marching modestly into Richmond, still the civilian, or riding triumphantly into City Point, in an odd German-made lithograph surely meant to celebrate Lincoln's arrival in the Confederate capital instead. And there could be no doubt that Lincoln had not only regained his claim to the mantle of Washington but had also emerged as his peer in the national pantheon in prints showing the two presidents together as equals, captions celebrating Lincoln for having "saved" what Washington "made." In the "coming days," one Lincoln eulogist said of the founder and preserver of the Union, "their portraits shall hang side by side." No prophecy about the American graphic arts was ever more quickly fulfilled.[30]

Of course, Jefferson Davis could never hope to achieve the image transformation that Abraham Lincoln earned with his assassination. But in prints Davis proved resilient; he was the Lazarus of Civil War iconography. Although his image died aborning with the decline of Confederate printmaking while the Southern cause lived, once the cause was lost, his image rose again from the dead.

Gibson & Company of Cincinnati was perhaps the first Northern firm to recognize this postwar commercial potential. Their 1865 lithograph, *The Last Act of the Drama of Secession,* was the only known separate-sheet print to treat the flight of Jefferson Davis without malice. Instead, Davis was shown in a dramatic torchlit scene taking leave of his despondent military family to keep the Confederate flag flying in exile. Surely this singular image could not compete with the sheer volume of hoopskirt depictions that convulsed the country with derisive laughter around the same time. But it may have been of more long-lasting importance, if only to reopen the national market for heroic images of Davis. Once Northern printmakers realized that Southerners still yearned for such portraits, they gladly filled the need.

Sometimes the competition for the reopened Southern market had comic consequences of which audiences remained unaware. One example could trace its origins almost perversely to A. H. Ritchie's influential engraving of Lincoln reading the preliminary Emancipation Proclamation to his cabinet (see Fig. 1.1, p. 10). Few images ever did more to illustrate — and perhaps enhance — Lincoln's enduring reputation as a liberator.[31]

The print proved so popular that it also inspired unauthorized copies whose creators were emboldened by the period's lax copyright enforcement. Typical was Thomas Kelly's *President Lincoln and His Cabinet/With General Grant in the Council Chamber of the Whitehouse* (Fig. 4.11), issued in New York in 1866. Here a few of the cabinet ministers were moved, Grant added, and the scene transformed from the first reading of the proclamation to a war council. But it was hardly as audacious a piracy as Kelly's second variation — *Jefferson Davis and His Cabinet. With General Lee in the Council Chamber at Richmond* (Fig. 4.12). It probably did not occur to Southern buyers that the room portrayed was unmistakably the Union White House, that the heads of Davis's ministers sat atop the bodies of Lincoln's, or that Davis's *own* head rested on Lincoln's frame. But both Davis and his admirers might well have objected had they known that the document he was shown

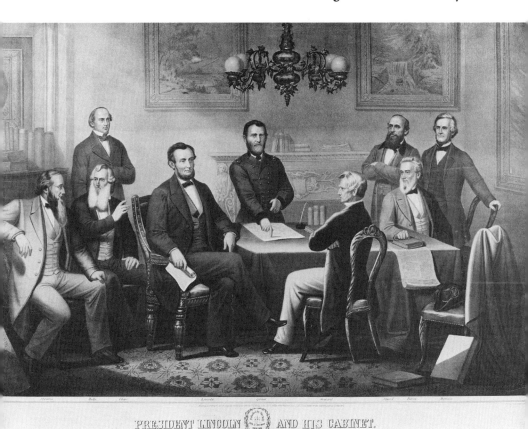

PRESIDENT LINCOLN AND HIS CABINET.

With General Grant in the Council Chamber of the Whitehouse

Fig. 4.11 Thomas Kelly, after A. H. Ritchie's engraving of a painting by Francis B. Carpenter, *First Reading of the Emancipation Proclamation Before the Cabinet, President Lincoln and His Cabinet/With General Grant in the Council Chamber of the Whitehouse* [*sic*]. Lithograph, New York, 1866.
   (The Lincoln Museum)

clutching in his right hand was, in its original incarnation, the Emancipation Proclamation.

The Davis image lived on as Davis lived on. In one last example of the mirror image phenomenon, Davis did what Lincoln had done in 1861, perhaps in a similar effort to soften his harsh image, or what remained of it. He grew a full beard to replace the devilish-looking goatee that had so long been his trademark. And he

Fig. 4.12 Thomas Kelly, after A. H. Ritchie's engraving of a painting by Francis B. Carpenter, *Jefferson Davis and His Cabinet./With General Lee in the Council Chamber at Richmond.* Lithograph, New York, 1866.
   (Library of Congress)

aged in popular prints into a benign-looking old man, an effective counterpoint to his own intensely unrepentant views about secession and the war.

   At last he was shown, too, with his family, given by Chicago lithographers Kurz & Allison in 1890 the same, softer, private image that had for twenty-five years been granted to Lincoln and his family in countless such pictures. Kurz & Allison's similar-looking Lincoln family group, produced a few years earlier, may even have served as the model for the Davis version. If so, it was the most fitting mirror image, since both Davis and Lincoln had in common the wartime loss of beloved young sons.

Further proof of Davis's rebounding image could be glimpsed, too, in a series of bizarre allegorical history prints by Kimmel & Forster of New York that may have sweetened the bitter history of war in order to appeal to Davis's admirers as well as Lincoln's. The first of these, *The Outbreak of the Rebellion,* seemed to propose that greedy capitalists, not hot-headed secessionists, had brought on the rebellion. Davis was included in the complicated scene, portrayed under a palmetto tree around which a serpent coiled. But his image was so small, and placed so deeply in the background, that it seemed almost an afterthought. Davis not only escaped blame, he may also have escaped notice.

As for the publisher's equally unusual companion piece, *The Last Offer of Reconciliation* implied only that Davis could have avoided further bloodshed at the end of the war by accepting Lincoln's invitation into a symbolic, eagle-festooned temple of liberty. Davis's gesture indicates that he rejects this offer, yet he is portrayed as dignified, not defiant. Such prints were principally designed to enhance Lincoln's reputation. But merely by allowing Davis to be portrayed side-by-side with Lincoln as his wartime equal, the prints subliminally encouraged the reconstruction of Davis's shattered image.

And shattered it certainly had been, a fate vivified in an 1862 card photograph of a "neglected picture" of Davis, a print whose glass has been broken by its presumably disgusted owner. Still the Davis image rose again. He remained a regional hero, of course, while Lincoln blossomed into national, even international fame. A substantial number of Northern-made prints continued to depict Davis as a traitor even as Lincoln entered the realm of national sainthood. And certainly the few examples examined here do not truly reflect the preponderance of Lincoln images throughout the war and into the twentieth century. There were countless more Lincoln prints than Davis prints, and after 1865 the image dominance was virtually overwhelming. Yet Davis and his image stubbornly endured, if only in the hearts of his most loyal followers; and what Roger Fischer has called "the struggle for the American soul" continued, in visual terms, in cartoon-laden humor magazines long after Appomattox and assassination suggested the possibility of sectional reconciliation.[32]

And not all postwar observers judged Davis harshly. Writing in 1868, *New York Tribune* editor Horace Greeley conceded that "each was thoroughly in earnest, thoroughly persuaded of the justice of the cayse whereof he stood forth." But he added, "Mr. Lincoln was remarkably devoid of that magnetic quality which thrills the masses with enthusiasm, rendering them heedless of sacrifice and sensible to danger; Mr. Davis was nowise distinguished by its possession. . . . But Mr. Davis carefully improved—as Mr. Lincoln did not—every opportunity to proclaim his own undoubting faith in the justice of his cause."[33]

In 1881, not long after his return to partial image respectability, Jefferson Davis published his own memoirs. Readers may have failed to notice his brief but almost poignant admission that once he had feared the burdens of the presidency because so few American presidents had ever "left the office as happy men." He knew "how darkly the shadows gathered around the setting sun" of former presidents, "and how eagerly the multitude would turn to gaze upon another orb . . . rising to take its place in the political firmament." "He must, indeed, be a self-confident man," Davis concluded, "who could hope to fill the chair of Washington" and feel "that the sacrifice of self had been compensated by the service rendered to his country."[34]

Davis never lacked for self-confidence. He could, like Lincoln, imagine himself a second George Washington. But in the end it was Lincoln who seized "the chair of Washington" as his own and Lincoln who made the ultimate sacrifice for his country. It was Lincoln to whom the multitudes turned to gaze upon, and it was Lincoln who came to dominate the political, historical, and pictorial firmament he had once shared with his mirror-image Confederate counterpart. So Davis had predicted. The father of his short-lived country fared far better in popular prints, and for far longer, than we have previously appreciated, in a country that ran out of paper and ink long before it ran out of patriotism. And while he lived, Lincoln probably fared worse than he deserved, the victim of a robust Northern printmaking industry as eager to sell caricatures to his critics as portraits to his admirers.

In a way, Lincoln's presidential image had risen from that of coward in disguise to that of military hero and latter-day Washington. Davis's image evolved precisely in reverse: from that of military hero and latter-day Washington to that of coward in disguise. Ultimately, Civil War iconography had room for many famous men, but for only one monument.

5

With Malice Toward One, or "Ridicule Without Much Malice"? Lincoln in Caricature Reconsidered

T WENTY YEARS before Abraham Lincoln ran for president, a New York print publisher, J. Childs, issued a lively cartoon sheet entitled *The Fox Chace* [*sic*]. It depicted President Martin Van Buren being hounded in the rear by rivals Daniel Webster and Henry Clay as he tries to scurry back into his foxhole—in this case, the safe haven of the White House. The Van Buren character does not realize it, but waiting for him there, armed with a sharp pitchfork, is William Henry Harrison. We know what will happen: Van Buren will be repelled by the hero of Tippecanoe, and the Whigs will take over the presidency.

The lithograph has no specific relevance to Lincoln, although the portrait of Harrison, dressed in his homespun (even though he was a former general), is something of a precursor to the Lincoln railsplitter image that emerged a gen-eration later. But the print is well worth remembering because it was owned, and displayed, by the very victim of its satirical assault: Martin Van Buren himself.

Touring Van Buren's estate in Kinderhook, New York, three years after his 1840 defeat, a visitor seemed delighted, but not terribly surprised, by the sight of it, alongside a number of other hostile cartoons, uninhibitedly on display in the former president's library. "I must not forget to remark," wrote the amused guest, "that I saw . . . scattered about the room a number of the vilest & funniest caricatures of himself. One, I recollect, exhibiting him as a fox hard chased by a pack of Whig Hounds!" This, of course, was the very image issued by J. Childs.[1]

Inventories of Van Buren's estate indicate that he owned a number of cari-catures of himself. This is an important revelation, since evidence of any kind attesting to how prints were used in nineteenth-century America is rare indeed. Information about how separate-sheet political cartoons were used is virtually nonexistent.

The Van Buren inventory offers an insight even more revealing: that the nation's eighth president, a man more often remembered as sly than as particularly good-humored, apparently boasted a healthy, thick skin where caricature was concerned, and perhaps a sense of fun, too. Certainly he seemed to handle such criticism far better than his counterparts in France; there the great pictorial satirist Daumier was fined and condemned to six months in prison merely for producing an unflattering cartoon of King Louis Philippe. The American tradition was more tolerant, and if Van Buren was able to laugh at himself it stands to reason that other subjects of political cartoons took them in stride, too, laughing along with them instead of regarding them as libelous.[2]

Unfortunately, we have no idea how Lincoln reacted to humorous prints. A visitor to his hometown on the eve of his departure for the presidential inauguration reported that Lincoln was well supplied with "wretched wood-cut representations," along with the occasional number of "indecent drawings." But there is nothing to prove that Lincoln was either convulsed or repulsed by them, that he tossed them angrily into the stove, or that he propped them up and examined them closely, much less laughed at them. There is no such proof at all.[3]

Nor is there any surviving evidence of how fellow Americans of Lincoln's era responded to these pictures. The galling absence of such documentation makes any examination of their impact on the Lincoln image at best speculative. And it makes sound judgment of their effect on popular opinion almost impossible. That may help explain why historians have barely nudged at the subject in nearly seven-score years of Lincoln biography. A writer and collector named Rufus Rockwell Wilson started it all in 1897 with two articles on Lincoln cartoons for a publication called *The Book Buyer*. Six years later, Wilson followed with a limited-edition portfolio presenting thirty-two unbound plates suitable for display, along with a brief eighteen-page commentary. Wrote Wilson in his introduction: "Lincoln in caricature is a phase of the career of the great war President that has thus far lacked adequate treatment." It still does. And a comprehensive study would require far more space, and far more illustrations, than this new analysis can possibly provide.[4]

It took more than forty years for Wilson's research to be expanded and published in a popular and accessible edition. That was in 1945, and there has not been a new study since. In 1929, Albert Shaw had produced two volumes entitled *Abraham Lincoln, A Cartoon History*. But despite the inclusion of a vast number of pictures, it was really an illustrated biography, presenting little analysis of the cartoons so liberally sprinkled on its pages. Besides, it never took its readers past 1861.[5]

More important, what little writing was done seemed fixated on portraying Lincoln as the undeserving victim of the most brutal pictorial assault in the long history of relationships between artists and leaders. To Rufus Rockwell Wilson, for example, Lincoln was nothing less than "the most bitterly assailed and savagely cartooned public man of his times." And to Stefan Lorant, the Hungarian-born photojournalist whose fascination with Lincoln images inspired a prodigious array of picture books, Lincoln was not only "treated more harshly than his predecessor had been," but he was lampooned with an unheard-of degree of "merciless fervor" and savagery. Lorant went so far as to conclude that "Lincoln withstood the attacks forthrightly, without a complaint. He bowed to the cartoonist's [*sic*] right of criticism, however cruel and unjust they were." [6] How did Lorant know this? The author never explained.

In 1984, Mark E. Neely Jr., Gabor S. Boritt, and I attempted to begin filling the void by supplying an occasional reference to caricatures in our study, *The Lincoln Image*. Inevitably, however, the cartoons we included were all but overwhelmed by the portrait prints that dominated our book. We were not surprised that one of the critics who reviewed the volume lamented the paucity of cartoons; we were more surprised that he was the only reviewer to do so. One of our team, Gabor S. Boritt, subsequently moved a step closer to broader scholarly evaluation of at least one distinct part of the Lincoln image in caricature with his paper for the Abraham Lincoln Association, "*Punch* Lincoln," planting rich seeds, one hopes, for a book yet to come. One yearns for the entire subject to be taken in hand by a scholar like Roger A. Fischer, who has written so incisively about "them damned pictures," as Boss Tweed later called them, particularly about the ways in which the monumental Lincoln has been used and misused by post–Civil War image-makers.[7]

But before the literature can mature, some long-overdue reassessment is required. Assumptions need to be challenged, and basic questions posed. For example, how were Lincoln caricatures first used? What political yearnings did they represent—both to their artists and to those who purchased them? Who exactly bought cartoons? Above all, do they prove that Lincoln was a uniquely beleaguered president, or do they simply represent part of the ongoing tradition of American press and artistic freedom, even in wartime? Exactly what, if anything, can the scores of surviving cartoons tell us about Lincoln's popularity and historical reputation?

The answer to the key question—do the cartoons serve as a gauge to Lincoln's popularity?—is: probably not. Previous studies have failed to point out factors that must be weighed in assessing the impact of political caricature on Lincoln and on the mid-nineteenth-century public. A new beginning is long overdue. It might usefully be preceded by seven truisms that a careful student of the nineteenth-century graphic arts might keep in mind when reexamining the caricatures and cartoons of Abraham Lincoln.

First, Lincoln was not singled out by caricaturists for unprecedented attack. The art of assailing American leaders in cartoons was already a well-established tradition by the time Lincoln won the presidency. Caricaturists had mocked not only Van Buren but all the presidents since Adams, and with no more or less disrespect than that with which they ultimately portrayed Lincoln. Jefferson might be shown spewing out a vomit of gold to purchase new American territories, Pierce as a rodent crawling out of a mousehole. It was business as usual from a free press in a free society. And Lincoln's opponents were as often maligned in caricature as he was. It should come as no surprise that Lincoln became the principal target of the 1860s; he was the leading personality of that decade.[8] But in the end, he was treated no more harshly than any of his rivals for the presidency, nor as brutally during his term of office than any previous, controversial occupant of the White House. Lampooned he certainly was, but as part of an established, albeit assaultive, American tradition.[9]

Second, despite hostile period cartoon prints like the well-known, frequently reproduced example of Lincoln literally letting the cat out of the bag—the cat being the campaign's "spirit of discord"—anti-Lincoln caricature never constituted the sole cartoon image of him, either during his campaigns for the presidency or during his administration. It was always accompanied, and its impact surely ameliorated, by pro-Lincoln caricature, occasionally issued by the same publishing company. But the existence of this counterbalancing body of work has seldom been recognized in the rush to judge Lincoln the victim of pictorial assault in the first degree. To begin redressing this long-standing historiographical imbalance, I will necessarily present a greater than usual number of more sympathetic Lincoln cartoons in this chapter.

Third, anti-Lincoln caricature thrived in the same realm as flattering Lincoln portraiture. There was hardly ever a period during Lincoln's national career in which print buyers could not choose to purchase either a critical lampoon or a handsome likeness. The marketplace was never dominated by negative imagery at the exclusion of positive imagery, and this has seldom been noted in the scant literature on the subject. Surely romanticized portraiture tempered the impact of acrid caricature, just as caricature most likely countered the charm of flattering portraits.

Fourth, we should acknowledge, just as Lincoln often did, that he possessed a face and a frame that seemed crafted for caricature; it hardly required exaggeration. The artist Daumier had to enlarge Louis Philippe into a "Gargantua" for effect, but the homely, unusually tall Lincoln looked rather funny just as he was. How could the cartoonists have resisted such a figure? As one comic "biography" of the period introduced him: "His head is shaped something like a ruta-bago, and his complexion is that of a Saratoga trunk. His hands and feet are plenty large enough, and in society he has the air of having too many of them." Some cartoons may have attempted to make Lincoln look ridiculous, but he entered the national stage looking rather ridiculous to begin with.[10]

Fifth, Lincoln also became an especially inviting target for lampooning because of his own, well-reported affection for funny stories. In a way, he violated what one historian later referred to cleverly as "the Republican law of gravity." Lincoln was widely known for his sense of humor — so much so that several treasuries allegedly featuring his favorite jokes were published during his lifetime. The Lincolnian catchphrase, "That reminds me of a funny story," was familiar enough to provoke one caricaturist to turn it against him in the brutal cartoon, *Columbia Demands Her Children* (Fig. 5.1), in which the furious national symbol demands the return of her 500,000 soldier "sons" killed in battle, only to be told by an appallingly insensitive Lincoln that their tragedy merely calls to mind another "story."[11]

Sixth, there has been a tendency among historians assessing these works to consider newspaper cartoons and separate-sheet political cartoons side by side. They were not quite the same. Notwithstanding the fact that a sufficient number of cartoons from *Harper's Weekly, Punch,* and *Vanity Fair* have survived, stoking private collections and illustrating modern books and magazine articles, the cuts in the weekly papers were inherently ephemeral, designed only to comment on the events of the moment and not for longtime display. The separate-sheet cartoon prints, issued for decoration, were intended for longer-term use, though they were not as permanent as portraiture.

Seventh, making cogent analysis even more vexing, separate-sheet prints were commercial ventures, more indicative of their publishers' marketing acumen than their political beliefs. Newspaper cartoons, on the other hand, did suggest an editorial point of view, but separate-sheet printmakers generally took no

COLUMBIA DEMANDS HER CHILDREN !

Fig. 5.1 J. E. Baker, *Columbia Demands Her Children!* Lithograph, Boston, ca. 1864.
  (Library of Congress)

sides; they took all sides. Their pictorial assaults were of the shotgun-blast variety, spraying at every potential victim in sight and targeted to appeal to as many customers as possible, not to support one or the other political party.

Perhaps the best way to explore these interweaving issues is to consider them concurrently as one traces the Lincoln image chronologically, keeping in mind these guiding principles: that Lincoln was applauded as often as he was assaulted, and his foes were assaulted as routinely as he was; that Lincoln's wit and physiognomy stoked the fires of cartoon by inviting lampooning; and that Lincoln was caricatured in two media at the same time, the picture press and separate sheets, each produced for a somewhat different audience.

No one can say for certain precisely which cartoon introduced Abraham Lincoln to America. Copyright registries for the period do not begin to reflect the huge number of caricatures the 1860 campaign inspired. But surely one of the very first was a crudely drawn lampoon, *Honest old Abe on the Stump* (Fig. 5.2), contrasting the Lincoln of the 1858 debates who denied presidential aspirations with his famous line, "In my poor, lean, lank face, nobody has ever seen that any Cabbages were sprouting out," to the more crassly ambitious Lincoln of the 1860 Illinois Republican ratifying convention, where he declared; "I come to see, and be seen." The result is a two-faced candidate whose self-deprecation cannot be trusted.[12]

Around the same time, a little-known Cincinnati printmaking firm, Rickey, Mallory & Company, began issuing a series of prints that have occasionally been cited to suggest the already growing hostility of cartoonists to the Republican nominee. Certainly, one of their prints, the frequently reproduced *The Undecided Political Prize Fight of 1860,* does suggest displeasure with Lincoln; he is shown being attended in his boxing match by a black man, suggesting his "dangerous" advocacy of racial equality. But it is instructive to note that his rival, Stephen A. Douglas, is shown with a drunken Irishman as his second in the ring, and Douglas's own bright-tipped nose leaves no doubt that he is inebriated, too. A clue to this unusual print's point of view can be glimpsed in the distant background: there, Constitutional Union candidate John Bell marches confidently toward the White House, cheered on by his sober supporters. This is actually a pro-Bell print.[13]

One of the firm's subsequent cartoons did warn of Lincoln's rising star in the Northeast by suggesting to the frustrated astronomer Bell (at left), as the figure of Stephen Douglas puts it, "John we better fuse." But it would be a mistake to assume from these pictures, published for ten cents each in 1860, that the firm of Rickey, Mallory "supported" John Bell. No print publisher was politically doctrinaire or commercially suicidal enough to take sides during the election of 1860; to do so would be to exclude too many customers from print sales, and above all, these printmakers were businessmen, not partisans. Besides, as election results showed that November, Bell had only 12,000 supporters in the publisher's home state of Ohio, compared to the more than 400,000 voters who cast ballots for either Lincoln or Douglas.[14]

Inevitably, Rickey, Mallory & Company came forward as well with a print showing a centrist Lincoln, well-dressed and carrying a log rail to remind viewers of his miraculous and admirable rise from poverty, dangling a pathetic Douglas from a string on one side and prodding a "no platform" Constitutional Union candidate with his rail, recognizable by the huge "Bell" covering his head to keep out troublesome discussions of the slavery issue. Perhaps the best of the Rickey, Mal-

Fig. 5.2 Printmaker unknown, *Honest old Abe on the Stump*. Lithograph, ca. 1860. *(Library of Congress)*

Fig. 5.3 Rickey, Mallory & Company, *A Political Race*. Lithograph, Cincinnati, 1860. *(The Lilly Library, Indiana University)*

lory prints—an emblem of the nonpartisan, pox-on-all-their-houses approach of nineteenth-century cartoon publishers—was the print *The Political Quadrille*. It suggested that the four presidential candidates were dancing wildly to the fiddle of Dred Scott: Lincoln with a black woman, John Bell with an American Indian, Stephen A. Douglas with a drunken squatter sovereign, and outgoing Pres. James Buchanan with the devil himself.

Another of their prints might laud Bell for patiently trying to paste the national map together while Lincoln, Douglas, and Breckinridge angrily rip it apart; and yet another, a particularly brilliant summation of *A Political Race* (Fig. 5.3), showed the long-legged Lincoln striding past his three midget rivals as cheering crowds welcome his election. (Here was one print in which Lincoln's unusual appearance worked to his advantage in caricature.)

Controversy and Public Memory

The bipartisan nature of the little-known Rickey, Mallory & Company oeuvre is not unusual. It neatly parallels the 1860 work of the far more famous lithographers, Currier & Ives of New York. On the one hand, Currier & Ives was capable of taking a pathetic Barnum sideshow attraction, the less-than-human "What Is It," and presenting him as *An Heir to the Throne*, a supposedly representative African American. The implicit, incendiary racist message was that such subhuman people would be Lincoln's probable successors in politics if voters were foolish enough to elect the Republican in 1860. Dressed disarmingly in homespun, leaning on his increasingly familiar symbolic log rail, Lincoln is depicted as a dangerous radical harboring secret plans for racial equality. "How fortunate," he remarks in the cartoon, "that this intellectual and noble creature should have been discovered just at this time, to prove to the world the superiority of the Colored over the Anglo Saxon race, he will be a worthy successor to carry out the policy which I shall inaugurate."[15]

Yet this is the same Currier & Ives who, Rufus Rockwell Wilson claimed, "played no inconsiderable part in the election of Mr. Lincoln." No doubt Wilson had in mind prints like the one that showed a log-wielding Lincoln, this time dressed in a celebratory Wide-Awake slicker, victoriously storming the White House as his three rivals fail to gain entry. Which was the true Currier & Ives? The answer is both. What was their impact on the election of 1860? Their body of work that year probably did benefit Lincoln, but not alone because of friendly cartoons (and not only in spite of hostile ones). Currier & Ives simultaneously introduced the virtually unknown Republican nominee with a series of flattering portraits, offering them for sale in catalogs, in the firm's Nassau Street emporium, and by itinerant salesmen all over the region.

Throughout the campaign, Currier & Ives proved as willing to applaud Lincoln, in one famous case reminding voters that he so dwarfed his opponents he could swallow them on the half shell, as they were willing to attack him, as in their print *The Great Exhibition of 1860*. In the latter, he was shown as suspiciously silent on the vexing issue of slavery, dancing to the tune of Horace Greeley's *New York Tribune* with no more independence than a leashed organ-grinder's monkey, his ubiquitous rail transformed into a hobby horse. The same firm that could suggest that Uncle Sam was "making new arrangements" for Lincoln to be the next tenant of the White House could also suggest, in a print from the same presses, indeed, probably by the same artist, Louis Maurer, that the only house to which Lincoln was headed was the "lunatic asylum."[16]

Lincoln might be shown tangled up in Currier & Ives's "political gymnasium," painfully straddling a wood-rail balance beam as a bandaged William Seward warns from nearby, "You'd better be careful friend, that you don't tumble off; as I did . . . for if you do you'll be as badly crippled as I am." And using a similar athletic metaphor, Currier & Ives could just as convincingly show Lincoln winning a game of baseball by using a rail bat labeled "equal rights and free territory," as the cartoon says, to strike "a 'fair ball' & a 'home run' " in the contest for the presidency.[17]

Clearly, one cannot make the argument persuasively that any publisher of caricature either helped or hurt Lincoln in 1860 — and certainly that none did so intentionally, no matter what the result of their efforts. And we still lack definitive evidence of how these separate-sheet cartoons were used, although they were probably sold in bulk by the publishers to political organizations, or to individual buyers by local newspapers aligned with one party or the other. We do know that they were offered in stores as well. Visiting New York that election season, a British journalist for Charles Dickens's weekly, *All the Year Round,* took note of a city consumed by politics — and, seemingly, by political caricature as well. His recollection reminds us that not only was there a pro-Lincoln cartoon for every anti-Lincoln cartoon, but that for every anti-Lincoln cartoon as well there was an anti-Douglas cartoon. The art of caricature spared no one. The only known contemporary description of how political caricatures were sold in the 1860 campaign suggests a haphazard marketing approach aimed at customers of all persuasions. But it succinctly and recognizably describes two well-known Currier & Ives lithographs from that image-rich 1860 campaign:

> All the way up Broadway the windows of the palatial shops are full of election caricatures. Yankee Notions shows us a rowdy in a silk hat, and boots over his trousers, taking boxing lessons ready for polling-day. Nick Nax presents us with Abe Lincoln spouting from a platform of rails, under which grins a half-concealed [slave] [Fig. 5.4]). . . . At the print-shops we see lithographs of Douglas being flogged by his mother for associating with the naughty "Nebraska Bill," [and also for defying tradition and campaigning directly for the White House] and on the other side of the door-post, a gaunt Abraham Lincoln trying to ford the Potomac and get into a very small "White House."[18]

Here again, it is instructive to point out that cartoonists did not burden Lincoln with the explosive race issue exclusively. Rickey, Mallory & Company also issued an 1860 campaign print crafted around the racist "nigger in the woodpile" theme, but in its version, a three-headed monster drawn to resemble Douglas,

Controversy and Public Memory

Fig. 5.4 Currier & Ives, *"The Nigger" in the Woodpile*. Lithograph, New York, 1860.
  (The Lincoln Museum)

Breckenridge, and Bell, not their opponent Lincoln, sat atop a pile of rails drawn
to look like a series of minstrelized African-American faces (Fig. 5.5).

Whatever their target, the questions remain of such graphics: who bought
them, how many were sold, and how did the buyers display them? Here the realm
of conjecture takes over. Two pioneering scholars of political caricature, Stephen
Hess and Milton Kaplan, estimated that such sheets were published in editions
of considerable size — 50,000 to 100,000 copies per print — and sold in the same
partisan newspaper offices that during political campaigns functioned the way
political clubhouses, and later, candidate headquarters, functioned in the twentieth century. Yet while Lincoln himself once told an admirer that he could certainly obtain copies of his Cooper Union Address in pamphlet form at the offices
of pro-Lincoln newspapers in New York or Springfield, no scholar has yet unearthed a similar piece of evidence from the candidate, or anyone else, to suggest

that Republicans could obtain pro-Lincoln, or anti-Douglas, prints at the same offices.[19]

We can conjecture that these separate-sheet cartoons were most likely displayed outside the realm of the family home. They might have been pasted to outdoor walls, like modern-day billboards, of course, or hoisted on poles, perhaps even thrown from windows, during parades and rallies. They might have been tacked up in saloons. Certainly, they decorated political headquarters across the country. (They seem often to have been sold in bulk quantities, suggesting that political organizations bought them for distribution to their faithful.) But just as surely, such corrosive caricatures never made it into the sacred family par-

Fig. 5.5 Rickey, Mallory & Company, *A Political Trinity./ Motto: there is a nigger in the wood pile.* Lithograph, Cincinnati, 1860.
(The Lilly Library, Indiana University)

lors where portraits and patriotic scenes were often displayed like sacred icons. At best, the use of separate-sheet cartoons remains something of a mystery. But surely enough clues — and enough pictures — survive to convince us that caricatures did not unfairly single out Lincoln or his party for derision and attack in 1860. They were commercially, not politically, motivated. There was enough derision to apply to all the candidates.

Moreover, although the 1860 election inspired a great many graphics, it generated no more than many previous, hotly contested national campaigns, notwithstanding the regional divisions and multitude of candidates characterizing the Lincoln-Douglas-Breckinridge-Bell election. The standard guide to the Library of Congress' collection, although by no means complete, confirms this, listing forty-four prints for the 1860 campaign, as opposed to fifty-eight in 1848 and sixty-five in 1840. The tradition of lampooning presidential candidates was an old one, and Lincoln was greeted by cartoonists no more viciously than his own rivals in 1860 and no more routinely than candidates in previous elections during the golden age of American printmaking. And it remains difficult to prove that separate-sheet cartoons designed principally to preach to the converted — that is, to anti-Lincoln cartoons for the Democrats, pro-Lincoln cartoons for the Republicans, pro-Douglas cartoons for the Democrats, anti-Douglas cartoons for the Republicans, and so on — made much of a difference in the outcome, aside from raising the entertainment value of the campaign. On the whole, the previously unknown Lincoln was helped by the print industry in 1860 because it also introduced him to the public in campaign portraits and banners. Even the cartoons that assailed him unavoidably reminded voters that he was a humble man whose ascent from the frontier was truly remarkable.[20]

It is true that Lincoln continued to inspire critical caricature after his election, but he might well have been spared some of the initial pictorial outcry had he not provided cartoonists with an irresistible opportunity to lampoon him by passing through Baltimore en route to his inauguration in disguise. *Harper's Weekly* quickly gave graphic vision to the story with its multipanel cartoon, *The Flight of Abraham* (Fig. 5.6), portraying Lincoln as a coward for fleeing Baltimore in disguise. This was a newspaper caricature, not a display sheet, but it exerted influence as the first of many to ridicule Lincoln for sneaking into Washington, and it undoubtedly inspired other printmakers. Perhaps, too, because the weekly illustrated papers reached a multitude of readers of differing political persuasions, including pro-Lincoln men, the print may have had a greater impact on fueling

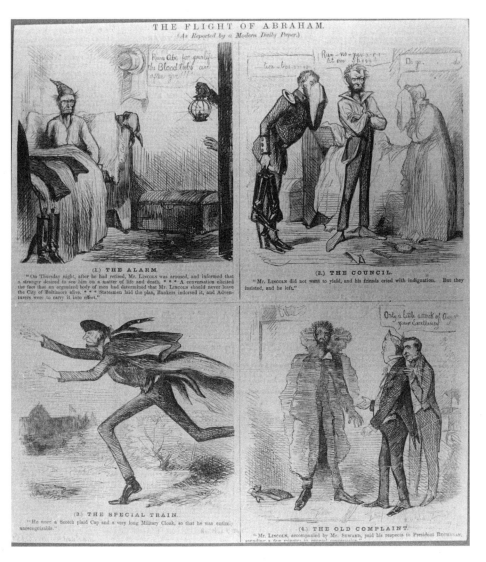

Fig. 5.6 Printmaker unknown, *The Flight of Abraham.* Woodcut engraving from *Harper's Weekly,* New York, March 9, 1861, in four panels: "The Alarm," "The Council," "The Special Train," and "The Old Complaint."

(*Author's collection*)

the anti-Lincoln image than the separate-sheet campaign cartoons designed for the Democratic party zealots.[21]

Yet, by the same token, a newspaper like *Harper's* was principally influential only until the next edition arrived, much as today's weekly magazines can cause a stir when first published, until the appearance of the subsequent issue, when the next celebrity, and the next tragedy, come to dominate coverage. Thus, in our own era, was boxer Mike Tyson's widely parodied ear-biting gambit eventually eclipsed by hagiographic cartoon tributes on the death of Princess Diana, which in turn yielded in frequency of coverage to the widely caricatured sexual proclivities of sports announcer Marv Albert, and ultimately to a relentless cartoon barrage commenting on President Clinton's dalliance with Monica Lewinsky. Overexposed by electronic coverage, such stories emerge in a burst of images and then just as quickly evaporate. Even in the nineteenth century, when pictures were less common and more prized, weekly cartoons surely drifted ultimately into memory as well, although the Scotch-cap symbol remained a prop in Confederate graphics, and some Northern-made prints as well, for years—the reminder of Lincoln fleeing in disguise an automatic accusation of his supposed lack of character.

But at the same time, some postinaugural cartoons celebrated Lincoln, particularly those issued in separate sheets for more permanent contemplation. He was the giant father figure trying to coax naughty secessionist bathers back to the comforting shores of the Union; or, in a series of cartoon-decorated patriotic envelopes, a prize-fighter confronting, and ultimately defeating, his Confederate counterpart, Jefferson Davis. Or, as Currier & Ives saw it, in one wartime cartoon sheet, Lincoln was capable of rendering Davis deeply humiliated in this early test of national resolve (see Figs. 4.8 and 4.7, respectively).

Over the next four years, the anti-Lincoln image assumed new dimensions and introduced potent new symbols into the nation's visual lexicon. As Americans came to know their president better, artists added new layers to the established Lincoln image of the railsplitter who rose from poverty to political success. But no matter how original each message, throughout the Civil War the anti-Lincoln image was inspired and propelled by four basic factors:

1. Impatience at home over the protracted rebellion and later opposition to the change in war aims from preservation of the Union to the destruction of slavery. This reaction was evidenced in pictorial commentary that ranged from loyal opposition to near-Copperheadism but, remarkably, seemed always to escape censorship by federal au-

thorities, even when nonpictorial newspapers were being shut down for being less offensive in words.

2. The natural hostility of the Confederacy, whose artists attacked Lincoln with a savagery unequaled anywhere else in the world, but usually with such minimal skill and such meager distribution that their pictures had little impact.

3. Old-fashioned American capitalism, as Northern printmakers continued throughout the war to churn out both pro- and anti-Lincoln display sheets, manufacturing pictures that appealed to audiences of every political persuasion.

4. Foreign opposition to the Northern side in the American Civil War, vivified in the picture press of Europe, particularly in England, where the *Illustrated London News* and *Punch* assailed Lincoln unrelentingly.

And Lincoln remained subject to vigorous visual criticism as well in the netherworld between Europe and America, between North and South. The most lively and ingenious lampoons came from German-born Baltimore artist Adalbert Volck, who contributed some of the best-known anti-Lincoln caricatures of the war. Volck's brilliant etchings included one of the best of the Scotch-cap prints, showing Lincoln traveling in a freight car, recoiling from the sight of a black cat, and the vitriolic *Worship of the North* (Fig. 5.7), in which a jesterlike Lincoln, clad in an armored helmet, presides over the ritual sacrifice of a white man on an altar of "Negro worship" and other radical ideas. However brilliant his work, though, Volck's influence was limited to the fellow local Confederate sympathizers he could enlist as subscribers to his secretly printed portfolios. Volck's impact on the anti-Lincoln image has long been overstated.[22]

So, in a way, has the influence of Confederate cartoonists operating within Confederate territory (see chapter 6). Needless to say, their work was stingingly and unrelentingly critical, and in some cases deeply malevolent. But their ambition far exceeded their reach. They were seen only in the Confederacy, where Lincoln's image was already in ruins. These efforts, pointed and poisonous alike, spoke directly to Lincoln's already-committed enemies. They surely influenced few and converted fewer. And their impact was certainly not enhanced by their lack of artistry.[23]

Any full consideration of British caricature of Lincoln would consume at least another entire study. There are many scalding works in this archive, such as the famous cartoons from *Punch* showing Lincoln shockingly indifferent to the pleas of a victimized black during the New York draft riots, or whipsawed by too much debt and too few soldiers. But it is important to remember that the British car-

Fig. 5.7 Adalbert Volck, *Worship of the North*. Etching, Baltimore, ca. 1862.
(*Harold Holzer*)

toonists might also acknowledge Lincoln as a warrior: either as the conqueror
of New Orleans or the classic Roman God of War. A systematic evaluation of
British-made Lincoln caricature is long overdue.[24]

When that comprehensive study is at last undertaken, the pictures should be
examined within the long, rich tradition of British caricature, whose own golden
age was, according to Diana Donald, often "abusive, scurrilous, and volatile" —
and gleefully so. It was an age in which "Grand Caricatura" exhibitions attracted
throngs of visitors, and eager patrons collected fancy volumes of bound cartoons
to display at home. Any new study of Lincoln's image in Britain, if it considers
the portrait prints issued there concurrently, will probably indicate a more even-
handed approach than we have previously been led to expect. And it will most

likely remind us as well that the influence of pro- and anti-Lincoln British cartoons alike was in the main restricted to the people who saw them — the British —
and never really filtered into American public opinion until twentieth-century
historians began positioning them as barometers of taste and popularity in Lincoln's era.[25]

A far more reliable test — offering renewed proof of the cartoonists' eagerness
to represent all things to all customers, to reinforce biases and appeal mostly to
the previously converted — came with the 1864 presidential reelection campaign.
Once again a full study of just this neglected slice of Lincoln iconography is both
justified and overdue. But even in its absence the case can again be made that
Lincoln was subjected to no more criticism than his opponent.[26]

True, Lincoln would be viciously assaulted in 1864 cartoon prints, occasionally with even more blatant cruelty than in 1860, but no more than was Democratic
challenger George B. McClellan, whose 1864 caricatures accused him of being a
coward. Once again, printmakers proved no less willing to criticize Lincoln than
his rival and were as likely in turn to praise one as the other.[27]

Two of the tougher assaults came from the anonymous printmaker who visu-
alized the libel that Lincoln had asked for music when visiting the casualty-strewn
battlefield of Antietam. A companion print to this work, showing Lincoln as a
hapless sportsman making pathetic efforts to secure peace (Fig. 5.8), could be
purchased at the offices of the *New York World,* the anti-Lincoln paper that had
invented the comic-song-at-Antietam story in the first place.[28]

Yet another series of critical images came from the imaginary character Maj.
Jack Dowling, a fictional political commentator invented in Boston during the
Jacksonian Era. The images were published by Bromley & Company in New York
at a price of twenty-five cents each, sixteen dollars per hundred, suggesting that
they were designed for bulk distribution to Democratic organizations throughout the country. And these, too, seem to have been issued in collaboration with
the busy *New York World.*[29] No less abusive, and far more ingenious, was an anonymous printmaker's provocative suggestion in *Behind the Scenes* (see Fig. 1.6, p. 21),
that Lincoln advanced the rights of African Americans because he was black himself. In a scene showing him playing Othello in a stage production (an appropriate
venue for a president whose love of the theater had become well known), Lincoln
declares, in lines from Shakespeare used here to turn against one of his most frequently praised virtues, "I am not valiant neither: — But why should honor outlive
honesty? Let it go all." Nearby is a trash basket crammed with discarded Supreme
Court decisions and the Constitution itself, while cabinet ministers assembled

Fig. 5.8 Printmaker unknown (monogrammed initials "CAL"), *The Sportsman upset by the Recoil of his own Gun.* Lithograph, New York, 1864.
(Library of Congress)

downstage comment darkly about ignoring election results and expanding arbitrary arrests.

Similar campaign prints portrayed Lincoln presiding over the burial of the Constitution in *The Grave of the Union* or introducing the shocking idea of the mingling of the races in *Miscegenation* (Fig. 5.9), in which Lincoln is accompanied by an African-American woman. The prints were hard-hitting, well drawn, and daring, but again it must be remembered that for every *Abolitionist Catastrophe* by Bromley, there was a Democratic *Catastrophe* print warning of very much the same doomsday scenario—from the opposite side of the political spectrum. Bromley & Company does, however, appear to be the only cartoon publisher of the Civil War era to do business exclusively in pro-Democratic, anti-Republican images. No example has yet been found of a Bromley print offering less than a villification of Abraham Lincoln.

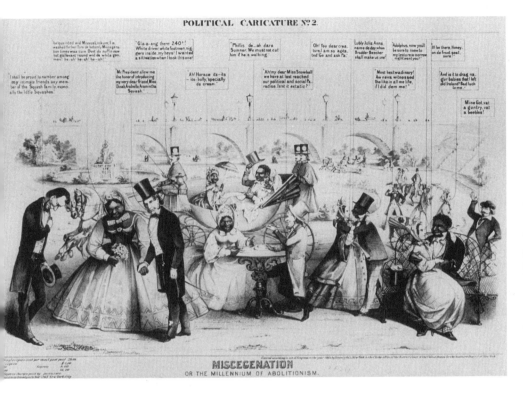

Fig. 5.9 Bromley & Company, *Miscegenation/Or the Millennium of Abolitionism*. Lithograph, New York, 1864.
(Library of Congress)

There is ample pictorial evidence to suggest that McClellan was similarly eviscerated in satirical prints of the campaign, whether assailed for his party's political platform, a frequent metaphor, or for consorting with the enemy. In the words of the caption to one such picture, McClellan promised the country "Union with Slavery." Lincoln promised "Union with Freedom." To some cartoonists, the campaign still seemed like a joke. Indeed, *Harper's Weekly* concluded in a memorable cartoon that "the Young Napoleon" reminded Lincoln of a joke (Fig. 5.10), a clever adaptation of the Gulliver theme that had been used in cartoons at least since the days of the first Napoleon. Here the diminutive general holds a little shovel, reminding voters that as a commander he had always seemed more eager to dig in than to attack.[30] Conversely, Lincoln might remind McClellan of a joke, though in J. H. Howard's brilliant campaign cartoon, placing both candidates into the gravedigger's scene of *Hamlet*, Lincoln appears as the grisly remains of a fellow of

WEEKLY. [SEPTEMBER 17, 1864.

Fig. 5.10 Printmaker unknown, *This reminds me of a little joke.* Woodcut engraving for
Harper's Weekly, New York, March 9, 1864.
  (The Lincoln Museum)

infinite jest while McClellan is shown playing the notoriously indecisive prince
who could never choose whether to be or not to be.[31]

    As in 1860, campaign cartoons were not the only graphics on view in 1864:
countless prints recalled Lincoln as the Great Emancipator, using his revolutionary document to break the backbone of rebellion or literally unshackling the slaves

from bondage. Some were extraordinarily powerful images, and they may have served to balance, or even render shallow and partisan, the pictorial criticism. Above all, one group of 1864 prints cannot be assessed without considering the other.

On election day, a nervous Lincoln had complained, "It is a little singular that I who am not a vindictive man, should have always been before the people for election in canvasses marked for their bitterness . . . [and] great rancor." But such experiences were not really unique to candidate Lincoln, even though he might well have felt so after the bruising 1864 campaign. It is likely that George B. McClellan felt he had been treated with malevolence, too.[32]

Lincoln decisively won the 1864 election, leading *Punch* to compare him to a phoenix rising from the ashes of American constitutional liberty, states' rights, and fiscal solvency. Here, in the words of the poem that accompanied the cartoon, was a new twist on the mythical bird, topped with "Old Abe's rueful phiz" and soaring "to new life from its fiery immersion":

> As the bird of Arabia sought resurrection
>> By a flame all whose virtues grew out of what fed it,
> So the Federal Phoenix has earned re-election
>> By a holocaust huge of rights, commerce, and credit.[33]

Perhaps *Punch* was also expressing frustration at its own inability to influence the American electorate—persuasive evidence in itself of the comic weekly's limited reach. And it is probably safe to say that Lincoln did not decisively lose the campaign of negative images that season, either, or, for that matter, the battle of caricature and cartoon that had been waged for nearly five long years.

Ultimately, with Lincoln's assassination and martyrdom in 1865, even *Punch* apologized for its years of criticism with its famous cartoon, *Britannia Sympathizes with Columbia,* accompanied, ironically, by a poem by Tom Taylor, the author of the play Lincoln was watching when he was murdered. Speaking for shamed cartoonists and "scurril-jester[s]" everywhere, the writer grieved that Lincoln

> had lived to shame me from my sneer,
>> To lame my pencil, and confute my pen—
> To make me own this hind of princes peer,
>> This rail-splitter a true born king of men.

The poem offered a belated tribute to the funny-looking man who had inspired so many lampoons:

Controversy and Public Memory

> You lay a wreath on murdered Lincoln's bier,
>   You, who with mocking pencil wont to trace,
> Broad for the self-complacent British sneer,
>   His length of shambling limb his furrowed face.[34]

But perhaps this frequently quoted apology was excessive and even a bit self-serving. British artists had criticized Lincoln no more frequently or viciously than American cartoonists. Here, as in England, artists had continually balanced their criticism with pictorial praise and, in the Union, with equally venomous caricatures of Lincoln's opponents. The "mocking pencil" had been much in evidence, but no more than the flattering crayon of the lithographers and the handsome steel plates of the engravers. Even before Lincoln's martyrdom, the print media had succeeded in creating an indelible persona for Lincoln—perhaps not precisely a king among men, as Tom Taylor's poem posthumously suggested, but certainly a giant among them—the great, tall westerner who had risen from the backwoods by virtue of hard work and honesty, to command the greatest army ever assembled, to fight to save American democracy, and to liberate the slaves.

Some caricatures may have castigated him, but Lincoln changed American iconography and iconology as surely as he changed America itself. Before Lincoln's prominence in both national life and popular prints, it is instructive to remember, the national symbol of Uncle Sam bore a close resemblance to the father of his country, George Washington. But during and after Lincoln's presidency, Uncle Sam slowly evolved into a figure who looked far less like the founder of the Union than the savior of the Union (see Fig. 2.7, p. 47). Caricature, the medium that supposedly treated Lincoln with unrelenting savagery, managed also to help transform his image into that of American icon.[35]

Lincoln's transfiguration ultimately convinced one French cartoonist, in yet another variation on the Gulliver theme, that in retrospect the American president had become even grander than Uncle Sam. As the artist accurately predicted in his drawing of a giant Lincoln examining a tiny Uncle Sam under a magnifying glass, American presidents, and America itself, would thenceforward be expected to live up to the standards of its sixteenth president. Despite caricatures, or perhaps, more accurately, with a little help from caricature, Lincoln had become the dominant figure not only of American history but of American visual memory. Writing to one of his favorite Shakespearean actors in 1863, Lincoln concluded, "I have endured a great deal of ridicule without much malice; and have received a great deal of kindness, not quite free from ridicule. I am used to it."[36]

Where caricature was concerned, praise never came quite free of ridicule, and ridicule seldom came with much malice, at least no more than what American audiences and American leaders alike had come to expect from the genre. Political caricature of the Lincoln era derived from a long-standing, good-humored, American free-press tradition. Lincoln caricature seems today as pointed and sharp and humorous as it must have been to American audiences of the Civil War era. Was Lincoln singled out as a particular victim of the caricaturists? No more than other leading figures of history.

One can only imagine him roaring with laughter at some of these pictures. One can only hope to yet find evidence that he did. It was, after all, "ridicule without much malice." And, as he admitted, he was "used to it." After generations of taking the joke far too seriously, we should become used to it, too.

Lincoln in Confederate Cartoons:
A "Lean-Sided Yankee," Seldom Seen

THE FAMILIAR FACE of Abraham Lincoln is juxtaposed on a woman's body, and the figure is shown struggling to restrain "the naughty boy Gotham who would not take the Draft." Lincoln wears satin shorts and circus tights as a "daring American acrobat" hanging perilously upside down from rings labeled "emancipation" and "paper money." Lincoln skulks through Baltimore garbed in a Scotch cap and ankle-length military cloak, regalia that evolved, thanks to such pictures, into a period metaphor for cowardice. A scandalously insensitive Lincoln calls for a comic song while walking indifferently among the dead and wounded of the Battle of Antietam. Or Lincoln is metamorphosed into a treed "coon" being held at bay by an angry, rifle-toting John Bull, the iconic symbol of England.

Throughout the Civil War, in these now-classic caricature designs, and in innumerable other inventive, satirical graphics, Abraham Lincoln was hilariously lampooned in engraved and lithographed cartoons. In many, he became the lightning rod of Civil War caricature, the symbolic scapegoat for the ills of a divided country. And such cartoons as the examples just described achieved, and maintained, wide twentieth-century visibility through frequent reproductions in biographies and histories of the war.

Seldom did such a leader seem more physically suited to pictorial lampoon. Although the political culture of nineteenth-century America routinely subjected its leaders to such artistic rough-housing, Lincoln seemed uniquely constructed for pictorial parody. As a contemporary recalled, "The peculiar characteristics of Mr. Lincoln made him a splendid subject . . . his long arms and legs, his leanness of flesh, his big nose and mouth, and his disheveled hair were distinguishing features for the exaggerations of the cartoonists" who, in turn, "labored to make him appear ridiculous." Their labors were often quite successful. The cartoonists' Lincoln legacy (see chapter 5) is provocative and memorable, and in many cases genuinely funny.[1]

But their work is also frequently misinterpreted. The now-classic composi-
tions just recounted were published either in the North or in England. (In fact,
the work produced in the *Illustrated London News* and *Punch* is among the richest,
most inventive, and surely the most frequently reproduced Lincoln caricature ever
produced anywhere.) And the output of Lincoln caricature was a no less lively
and ubiquitous genre in that section of America where Lincoln maintained executive authority. Even though that authority occasionally extended to the imprison-
ment of critics who overstepped the administration's boundaries of lawful dissent,
Northern cartoonists maintained a lively political attack on Lincoln throughout
his presidency. Yet such was decidedly not the case in the states that separated
from the Union in 1861. The fact is, although some modern illustrated books and
magazines occasionally make it appear otherwise, Lincoln caricatures and cartoons produced in the Confederacy itself, where opposition to him arguably ran
fiercest, were a rare genre indeed during the Civil War.

Moreover, when such work was created, it was almost always uninspired in
message and crude in execution. Although understandably bitter in tone, Southern caricatures lacked the deftness and wit exemplified during the war by Matt
Morgan and John Tenniel in *Punch*, Henry L. Stephens in *Vanity Fair*, or the lithographers who issued separate-sheet cartoons in the Union. Even the most widely
read modern Civil War aficionados would most likely be hard-pressed to name
the leading lights of Confederate caricature. The truth is, there were none.

In a way, the dearth and ineptitude of Confederate caricature is somewhat
surprising, since, as Robert Philippe has noted, such art traditionally "flourishes
at periods of crisis in the established order." Caricature, Philippe stresses, proves
a potent "weapon" during such times, capable of "synthesizing power" through
"dynamic, aggressive, fertile and creative" attempts to "enlarge, shrink, or disguise people to reveal their many faces at a glance." Capable of "bolstering hope,"
Philippe points out, caricature can temper "the depression of defeat with the sweet
consolation of revenge." Yet Confederate cartoon artists, by and large, took no
notable revenge on Abraham Lincoln and sought little consolation for their military setbacks and civilian suffering by attacking him pictorially.[2]

This is not to suggest that Confederate caricature of Lincoln was nonexistent.
A noteworthy body of graphic material survives, and it certainly merits attention
within any analysis of the iconography of the Civil War. But examples were so few
that when Martin Abbott gathered a study of "President Lincoln in Confederate
Caricature" in the 1950s, he sidestepped the puzzle entirely by interpreting the

term "caricature" as applying exclusively to the nonpictorial attacks on Lincoln "in Confederate newspapers." According to Abbott:

> Of all these efforts at inspiring loyalty, probably none was more effective . . . than that originated by newspaper editors in their depictions of Lincoln, through caricature, as the embodiment of all that was coarse, brutal, boorish, and crude among their foes. By lampooning every foible, some real and many imagined, they fashioned a stereotype which, though seldom subtle and often grotesque became the popular image . . . the symbol toward which Southerners directed their venom and spite for the Northern enemy.[3]

Aside from missing the obvious point — that Confederate cartoonists created a body of work that needs to be judged outside the realm of written material produced by "newspaper editors" — Abbott raised another questionable issue. He claimed that Southern anti-Lincoln caricature was effective. Judged by ubiquity alone, such a claim would be difficult to prove.

Precisely applied, the word "caricature" means a distortion of character (from the Italian verb *caricare:* to overload or burden). As a medium of editorial criticism, caricatures predate even newspapers. From the time of the Renaissance, in the words of Ron Tyler, "Caricature and cartoon were long-practiced and sophisticated methods of expression."[4]

By the time of the American Revolution, some colonial newspapers had already published caricatures; and separate-sheet cartoons, issued as display pieces, began appearing with some regularity before the beginning of the nineteenth century. At the outset, in the absence of a native tradition, artists tended to copy the style of European caricaturists. But by the Jacksonian Era, American themes were being richly and routinely mined by American artists. The development of lithography, a faster and cheaper process than that of steel engraving, sped the proliferation of separate-sheet caricatures (which, as newsworthy commentary, required timely publication to ensure sales interest). In Lincoln, ultimately, artists were presented with the most irresistibly comical political face and figure since Old Hickory himself. One would have expected the impulse to lampoon would have flowered most richly in the region where he was the most unpopular.[5]

Certainly, as Abbott has noted, the editorial criticisms of Lincoln in the South were swift and severe. As the *Houston Telegraph* commented in summer 1860: "Lincoln is the leanest, lankiest, most ungainly mass of legs, arms and hatchet face ever strung upon a single frame. He has most unwarrantably abused the privilege which all politicians have of being ugly." The *Richmond Examiner* remarked that

Lincoln seemed the "delightful combination of Western country lawyer with a Yankee bar-keeper." And the *Southern Confederacy* offered a similar assessment, this time in rhyme:

> His cheek bones were high, and his visage was rough,
> > Like a middling of bacon — all wrinkled and tough;
> His nose was as long, and as ugly and big,
> > As the snout of a half-starved Illinois pig;
> He was *long* in the legs, and *long* in the arms —
> > A *Longfellow,* indeed, save the poetic charms.

Commenting on a newly published woodcut of Lincoln that appeared that campaign summer in *Harper's Weekly* — not coincidentally, it might be noted, a Northern publication — the *Charleston Mercury* declared of the Republican candidate: "A horrid looking wretch he is, sooty and scoundrely in aspect, a cross between the nutmeg dealer, the horse-swapper, and the night man, a creature fit evidently for petty treasons, small strategems and all sorts of spoils. He is a lank-sided Yankee of the unlovliest and of the dirtiest complexion."[6]

The mere sight of Lincoln's visage staring back from that same *Harper's Weekly* edition was enough to inspire postal workers in yet another Southern city to refuse to deliver copies of the issue bearing the nominee's portrait. Unquestionably, the power of pictures was deeply felt in the prewar South. The only problem was that the feeling did not prove strong enough to inspire a regional graphic response once the war was under way.

And that has begged the baffling question: Why are Confederate caricatures so rare — despite such passionate hatred of Lincoln — and especially when such art might have proven an effective weapon for maintaining Confederate morale by rallying what Robert Philippe has called "visual irreverence"? Finally, why do the Confederate Lincoln caricatures that were produced seem so artistically inferior to the product appearing simultaneously in New York, Philadelphia, Boston, and even London?

The problem, like so many other issues facing the country in 1860, was purely sectional. Confederate artists did not abandon Lincoln as a subject because of lack of interest or will, but because of lack of resources and talent. Just as the war might be said, on one level, to have represented a struggle between agrarian and industrial societies, in which victory by the technologically superior North seemed almost inevitable, the war of art was also stacked heavily on the side that boasted the most weapons: the North, whose cities housed by far the greatest number of print publishers. The South simply did not have an equally thriving publishing industry at the outbreak of the Civil War. New York City led in the publication of caricature-rich picture weeklies and separate-sheet engravings and lithographs, with other Northeastern cities boasting considerable picture publishing business as well (Louis Prang in Boston, the Sartain family in Philadelphia, and Louis Kurz in Chicago, to name but three examples).

The Old South did have three significant antebellum printmaking centers. But one, New Orleans, fell to the Union early in the war, and Confederate publishing there died aborning. Baltimore, home to perhaps the region's strongest picture-publishing industry, remained with Maryland in the Union; and while federal troops occupied it, anti-Lincoln printmaking was forced to retreat underground. Finally, there was Richmond; but once that city became the capital of the Confederacy, printmaking energies there began focusing exclusively on the production of "official" prints — the portraits for new national currency and postage stamps — and independent, for-profit, and certainly for-amusement printing dwindled.[7]

Besides, many printmakers were immigrants, most lithographers German. And like the preponderant majority of all such newcomers to America, they had settled in the North. Louis Kurz migrated from Germany to Chicago. German-born Louis Maurer, who designed many of the 1860 anti-Lincoln cartoon sheets for Currier & Ives, moved to New York. German Louis Prang ended up in Boston and Anton Hohenstein in Philadelphia.

It should be remembered that many Southern picture patrons had by the outbreak of the war grown accustomed to the products of Northern and European illustrated presses, to which residents of even the most remote outposts could subscribe by mail. Understandably, little thought was given to developing a regional counterpart. In a peculiarly logical way, it probably no more occurred to political partisans in, say, prewar Louisiana, to set up a picture press capable of national distribution, than it would have occurred to a Bostonian to build a plantation and grow tobacco. The work was being done well enough elsewhere.

Certainly Northern caricaturists were kept busy lampooning Lincoln during the 1860 presidential campaign, and their work may have been exported to the South. Yet the market for such pictures surely dwindled in those states where Lincoln's name did not even appear on the November ballot. These prints were meant as tools for electioneering within the two-party system, and the curious canvas of 1860, listing four candidates, two of whom (Lincoln and John C. Breckinridge) proved regional, not national, probably limited the normal demand for and flow of campaign prints, including caricatures. Why buy an anti-Lincoln campaign print in a state in which Lincoln was not even a candidate? In those Southern states in which his name did appear, Lincoln was thoroughly routed, but there is no way to know whether Northern-made caricatures made a difference, or even whether they enjoyed local distribution. Print-publishing records, notoriously scarce, are even less conclusive where cartoons and caricatures are concerned.

After the 1860 election, the print-buying marketplace changed abruptly. Lincoln took office, Southern states began seceding, and with commerce in all goods inhibited, the circulation of anti-Lincoln caricature from the North slowed to a trickle, even though Southern demand might have been increasing. The time had arrived at last for development of a home-bred alternative. The demand never slackened, but the supply did.

One of the first indigenous, separate-sheet Confederate caricatures of this period appeared soon afterward, an anonymous lithographed cartoon, probably issued in Richmond, *Virginia Paw-sing*. In the print, the seceding Southern states were portrayed, oddly enough, as rats fleeing from a tomcat identified as "Uncle Abe." As the cat offers an "enduring thought"—that "Nothing is going Wrong, Nothing really hurts Anybody, Nobody is suffering anything" (paraphrasing Lincoln's awkward words of reassurance en route to his inauguration)—he reaches out and nabs "Virginia" with his paw while the other states escape. Though snared, the Virginia rat insists, "We can get out on the 4th of July as well as on the 4th of March (Lincoln's inauguration day), a reference to the state's initial reluctance to join the secession bandwagon, coupled with a challenge to use the forthcoming Independence Day to declare independence for the Old Dominion. But with the largest rat in the composition, one labeled with the Lincolnian credo, "The Union Must and Shall Be Preserved," lying on its back, dead, impaled by an American flag, the message is clearly that the Union has already been effectively dissolved and that Virginia's "paw-sing" on the brink of secession could no longer be tolerated.

Virginia eventually followed her sister states into the Confederacy, of course. And with Southerners cut off from their Northern illustrated weeklies, with their dependable access to European papers subject to Union blockade of the region's ports, and with export restrictions effectively embargoing the sale of Northern-made separate-sheet prints, the Confederacy finally began developing a regional publishing industry to meet demand for images, caricature included. A major Richmond-based illustrated weekly soon appeared, but considering the market potential, not as soon as might have been expected.

Controversy and Public Memory

The *Southern Illustrated News* did not publish its maiden issue until September 13, 1862, eighteen months after Lincoln's inauguration. For the next two years, it offered its readers pallid but earnest imitations of *Harper's Weekly* and *Frank Leslie's Illustrated Newspaper*, despite high hopes for success at the outset, which prompted even the potential competition at *Leslie's* to marvel, "The South is . . . resolved to have pictures of its own. By one bound it leaps to the dignity of an illustrated newspaper." This journal alone constituted the sole source of regularly published Southern political caricature during the Civil War.[8]

With the new nation mobilized for defense and survival, there was little likelihood that the Confederacy could overnight develop a profitable picture-publishing industry, audience demand notwithstanding. Predictably, chronic shortages in talent and supplies eventually took their toll. Artists and printmakers were conscripted into military service or assigned to government printing. The *Southern Illustrated News* began using its own pages to advertise unashamedly for engravers. As for raw materials, an agent for the Marietta Paper Mill admitted in 1863, "I have on hand a few bundles of paper . . . and this will be the last for some time," adding, "you know Paper Makers are not to be had in the South." Another Georgia mill, destroyed by fire, started advertising for recyclable raw material: "old ledgers, old cash books, old journals, old bank books, of any kind either all written over, partly written over, or not written over at all." But there was nothing available, not even for government presses "urgent for paper."[9]

The supply of ink dried up, too. Southern printers were compelled to experiment with shoe black, fig juice, pomegranate, and other unsatisfactory substitutes. One observer vividly remembered one such futile effort, providing a rare firsthand glimpse into the frustrating art and commerce of Confederate printmaking, working against huge odds to create pictures for their potential customers (and with it, a priceless social comment on forced labor in the Confederacy):

> There was a large room in the building set apart for that purpose and in it benches were set up with slabs to grind up lamp black. The varnish was made up in a large iron kettle and the litho[grapher]s had to take turns superintending it. They were assisted by darkies who were nearly all slaves. It was quite a sight to see them stripped to the waist, mixing and grinding ink. Of course, the ink was only half ground and it was with some difficulty that we could print and keep it on the stone.[10]

Some books and journals continued to trickle in from Europe (diarist Mary Chesnut recorded reading an issue of *London Punch* as late as July 1864). Some

Southern painters, meanwhile, continued efforts to portray new Confederate heroes. But for many artists, the North remained the place to live and work. David H. Strother, for example, born in Virginia and celebrated under the pseudonym "Porte Crayon" as a chronicler of the Old South, chose to work for *Harper's New Illustrated Monthly Magazine* during the war and eventually joined the Union army. He remained capable of producing anti-Lincoln caricature (his lampoons of the disastrous 1862 Peninsular campaign twitted both the commander in chief and his general, George B. McClellan), but as one Southern critic pointed out angrily, Strother had become to his native section "a cowardly renegade, who after having offered his services to the Governor of Virginia to help her in her need, became alarmed over the prospect of losing his gains as a writer and caricaturist in the Northern journals . . . [and] went to the enemy because they offered him better pay and higher rank."[11] By 1862, with the pool of artistic talent drained and supplies gone, the Confederate separate-sheet printmaking industry collapsed. And the *Southern Illustrated News,* its woodcut illustrations dwindling in number and eroding in quality as the months went by, failed even to survive through the penultimate year of the war, 1864.

In a sense, that the chronically deprived Confederate graphics industry was able to produce any Lincoln caricatures at all under such circumstances is remarkable. Had not its output been so routinely exaggerated by previous scholarship, it might be tempting to marvel at the results without commenting on their failings: the efforts proved neither bright nor artistically mature; at best they were poorly drawn and uninspired, and at worst, went beyond satire into the realm of illustrated invective.

John H. Parrott's lithographed sheet-music cover for a curious composition, *The Abe-Iad,* for example, published in 1861 in Alexandria, Virginia, fell into the former class of rudimentary artistry. The composition featured a crude stick figure of Lincoln in Scotch cap and military cloak, fleeing from a lone Confederate soldier firing a weak cannonball toward his rear as Lincoln cries, inexplicably, "Catch who." The caricature concludes in verse: "The former place, the changing face / The Midnight race, the present place / of Honest Abe." The music inside by one F. Bartenstein featured lyrics by a "J. P. McRebel." Only a single known copy survives, which suggests that audiences of the day were as mystified by the hodgepodge as are those attempting to parse it today.[12]

Its appearance, however, did signal the fact that Lincoln's increasingly notorious nighttime passage through Baltimore en route to his inauguration was inspiring caricaturists South as well as North. But although lampoons continued into 1864 routinely to accoutre Lincoln in the trappings of the Baltimore episode, Confederate cartoonists abandoned the potent symbols, an error of omission sufficient on its own to cast their understanding of the medium into serious doubt.

Even cruder was a poster cartoon issued in Richmond in 1861 by an unknown artist, *The Fate of the Rail-Splitter, Abe Lincoln* (see Fig. 4.4, p. 85). The print depicted a military hanging, the victim presumably Lincoln (although he was portrayed as clean shaven, probably because no photographs of the newly bearded president had reached the South, and its artists simply did not know what he looked like). The only clever device in the cartoon was the insertion of a wooden gallows made of Lincolnian log rails, a reference to those products of Lincoln's backwoods past that so often had been used, both as positive and negative symbols, in Northern-made cartoons. A similarly crude effort, *Abduction of the Yankee Goddess of Liberty*, offered a malevolent portrayal of Lincoln as the "Prince of Darkness" and the "monster of perdition," an attack that approached overkill without sufficient skill to bring off its point.

Woodcuts in the Confederate press were no more sophisticated. The *Southern Illustrated News'* November 8, 1862 effort, *Masks and Faces: King Abraham before and after issuing the Emancipation Proclamation* (Fig. 6.1), managed to suggest Satanic influences on Lincoln as well as the president's supposed monarchical despotism. Unmasked as the devil incarnate, he triumphs over a barren landscape wasted by war, in the background of which a gallows waits at the ready atop the unfinished stump of the Washington Monument, cleverly suggestive of the Union's lack of commitment to the memory and ideals of the Founders (especially powerful at a time Confederate President Davis was being compared to George Washington). Visible in the foreground is a scroll labeled "January 1, 1863," a reference to the day on which Lincoln's Emancipation Proclamation was scheduled to take effect (thus revealing his deviltry and justifying punishment by hanging).[13]

The January 31, 1863 issue of the news weekly featured another prototypical Confederate caricature, *Schoolmaster Lincoln and His Boys* (Fig. 6.2), showing the president (again, inexplicably, clean shaven) about to rap with a ruler labeled "Constitution" his battle-scarred field commanders. Here again, a rich pictorial idea went unfulfilled at the hands of an engraver of minimal skill. None of the bandaged and hobbled generals bears the slightest resemblance to identifiable generals. The figure-drawing is poor, the perspective weak, and the background all but indecipherable. Once again, a small detail offers a saving grace: a spittoon on the floor near "schoolmaster" Lincoln, suggesting his incurable crudeness. Yet

MASKS AND FACES.

King Abraham before and after issuing the EMANCIPATION PROCLAMATION.

Fig. 6.1 Printmaker unknown, *Masks and Faces./King Abraham before and after issuing the EMANCIPATION PROCLAMATION*. Wood engraving, published in the *Southern Illustrated News*, Richmond, November 8, 1862.
  (*The New York Public Library, Astor, Lenox, and Tilden Foundations*)

Controversy and Public Memory

THE SOUTHERN ILLUSTRATED NEWS.

SCHOOLMASTER LINCOLN AND HIS BOYS.—*Lincoln*—Waal, boys, what's the matter with yer; you haint been hurt, hev yer? *McClellan.*

Fig. 6.2 Printmaker unknown, *Schoolmaster Lincoln and His Boys*— Lincoln— *Waal, boys, what's the matter with yer; you h'aint been hurt, hev yer?* Wood engraving, published in the *Southern Illustrated News*, Richmond, January 31, 1863. *(The New York Public Library, Astor, Lenox, and Tilden Foundations)*

Confederate caricaturists were still producing work that seemed a century or more behind that of their Union counterparts in style and sensibility.

Only occasionally did Southern cartoonists during the war show glimmers of inventiveness and advanced technique. The *Southern Illustrated News*' February 28, 1863 classic, *Master Abraham Lincoln Gets a New Toy* (Fig. 6.3), ingeniously presented Lincoln (yet again beardless) as a hapless puppeteer touting the potential of his latest creation, "Fighting Joe" Hooker, oblivious of the nearby storage shelves stacked with now-useless puppets named Scott, McDowell, Frémont,

Banks, Burnside, and McClellan. Here, though the execution was again inferior, the concept might be called inspired.

A more muddled effort was *John Bull-ied!* (Fig. 6.4), published November 14, 1863, a cartoon showing an armed but presumably not terribly dangerous Lincoln threatening the prime minister of England "with unparalleled ferocity" in order

Fig. 6.3 Printmaker unknown, *Master Abraham Lincoln Gets a New Toy.* Wood engraving, published in the *Southern Illustrated News,* Richmond, February 28, 1863. *(The New York Public Library, Astor, Lenox, and Tilden Foundations)*

Controversy and Public Memory

Fig. 6.4 Printmaker unknown, *John Bull-ied!* (Lincoln and Lord Russell). Wood engraving, published in the *Southern Illustrated News*, Richmond, November 14, 1863. *(The New York Public Library, Astor, Lenox, and Tilden Foundations)*

to thwart the export of weapons to the Confederacy, while he appears eager to accept them himself. Here, as in most *Southern Illustrated News* caricatures, the cartoon's ambition far exceeded its artistic reach.

But *I Wish I Was in Dixie* (Fig. 6.5), published February 27, 1864, achieved a measure of brilliance by utter simplicity, and its late appearance suggests that dearth of engravers notwithstanding, *Southern Illustrated News* artists were on their way to producing more mature work had the paper endured. Here the *News* portrayed Lincoln as a melancholy troubadour (a familiar motif in American and European caricature), dressed in a Union suit, an old swallowtail coat, and a battered hat as he strums a banjo and sings a "plaintive air." Before an outsized map of the capital he has failed to conquer, Lincoln sings of lost opportunities, an unused amnesty proclamation stuffed into his jacket pocket, and an ax and maul, symbols of his railsplitting days on the prairie, piled uselessly against the wall. This stellar February 27, 1864 cartoon may be unique in Confederate iconography—beyond even the concession, at last, to Lincoln's bewhiskered appearance. It employed subtle imagery and confident restraint. But it was the exception, not the rule.

It is instructive to note that the best cartoon ever published in the *Southern Illustrated News, One Good Turn Deserves Another* (Fig. 6.6), appearing March 14, 1863, and showing a Scotch-capped Lincoln offering arms to a reluctant slave in

PLAINTIVE AIR—Sung nightly in Washington by that Celebrated Delineator, ABRAHAM LINCOLN.

Fig. 6.5 Printmaker unknown, *"I Wish I Was in Dixie!"* Wood engraving, published in the *Southern Illustrated News,* Richmond, February 27, 1864.

(The New York Public Library, Astor, Lenox, and Tilden Foundations)

ONE GOOD TURN DESERVES ANOTHER.

Fig. 6.6 Printmaker unknown, *One Good Turn Deserves Another*. Wood engraving, first published in the *Illustrated London News* and reprinted in the *Southern Illustrated News*, Richmond, March 14, 1863.

(The New York Public Library, Astor, Lenox, and Tilden Foundations)

return for his freedom, did not originate with the Richmond weekly itself. Rather, it was adapted from the *Illustrated London News* of August 9, 1862 — (the addition of the ubiquitous Scotch cap the one original modification from the English original) in what might be inferred to be a pictorial admission that, vitriol notwithstanding, Confederate caricaturists had failed in their efforts to build a strong visual case of their own against Abraham Lincoln. In the end, judged alone by the tiny body of anti-Lincoln work produced during the Civil War, they barely tried.

The pervasive myth of a vigorous anti-Lincoln graphic tradition in the Confederacy may be largely attributable to the work of one proficient and prolific artist: Adalbert Johann Volck, whose cleverly rendered etchings mocked Lincoln brilliantly. But contrary to overzealous early biography, Volck was no Confederate artist, and it is his frequent and unjustifiable inclusion in that category that is the probable cause of the relentless inflation of the reputation of wartime Confederate caricature. Rather, Volck was a Confederate sympathizer — a Copperhead artist who lived and worked in occupied Baltimore and was thus compelled to publish his work secretly, and to only a small handful of local subscribers, while the war raged. Described by a recent biographer as a "violent" rebel partisan, Volck issued a large body of brilliant pro-Confederate, anti-Lincoln prints under the pseudonym "V. Blada," a thinly disguised, abbreviated anagram of his name spelled backward. But the deserved fame of his oeuvre came with its postwar republication and by frequent reproduction of his plates as illustrations in twentieth-century books.[14]

That said, Volck's genius should not be underestimated. Had he enjoyed the unfettered publishing freedom of Northern artists like Thomas Nast or Frank Bellew, he might well have emerged as one of the Union's most acclaimed and influential caricaturists; had he lived in the Confederacy, he would surely have taken his place as the greatest of its practitioners of that art. But recognition and influence eluded Volck while he worked.

His *Sketches from the Civil War in North America,* seen by few contemporaries, featured some of the most caustic but ingeniously devised and cleverly rendered Lincoln caricatures in all of Civil War iconography: the president-elect, disguised in Scotch cap and military greatcoat, recoiling from the sight of a black cat in *Passage Through Baltimore;* a satanically inspired devil in *Writing the Emancipation Proclamation;* and a bumbling commander in quest of an impossible dream of conquest, along with the reviled Gen. Benjamin F. Butler, in *Don Quixote and Sancho Panza* (Fig. 6.7).

In perhaps the quintessential Volck etching, Lincoln is seen as an idol in the

Fig. 6.7 Adalbert Volck, *Don Quixote and Sancho Panza*. Etching, Baltimore, ca. 1864. *(Harold Holzer)*

form of a court jester, consecrating the bloody sacrifice of a white man on the altar of "Negro Worship" in the complex, inspired composition, *Worship of the North* (see Fig. 5.7, p. 120). As the blasphemous ritual unfolds, abolitionist Henry Ward Beecher wields the sacrificial knife, Generals Halleck, Frémont, and Scott look on, and Horace Greeley prays toward a statue of John Brown.

Despite such profoundly demonstrated ingenuity, however, Adalbert Volck's artistic skill far exceeded his public reach. Later in life, he ironically voiced "the greatest regret ever to have aimed ridicule at that great and good Lincoln." Yet had he published freely outside the Union during the Civil War, he alone might have elevated the craft of Confederate caricature to that of an art. But he had no opportunity to do so, and claims by historians such as William Murell, who argued that Volck made "the most important contribution to American graphic humor in the South," are wildly exaggerated. The Confederacy had no Volck, least of all Volck himself.[15]

Early in the Civil War, the *Charleston Daily Courier* had predicted laughingly that the initials "C.S.A." would come eventually to signify "Couldn't Stand Abe." But even if Confederate audiences could not, their hatred would never be fueled by hostile graphic art equal to their contempt for the subject. And then, only a week after the war ended, Lincoln was idealized as a martyr, a metamorphosis recorded as well as influenced by a rush of heroic portraiture and repentant caricature from the North and abroad. In the end, the North prevailed artistically as well as militarily.

As for the greatest of all "Confederate" caricaturists, Adalbert Volck lived on until 1912. He was buried in Baltimore's Loudon Park Cemetery, "in the shadow" of the local monument to Stonewall Jackson, a symbol of the Confederate lost cause. Ultimately, that cause was lost in art as surely as it was lost on the battlefield.[16]

Part Three

The Gift of Language and the Language of Gifts

7

"Tokens of Respect" and "Heartfelt Thanks": How Lincoln Coped with Presidential Gifts

I N SPRING 1982 President Ronald Reagan filed his income tax return for the previous year and, in making it public, unleashed a flurry of press coverage of a fascinating but seldom-discussed topic: the many gifts, both valuable and sentimental, that our chief executives seem inevitably to amass while in office. President Reagan's returns showed that he had received (and was prepared to declare as income) some $31,000 in gifts, including such items as silver picture frames, a crystal wine cooler, three pairs of boots, a Chinese porcelain dinner service, and a horse blanket.[1]

While it lasted, the gift controversy was closely watched by the press. Overlooked, however, was the fact that presidential gift hoarding was not a new—not even a twentieth-century—phenomenon. And it would probably have surprised many observers that among the presidents who cheerfully accepted valuable presents while in office was Abraham Lincoln, who not only never disclosed them publicly (he was not required to do so), but occasionally forgot even to thank his admirers and benefactors. Had the tax and disclosure laws of the 1980s prevailed during the 1860s, the Lincolns would surely have had to contend with embarrassing revelations of their own. But such scrutiny was unheard of during Lincoln's time, as was the ethic that today seems automatically to link such presentations to ulterior motives by their donors. Coincidentally, the news of the Reagan family's gift controversies broke in the press exactly 120 years after the daughter of a Dakota judge gave Lincoln a pair of pipestone shirt studs. Lincoln freely and without inhibition accepted them, thanking her for her "kindness" and telling his "dear young friend" that he thought the studs "elegant."[2]

Among the countless other items, including edibles and potables, that Lincoln collected during his presidency were things he could not possibly have wanted or needed, even cases of alcoholic beverages. As his friend Ward Hill Lamon remembered, Lincoln "abstained himself, not so much upon principle, as because of a total lack of appetite." Once, nonetheless, a group of New York admirers "clubbed together to send him a fine assortment of wines and liquors," a White House secretary recalled. A dismayed Mary Lincoln was sure that her husband would object to keeping the gift at home, and so she donated the spirits to local hospitals. There, she hoped, doctors and nurses could "take the responsibility of their future."[3]

Edible gifts, fruits and dairy products, for example, the Lincolns seemed more than willing to keep and consume. And then there were the attractive and valuable presents—pictures, books, animals, garments, and accessories—which Lincoln almost always kept for himself. The following litany could be said, in a sense, to constitute Lincoln's own retrospective public accounting. The list serves also as a reminder of how much the rules of conduct for public figures have changed.

For this reason, this chapter is in no way intended as an indictment. No one who observed Lincoln ever thought him obsessed with personal gain or fashion. As Lamon said, "He was not avaricious, never appropriated a cent wrongfully, and did not think money for its own sake a fit object of any man's ambition." But as Lamon added, Lincoln also "knew its value, its power, and liked to keep it when he had it." Lincoln did, in fact, defend the aspiration to wealth, declaring once that "property is desirable . . . a positive good in the world."[4] He had even admitted, half-jokingly, in 1836, "No one has needed favours more than I, and generally, few have been less unwilling to accept them."[5] That attitude also characterized his policy where gifts were concerned—gifts that began arriving soon after his nomination to the presidency and that continued arriving until the day of his assassination.

The gifts came from sincere admirers and blatant favor-seekers, princes and patriots, children and old women. Some people made presentations in person; others sent their presents by express. On at least one occasion, a simply wrapped little package looked so suspicious that Lincoln seriously entertained the notion that it had been designed to explode in his face.

But most of the gifts, from modest shawls and socks to expensive watches and canes, seemed to reflect a deep and widespread desire among Lincoln's admirers, chiefly strangers, to reach out to the troubled president and to be touched back in return by the acknowledgment that was certain to follow. It is difficult for the modern American living in the era of the so-called imperial presidency to comprehend the emotional and political simplicity inherent in these gestures. The inviting intimacy of the nineteenth-century presidency—not to mention the code of conduct that encouraged such expressions of generosity—seems to have vanished. In Lincoln's day it thrived. And so the gifts began arriving after Lincoln won the Republican presidential nomination in 1860.

Lincoln received dozens of presents during the campaign, ranging from the potentially compromising to the presumptuous. In the former category was a barrel of flour that arrived "as a small token of respect for your able support of the Tariff." [6] In the latter was a newfangled soap that inspired Lincoln to write self-deprecatingly to its inventor: "Mrs. L. declares it is a superb article. She at the same time protests that *I* have never given sufficient attention to the 'soap question' to be a competent judge." Nonetheless, Lincoln admitted that "your Soap . . . [has] been used at our house." [7]

Whether the soap improved Lincoln's appearance can only be judged by looking at period pictures — and the candidate received a number of those as gifts also. "Artists express their happiness in supplying him with wretched wood-cut representations," reported journalist Henry Villard. Lincoln admitted that his "judgment" was "worth nothing" when it came to art, but that did not stop art publishers from sending him examples of their work, possibly eager for endorsements that could be marketed to enhance sales. Engraver Thomas Doney, for example, sent a copy of his mezzotint portrait of the nominee, and Lincoln admitted that he thought it "a very excellent one." But he cautioned, "I am a very indifferent judge." Chicago lithographer Edward Mendel won a more enthusiastic endorsement (written by a secretary, signed by Lincoln) for his so-called "Great Picture" of the nominee. Acknowledging its receipt, Lincoln called it "a *truthful* Lithograph Portrait of myself." A month later, the full text of his letter was reprinted in a newspaper advertisement offering the print for sale. A possibly more wary Lincoln signed a more noncommittal acknowledgment when a Pennsylvania jurist shipped copies of an engraving whose costly production he had underwritten. Though it was a far better print portrait than any other received by the president, and was the only one based on life sittings, Lincoln expressed thanks but no opinion. Perhaps he truly was a "very indifferent judge." [8]

What Lincoln really thought about some of the odder gifts that arrived in Springfield in summer 1860 can only be imagined. The "Daughters of Abraham" sent what Lincoln described as "a box of fine peaches," accepted with "grateful acknowledgment." A "bag of books" arrived in the mail. From Pittsburgh came a "Lincoln nail," which had been manufactured, according to its presenter, "in a moving procession of 50,000 Republican Freemen" on "a belt run from the wheel of a wagon connected with a nail machine." Each of the Lincoln nails had the initial *L* carved on the nailhead. "Show it to your little wife, I think it will please

The Gift of Language and the Language of Gifts

her curiosity," wrote the Pittsburgh man, adding, "I hope God that the American people may hit the nail on the head this time in your election — please accept this little token enclosed [as] a tribute of respect to yourself & the greate cause of Truth and Justice which you represent."[9] With similar gifts arriving almost daily, Lincoln's temporary office in the Springfield State House began soon to look like "a museum, so many axes and wedges and log-chains were sent the candidate." According to the daughter of Lincoln's private secretary John G. Nicolay, the future president "used them in his explanations and anecdotes of pioneer days, making them serve the double purpose of amusing his visitors and keeping the conversation away from dangerous political reefs." Perhaps the best known of the office props — a familiar accessory visible in the background of period engravings — was an oversized wood-link chain, "sent to Mr. Lincoln by some man in Wisconsin," Nicolay wrote, "who . . . being a cripple and unable to leave his bed . . . had the rail brought in from the fence, and amused himself by whittling it out." The resulting "neat wooden chain," the *New York Tribune* cautioned, though made from a rail, was not made from "a Lincoln rail, as everybody is disposed to think." Another gift received around the same time, "a pair of first-class improved wedges, for splitting logs," proved similarly misleading. "Everybody persists in looking upon [them] as relics of Mr. Lincoln's early life," the *Tribune* observed, "but which really were sent to him only about a fortnight ago, together with a fine ax."[10]

In June came a historic relic, a "rustic chair" that had stood on the platform of Chicago's Wigwam when Lincoln was nominated. It was made of thirty-four different kinds of wood, "symbolizing the *union* of the Several States, including Kansas," explained the college professor assigned to forward the memento to the candidate. "Though rude in form," the chair was meant to serve as "an Emblem of the '*Chair of State*,' which . . . it is believed you are destined soon to occupy." Lincoln "gratefully accepted" both the chair and "the sentiment" but, with secession no doubt much on his mind, wondered, "In view of what it symbolizes, might it not be called the 'chair of State and the Union of States?' The conception of the maker is a pretty, a patriotic, and a national one."[11]

Many gifts were similarly inspiring, or at the very least, friendly. If ever there was danger to Lincoln in accepting every package that came through the mails, it could never have been more apparent than on October 17, when he received this warning from a Kansas man: "As I have every reason to Expect that you will be our next President — I want to warn you of one thing — that you be Exceeding [*sic*] Careful what you Eat or Drink as you may be Poisoned by your Enemys as was

President Harrison and President Taylor." That same day, a Quincy, Illinois, man sent Lincoln "a Mississippi River Salmon," with the hope that "the fish . . . caught this morning will grace the table of the next President of the United States."[12] There is no record that Lincoln responded to either letter, but it is amusing to wonder how he reacted to the receipt of the food concurrently with the receipt of the warning.

After Lincoln's election three weeks later, the steady stream of gifts grew into a flood. "A pile of letters greeted him daily," wrote Villard, and many packages bore gifts. Books, for example, arrived frequently. "Authors and speculative booksellers freely send their congratulations," Villard explained, "accompanied by complimentary volumes." Many of the other gifts were homespun, others merely "odd."[13]

In December one New York "stranger" sent two specially made hats.[14] "A veritable *eagle quill*" arrived from Pennsylvania, plucked from a bird shot in 1844 in the hope that the pen fashioned from it would be used by Henry Clay to write his inaugural address. For sixteen years its owner had waited for a candidate of equal stature to win the presidency. And thus he wrote to Lincoln:

> I . . . have the honor of presenting it to you in your character of President elect, to be used for the purpose it was originally designed.
> What a pleasing, and majestic thought! The inaugural address . . . written with a pen made from a quill taken from the proud and soaring emblem of our liberties.
> If it be devoted in whole or in part, to the purpose indicated, would not the fact, and the incident be sufficiently potent to "Save the the [*sic*] Union."[15]

The new year of 1861 brought more valuable gifts, including several canes. One redwood, gold, and quartz-handled example was judged "highly artistic and in very good taste" by the visiting sculptor, Thomas Dow Jones.[16] Mrs. Lincoln received a sewing machine; some Cleveland millworkers sent Lincoln a Model T-rail; and Chicago City Clerk Abraham Kohn sent a watercolor he had painted, complete with Hebrew inscriptions.[17]

A poignant allusion to Lincoln's "beau ideal," Henry Clay, was offered with the arrival in February of a decades-old portrait medallion from a limited run of 150. One had been "reserved, at the time," explained the presenter, "with the intention . . . of presenting it to the citizen of the school of Henry Clay, who should first be elected to the Presidency. . . . I rejoice that that event has, at last, occurred." Lincoln replied with "heartfelt thanks for your goodness in sending me this valu-

The Gift of Language and the Language of Gifts

able present," expressing the "extreme gratification I feel in possessing so beautiful a memento of him whom, during my whole political life, I have loved and revered as a teacher and leader."[18]

More clothing arrived as well. A Boston wholesaler sent what Lincoln acknowledged as "a very substantial and handsome overcoat," an "elegant and valuable New Year's Gift." A westerner sent "an Union grey shawl, made of California wool ... together with a pair of family blankets" as samples of "Pacific State weaving." Thanking the donor for the "favour," Lincoln noted the "forward state of California manufactures which those articles exhibit."[19] Shortly before leaving for Washington, as he stared into a mirror admiring a new topper sent by a Brooklyn hatter, Lincoln reportedly remarked to Mary Lincoln, "Well, wife, there is one thing likely to come out of this scrape, any how. We are going to have some *new clothes!*" As he had predicted, three days before his fifty-second birthday, Titsworth & Brothers, Chicago clothiers, donated an expensive suit for Lincoln to wear at his inauguration.[20]

That same day he received a more peculiar gift, one that arrived in a package so "suspicious" looking that Thomas D. Jones, for whom Lincoln was then sitting for a sculpture, worried at first that it might contain "an infernal machine or torpedo." Jones placed it "at the back of the clay model" of Lincoln's head, "using it as an earthwork, so, in case it exploded, it would not harm either of us." It turned out to be a whistle fashioned from a pig's tail, which Tad Lincoln was soon using "to make the house vocal, if not musical ... blowing blasts that would have astonished Roderick Dhu." Both the suit and whistle inspired Villard to file this report on February 9:

> A large number of presents have been received by Mr. Lincoln within the last few days. The more noteworthy among them are a complete suit ... to be worn by his excellency on the 4th of March. . . . The inauguration clothes, after being on exhibition for two days, will be tried on this evening—a most momentous event to be sure. . . . The oddest of all gifts to the President-elect came to hand, however, in the course of yesterday morning. It was no more or less than a whistle, made out of a pig's tail. There is no "sell" in this. Your correspondent has seen the tangible refutation of the time-honored saying, "no whistle can be made out of a pig's tail" with his own eyes. The donor of the novel instrument is a prominent Ohio politician. . . . Mr. Lincoln enjoyed the joke hugely. After practicing upon this masterpiece of human ingenuity for nearly an hour, this morning, he jocosely remarked, that he had never suspected, up to this time, that "there was music in such a thing as that."[21]

Even as Lincoln prepared to leave for Washington the following day, he was asked to accept one more gift — specially designed for the inaugural journey. A Burlington, Iowa, man proposed making a mail-armored shirt for Lincoln to wear for protection. He even offered to plate it "with gold, so that perspiration shall not affect it." The instructions continued: "It could be covered with silk and worn over an ordinary undershirt. . . . I am told that Napoleon III is constantly protected in this way." Lincoln declined the offer, and left Springfield armorless. But he was not long without other sorts of gifts. En route to Washington he was routinely given baskets of fruit and flowers. And in New York he was given silk top hats from both Knox and Leary, rival hatters. Asked to compare them, Lincoln diplomatically told the *New York World* that they "mutually surpassed each other." [22]

Lincoln moved into the White House on March 3. But the flood of gifts only increased. A carriage came from some New York friends, and a pair of carriage horses was reportedly sent to Mrs. Lincoln. Presumably, they were hitched to-gether.[23] A more modest donor, disclaiming personal ambition but hearing that Lincoln was "constantly besieged with applications for office," thought "that something nice & palatable in the way of good Butter might do you good, & help to preserve your strength to perform your arduous duties." Along with the tub of butter came this advice: "Keep a good strong pickle in this butter & in a cool place then it will keep sweet till July." [24] There is no record of whether the butter stayed fresh through the summer, but during the same hot months, Secretary of State William H. Seward gave the Lincolns a quite different gift: kittens. The pets were intended for the Lincoln children, but the president reportedly liked to have them "climb all over him" and grew "quite fond of them" himself.[25]

John Hancock's niece sent Lincoln "an interesting relic of the past, an auto-graph of my uncle, having the endorsement of your ancestor, Abraham Lincoln, written nearly a century ago: humbly trusting it may prove an happy augury of our countrys future history." Lincoln returned his "cordial thanks" for both the relic and "the flattering sentiment with which it was accompanied." [26] There were gifts to warm the spirit and spirits to warm the president. A "poor humble Mechanic" from Ohio forwarded "one pair" of slippers worked by my Little Daughter as a present for you from her." A Cincinnati man recommended the "quick and whole-some nourishment" of "pure wine" made from grapes he had planted himself. He sent a case.[27]

Some gifts were meant to preserve honor. When a Brooklyn man read that no American flag flew over the White House, he asked for "the privilege, the honor, the glory" of presenting one. The "ladies of Washington" made a similar offer a few days later. No reply to either has been found.[28] Nor did the president respond to an offer of toll-free carriage rides on the Seventh Street Turnpike or to the gift of "Dr. E. Cooper's Universal Magnetic Balm," good for "*Paralysis,* Cramps, Colics, Burns, Bruises, Wounds, Fevers, Cholera, Morbus, Camp Disease, &c. &c. &c.," despite advice that Lincoln "trust it as you would a true friend, — administer it to your own family and friends (especially to Gen. Scott)." But he did respond to the gift of "a pair of socks so fine, and soft, and warm" that they "could hardly have been manufactured in any other way than the old Kentucky fashion." [29]

Foreign dignitaries usually sent far more exotic presents, some so valuable that Lincoln decided he could not accept them. When the king of Siam, for example, presented "a sword of costly materials and exquisite workmanship" along with two huge elephant tusks, Lincoln replied, "Our laws forbid the President from receiving these rich presents as personal treasures. They are therefore accepted . . . as tokens of your good will and friendship for the American people." Lincoln asked Congress to decide upon a suitable repository, and it chose the "collection of curiosities" at the Interior Department. Yet another gift offer from the king of Siam — a herd of elephants to breed in America — was refused outright, with Lincoln explaining dryly, "Our political jurisdiction . . . does not reach a latitude so low as to favor the multiplication of the elephants." [30]

Gifts from domestic sources were not only less cumbersome but also proper to accept. White rabbits arrived for Tad, and in the ultimate expression of faith that Lincoln had attained the stature of his political hero, Henry Clay, Clay's own snuffbox was presented by Clay's son.[31] Earlier, when a Massachusetts delegation presented Lincoln with an "elegant whip," the ivory handle of which bore a cameo medallion of the president, he replied, according to Nathaniel Hawthorne, who witnessed the scene, with "an address . . . shorter than the whip, but equally well made":

> I might . . . follow your idea that it is . . . evidently expected that a good deal whipping is to be done. But, as we meet her socially, let us not think only of whipping rebels, or of those who seem to think only of whipping negroes, but of those pleasant days which it is to be hoped are in store for us, when, seated behind a good pair of horses, we can crack our whips and drive through a peaceful, happy and prosperous land.[32]

"There were of course a great many curious books sent to him," Francis Bicknell Carpenter recalled, "and it seemed to be one of the special delights of his life to open these books at such an hour, that his boy [Tad] could stand beside him, and they could talk as he turned over the pages." Some books, however, proved troublesome. Such proved the case when actor James H. Hackett sent his *Notes and Comments upon Certain Plays and Actors of Shakespeare*. Lincoln had seen Hackett perform Falstaff in *Henry IV* at Ford's Theatre, but when he acknowledged the gift the president admitted, "I have seen very little of the drama." A proud Hackett published the letter for his "personal friends" only, but the press got hold of it and quoted it liberally to illustrate Lincoln's cultural ignorance. Hackett later apologized.

Canes were sent in abundance as well, typically hewn from some hallowed wood. Lincoln received one cane made from the hull of a destroyed Confederate ship, *Merrimac,* and another from a sunken Revolutionary War ship, *Alliance.* Yet another, featuring a head carved in the shape of an eagle, was made from wood gathered in the vicinity of the 1863 Battle of Lookout Mountain. Journeying to Philadelphia in June 1864 to attend the Great Central Sanitary Fair, Lincoln was given a staff made from the wood of the arch under which George Washington had passed at Trenton, New Jersey, en route to his inauguration.[33]

Were all these gifts made with no ulterior motive in mind? It is impossible to say—although Lincoln might have sniffed out one potentially compromising situation in 1863 when Christopher M. Spencer gave him a new Spencer rifle and offered a demonstration of the proper way to assemble it. A large War Department order could make a munitions man wealthy overnight, and there was no shortage of new military gadgetry sent to the White House. Presidential clerk William Stoddard reported that his own office eventually "looked like a gunshop."[34] Similarly, when an Indian agent, fighting a theft charge, petitioned Lincoln to intervene for him, enclosing quilled moccasins as a gift, Lincoln took off his boots and tried them on with a smile. But he did not intervene in the case. Later, when California railroad men presented Lincoln with an exquisite, thirteen-inch-long spun-gold watch chain, it was quite possible the delegation was thinking not so much about how elegant the adornment would look on the presidential waistcoat but how lucrative would be government support for the building of roadbeds in the West. Lincoln apparently did not much care. He posed for his most famous photographs wearing the ornament.[35] An ideal companion piece, a gold watch, arrived in late 1863, forwarded by a Chicago jeweler in behalf of the local Sanitary Commission. Lincoln expressed thanks for the "humanity and generosity" of which he had "unexpectedly become the beneficiary." It seemed the jeweler had promised the watch to the largest contributor to the recent Ladies North Western Fair. Lincoln had donated a copy of the Emancipation Proclamation, which sold for $3,000, winning him the prize.[36] Lincoln seemed pleased also by a rather hideous chair presented by a frontiersman, Seth Kinman (Fig. 7.1); his wife even kept a carte-de-visite of the chair in the White House family album, and the wear and tear it reveals suggests it was handled and examined often.[37] He admired an afghan made by two New York girls ("I am glad you remember me for the country's sake"), and the Vermont cheese forwarded by an admirer from Danby ("superior and delicious"). He liked the book of funny lectures he received from a comic "mountebank" and the "very excellent . . . very comfortable" socks knitted by an eighty-seven-year-old Massachusetts woman. Lincoln thought these "evidence, of the patriotic devotion which, at your advanced age, you bear to our great and just cause." [38]

There was much more: a "very comfortable" chair from the Shakers; a fine "suit of garments" made to Lincoln's order by Rockhill and Wilson clothiers and displayed for a while at a Sanitary Fair; a "pretty and useful" shepherd-check Scotch plaid from an eighty-one-year-old admirer in Edinburgh; a "handsome and ingenious pocket knife" (acknowledged not once but twice); a red, white, and blue silk bedspread emblazoned with stars and stripes and the American eagle; an exquisite gold box decorated with his own likeness and filled with quartz crystal — all of these received and acknowledged in 1864.[39]

More art came to hand as well. Sculptor John Rogers sent his statuary group, *Wounded Scout—A Friend in the Swamp,* which Lincoln thought "very pretty and suggestive." The president found "pretty and acceptable" a gift of photographic views of Central Park in New York City, which its senders, E. & H. T. Anthony & Company, hoped would "afford you a relaxation from the turmoil and cares of office." Photographer Alexander Gardner sent along the results of an 1863 presidential sitting, which Lincoln thought "generally very successful," adding, "The imperial photograph, in which the head leans upon the hand, I regard as the best that I have yet seen." Lincoln seemed less taken with a photographic copy of an allegorical sketch by Charles E. H. Richardson, *The Anteitam* [sic] *Gem.* As a contemporary described the scene: "Twilight is seen scattering the murky clouds which enveloped and struck terror to the people in the days of Fort Sumter." The Union was shown "crushing out Secession, unloosening its folds from around the Fasces of the Republic." The carte-de-visite copy had been sent in the hope that Lincoln would want the original after the conclusion of its display at a Philadelphia charity exposition. Instead, Lincoln suggested tactfully that it be "sold for the benefit of the Fair." Despite his apparent aversion to such symbolic works of art, the president did once endure the presentation of an allegorical tribute

Fig. 7.1 Photograph of the *Elk-Horn Chair* given to Lincoln at the White House by frontiersman Seth Kinsman on November 26, 1864. This battered carte-de-visite was owned by the Lincolns and displayed in their family photo album.
(The Lincoln Museum)

to emancipation "in a massive carved frame." Lincoln "kindly accorded the desired opportunity to make the presentation, which occupied but a few minutes," remembered Francis B. Carpenter, who witnessed the scene. After it was over, Lincoln confided to Carpenter precisely how he felt about the gift. "It is what I call *ingenious nonsense*," he declared.[40]

According to Carpenter, of all the gifts Lincoln ever received, none gave him "more sincere pleasure" than the presentation by the "colored people of Baltimore" of an especially handsome pulpit-size Bible, bound in violet velvet with solid gold cornerbands. "Upon the left-hand corner," Carpenter observed, "was a design representing the President in a cotton-field knocking the shackles off the wrists of a slave, who held one hand aloft as if invoking blessings upon the head of his benefactor." The Bible was inscribed to Lincoln as "a token of respect and gratitude" to the "friends of Universal Freedom." The Reverend S. W. Chase, in making the presentation, declared, "In the future, when our sons shall ask what means these tokens, they will be told of your mighty acts, and rise up and call you blessed." Lincoln replied, "I return my sincere thanks for this very elegant copy of the great book of God . . . the best gift which God has ever given man."[41]

Another touching ceremony took place the next year, when a Philadelphia delegation gave Lincoln "a truly beautiful and superb vase of skeleton leaves, gathered from the battle-fields of Gettysburg." Lincoln told the group that "so much has been said about Gettysburg, and so well said, that for me to attempt to say more may, perhaps, only serve to weaken the force of that which has already been said." Interestingly, he was referring not to his own words spoken November 19, 1863, but to those of principal orator Edward Everett, who had died just nine days before the presentation of the vase.[42]

Lincoln was deeply moved as well when Caroline Johnson, a former slave who had become a nurse in a Philadelphia hospital, arrived at the White House to express her "reverence and affection" for Lincoln by presenting him with a beautifully made collection of wax fruits and an ornamented stem table-stand. Together with her minister, she arrived in Lincoln's office, unpacked the materials, and set up the stand and fruits in the center of the room as the president and First Lady looked on. Then she was invited to say a few words, and as she later recalled, made an emotional speech that not only echoed with gratitude but also suggested that Lincoln had never been influenced by the gifts which he had been given:

> I looked down to the floor, and felt that I had not a word to say, but after a moment or two, the fire began to burn, . . . and it burned and burned

till it went all over me. I think it was the Spirit, and I looked up to him and said: "Mr. President, I believe God has hewn you out of a rock, for this great and mighty purpose. Many have been led away by bribes of gold, of silver, of presents; but you have stood firm, because God was with you, and if you are faithful to the end, he will be with you." With his eyes full of tears, he walked round and examined the present, pronounced it beautiful, thanked me kindly, but said: "You must not give me the praise — It belongs to God."[43]

By the last few months of his life, the novelty of presidential gifts seemed finally to wear off for Lincoln. When in late 1864 the organizers of a charity fair asked him to contribute the mammoth ox, "General Grant," recently sent by a Boston donor, Lincoln seemed totally unaware that he had even been given the beast. "If it be really [mine] . . . I present it," he wrote incredulously. It was auctioned off for $3,200. A new pattern had been established. Gifts were still arriving, but Lincoln was no longer taking notice. There is no record of any acknowledgments, for example, for the many Thanksgiving gifts received in November 1864.[44]

Then, only two months before the assassination, Lincoln had to be reminded by abolitionist leader William Lloyd Garrison that he had also failed to acknowledge the gift a full year before of a "spirited" painting depicting blacks awaiting the precise moment of their emancipation. "As the money was raised," Garrison wrote testily, "by ladies who desire that the donors may be officially apprised of its legitimate application, I write in their behalf." Noting that visitors had "seen the picture again and again at the White House," Garrison pressed Lincoln to avoid further "embarrassment" by taking note that "the painting . . . was duly received." A weary Lincoln apologized for his "seeming neglect," explaining weakly that he had intended "to make my personal acknowledgment . . . and waiting for some leisure hour, I have committed the discourtesy of not replying at all. I hope you will believe that my thanks though late, are most cordial." The letter was written by secretary John Hay; Lincoln merely signed it.[45]

The very last recorded gift presented to Lincoln came from a delegation of fifteen visitors only hours before the president left on his fateful visit to Ford's Theatre. Anticlimactically, the presentation ceremony, such as it was, took place in a hallway. A spokesman made a brief impromptu speech, and Lincoln was handed a picture of himself in a silver frame. There is no record of his reply.[46] But by then, Lincoln had been given a far more precious gift: the surrender of Lee's army at Appomattox. Before he had very much time to savor it, however, he was dead.

8

"Avoid Saying Foolish Things":
The Legacy of Lincoln's Impromptu Oratory

IN 1862 a Union brigadier general named George Lucas Hartsuff was wounded at Antietam and sent to nearby Frederick, Maryland, to recover. There, on October 4, Pres. Abraham Lincoln, en route home from a visit with the Army of the Potomac in the field, stopped to pay a visit to the general at his bedside.[1]

No one knows what the commander in chief whispered into the general's ear that day, although, conceivably, it inspired Hartsuff to his remarkable recovery. But what Lincoln said that same day to a group of well-wishers gathered outside the house where the general was recuperating was transcribed. Waiting until Lincoln emerged, they called for what well-wishers usually demanded when they saw Lincoln in the flesh. They wanted a speech. It is doubtful if any of the townspeople who heard the president that day were as inspired by his words as was the bedridden general; Lincoln said, "In my present position it is hardly proper for me to make speeches. Every word is so closely noted that it will not do to make trivial ones, and I cannot be expected to be prepared to make a matured one just now. If I were as I have been for most of my life, I might perhaps talk amusing to you for half an hour, and it wouldn't hurt anybody, but as it is, I can only return my sincere thanks for the compliment paid our cause and our common country."[2] Neither Lincoln's ordeal — nor that of his listeners — was quite over. Minutes later, he arrived at the local railroad station, where he was compelled to orate again. "Fellow-Citizens," he began, "I see myself surrounded by soldiers and a little further off I note the citizens of this good city of Frederick anxious to hear something from me. I can only say, as I did five minutes ago, it is not proper for me to make speeches in my present position."[3]

Think of it: "*Not proper for me to make speeches*"! This, from the fabled orator who delivered a Gettysburg Address and a Second Inaugural Address destined to live in the annals of both history and literature; this from the westerner who had earned a huge reputation as an orator and a debater in Illinois. The voice was the same, but the syntax was different, along with the protestations that encouraged his listeners at Frederick to believe that he was inadequate to the task of public speaking or that any effort at all smacked somehow of impropriety. There was still another obvious difference: preparation.

Abraham Lincoln, whose ascent to the presidency owed a major debt to his accomplishments as a public speaker, was an oratorical enigma. He could, of course, soar. But he could also sink. And more often than not, he was little better than dreadful when he spoke extemporaneously. At least that is the inevitable conclusion after a careful review of Lincoln's impromptu talks *on paper,* the transcriptions that stenographers recorded on the spot for publication in newspapers. With few exceptions, these show a Lincoln at the nadir of his oratorical skills. The surprise is that the worst of these talks proliferated at the peak of his powers as a writer, from 1861 to 1865.

Ironically, once he became president, the man who had inspired and amused audiences so successfully as a public speaker and courtroom lawyer in Illinois decided it was no longer proper for him to make speeches at all, impromptu or prepared. And with rare exceptions, it is seldom remembered, he did not. As he said in Pittsburgh as president-elect, "I am rather inclined to silence, and whether that be wise or not, it is at least more unusual now-a-days to find a man who can hold his tongue than to find one who cannot." True, Lincoln was then and throughout the long and difficult interregnum between his election and his inauguration avoiding policy statements, trying through silence to keep the Union together, at least so some historians have concluded. But in so doing he was also forfeiting a precious opportunity to use his newly expanded rostrum — the bully pulpit of the presidency — to keep additional states from seceding. Lincoln either did not know of or ignored the precedents for so doing. Even George Washington, who had also wanted what he called "a quiet entry devoid of ceremony," was instead repeatedly honored and called upon to speak en route to his inaugural. The historian J. G. Randall argued that Lincoln instead sought to "make no mistakes before taking further bearings." Randall did not add that Lincoln undoubtedly knew all too well that when he spoke extemporaneously he was prone to "mistakes."[4] Garry Wills has contended that Lincoln's greatest words profoundly changed a nation that was already fourscore and seven years old; if so, then it is not altogether unreasonable to speculate that preinaugural words by Lincoln might have changed another nation — the Confederacy — that was only two months old. They did not.[5]

In his defense, Lincoln had spent days before leaving for the capital meticulously preparing the one speech he knew would be the most closely read and important of his career: his inaugural address. The result unquestionably benefited from the close attention he paid to its preparation. But it was too late to preserve the Union with words. His impromptu speeches en route to that inaugural were potentially more timely but nowhere near as effective, or so their transcripts suggest.

Of course not all of Lincoln's impromptu speeches were transcribed accurately. His legendary "lost speech" in Bloomington was not recorded at all, although most historians now doubt the stubborn myth that reporters dropped their pens in awe, transfixed by Lincoln's golden oratory. We cannot completely dismiss charges by Lincoln's supporters that Democratic party stenographers worked to "garble the speeches of Mr. Lincoln" at the 1858 debates with Douglas. But neither can we totally ignore the Democratic argument that in Lincoln, Republicans had "a candidate for the Senate of whose bad rhetoric and horrible jargon they are ashamed, upon which before they would publish it, they called a council of 'literary' men to discuss, reconstruct, and rewrite." Nor should it be forgotten that Lincoln once reacted to a supporter's, not an opponent's, transcript of an 1858 speech by admitting, "Well, those are my views, and if I said anything on the subject, I must have said substantially that, but not nearly so well as that." In other words, Lincoln's impromptu rhetoric often needed the ameliorating help of sympathetic transcribers, for which he might be grateful. Stenographic reports could surely distort, but they could also improve. Unfortunately, there is no better record on which to rely.[6]

Admittedly, there are also qualities in spoken speech, especially extemporaneous speech, that no transcriber can capture. Such idiosyncratic touches are apparent only to on-the-spot listeners but are unavoidably lost to time and history. Such words might sound perfectly lucid as they are spoken but later look garbled in print. The *New York Tribune,* for example, acknowledged after his Cooper Union Address that Lincoln's "tones, [and] gestures, the kindling eye, and the mirth-provoking look defy the reporter's skill." John Locke Scripps remembered "the intense irony of his invective, and the deep earnestness . . . of his eloquence." And a Massachusetts newspaper marveled at "that perfect command of manner and matter which so eminently distinguishes the western orators." If accurately recalled, these were characteristics Lincoln may well have learned from one of his heroes. He believed that Henry Clay's eloquence consisted of a "deeply earnest and impassioned tone, and manner, which can proceed only from great sincerity." But if Lincoln tried to emulate Clay's style, his own manner often defeated him. A Cincinnati newspaper, for example, complained that Lincoln pronounced "words in a manner that puzzles the ear sometimes to determine whether he is speaking his own or a foreign tongue."[7]

Even with his unique accent tempered by the undeniable effects of gestures and expressions we cannot re-create, there is still little of a charitable nature that can be said about Lincoln's performances in the towns and cities on his inaugural train journey. "I do not . . . expect, on any occasion, till after I get to Washington, to attempt any lengthy speech," he vowed in Indianapolis. He might have extended his ban to speeches of any length at any of the stops where, as he put it during the trip, his "iron horse" stopped "to water himself." Journalist Henry Villard had perceptively noted as Lincoln prepared to depart Springfield that "the grandeur of the mission he will be called upon to fulfill" was more "a source of anxiety and embarrassment than of hopeful and exciting emotion to him." Villard believed that "his lips must be trained to less ready and unqualified responses." But the ensuing inaugural journey suggested that Lincoln's "training" had been insufficient.[8]

At one of his first stops along the long rail trip he said, "I hope that our national difficulties will pass away, and I hope we shall see in the streets of Cincinnati — good old Cincinnati — for centuries to come, once every four years her people give such a reception as this to the constitutionally elected President of the whole United States." It was a noble expression, but a tortured one, too.[9] At Steubenville, he declared, "If anything goes wrong . . . and you find you have made a mistake, elect a better man next time. There are plenty of them." Listeners probably wondered whether they *had* made a mistake.[10] And in Columbus, he assessed the disunion crisis by declaring, "It is a good thing that there is no more than anxiety, for there is nothing going wrong . . . nothing that really hurts anybody," careless words that were widely reprinted in the newspapers to show that Lincoln was not up to the task before him. He preached merely "patience and a reliance on . . . God," and supposedly a local citizen approached him afterward and declared, "You've got to give them Rebels a hotter shot than that before they're licked." As *Vanity Fair* observed with perhaps more insight than the writer realized, "Abe is becoming more grave. He don't construct as many jokes as he did. He fears that he will get things mixed up if he don't look out."[11]

By the time Lincoln got to New York he had probably heard about such criticism, but if he sought to alleviate growing concern over his abilities with a reassuring address in that hostile city he did not succeed. Yet he did come close to excusing his lackluster, inconsistent performances by admitting the wide gulf of ability that separated Lincoln the speech reader from Lincoln the speech giver.

The Gift of Language and the Language of Gifts

> I have been in the habit of thinking and speaking for some time upon
> political questions that have for some years past agitated the country,
> and if I were disposed to do so, and we could take up some of the issues as
> the lawyers call them, and I were called upon to make an argument about
> it to the best of my ability, I could do that without much preparation. But
> that is not what you desire. . . . I have been occupying a position, since
> the Presidential election, of silence, of avoiding public speaking . . . be-
> cause I thought, upon full consideration, that was the proper course for
> me to take . . . not . . . for any party wantonness, or from my indifference
> to the anxiety that pervades the minds of men. . . . I have kept silence
> for the reason that I supposed it was peculiarly proper that I should do
> so until the time came, according to the custom of the country, I should
> speak officially.[12]

Here at least was insight into the "position" Lincoln maintained throughout
his presidency, even if he was unable to adhere to it on his inaugural journey: he
believed that presidents properly spoke publicly, when they spoke publicly at all,
"officially"—that is, from text. Issues might be debated by lawyers or politicians
"without much preparation" but not by presidential candidates, presidents-elect,
or presidents. For one reason, their words were watched too closely; for another,
events moved too quickly. As Lincoln told his New York audience, the "political
drama" was "shifting its scenes" so rapidly even then that if he did not hold his
tongue he "might be disposed by the shifting . . . afterwards to shift" himself. Besides, as Lincoln pointed out in Indiana, if he gave too many speeches, he "should
be entirely worn out."[13]

To be sure, Lincoln eventually did produce some fine oratorical moments as
he neared Washington, although it is possible that by then he had learned the bitter lessons of Indianapolis, Columbus, and New York and had begun writing out
his thoughts in advance or at least preparing notes, as he probably had done for the
best of his so-called extemporaneous speeches in Illinois, including the debates
with Douglas. But by then the prosecession *Charleston Mercury* had already dismissed Lincoln's cumulative efforts as mere "fiddle-faddle," a "weak compound
of blockhead and blackguard." Even in the North, no less ardent a Unionist than
Charles Francis Adams worried that Lincoln's talks had "fallen like a wet blanket,"
putting "to flight all notions of greatness."[14]

Those preinaugural speeches—Lincoln's last prolonged exercise in impromptu oratory—probably taught him a valuable lesson. Accepting his limita-
tions as an extemporaneous speaker, he wisely curtailed such opportunities thereafter. Or, once spoken, he altered the results as he had done at the outset of his

inaugural journey, as perhaps he had first learned to do as a congressman by revising his remarks, as other congressmen did and do, for official publication. Proof that Lincoln subjected his extemporaneous remarks to after-the-fact editing was unearthed with the discovery of a long-lost scrapbook in which Lincoln's assistant private secretary, John M. Hay, meticulously pasted newspaper accounts of the president-elect's journey eastward. In one such clipping, headlined "Mr. Lincoln's Speeches at Indianapolis," the text is revealingly prefaced: "The following are the speeches delivered by Mr Lincoln in Indianapolis, *as revised by himself* [emphasis added] for the Indianapolis Journal." Lincoln was apparently a willing conspirator in the effort to improve for posterity what he said extemporaneously.[15]

In an earlier example, we all remember, or at least think we remember, the achingly beautiful words Lincoln spoke before his departure from Springfield. "No one, not in my situation, can appreciate my feeling of sadness at this parting," he began. Or did he? Not according to a stenographer whose version appeared the next morning in the *Illinois State Journal.* In that transcript, Lincoln began a good deal more awkwardly: "No one who has never been placed in a like position, can understand my feelings at this hour, nor the oppressive sadness I feel at this parting." The pristine text admired by generations of readers continued: "Here I have lived a quarter of a century, and have passed from a young to an old man." But as the stenographer recorded it: "For more than a quarter of a century, I have lived among you, and during all that time I have received nothing but kindness at your hands. Here I have lived from my youth until now I am an old man." And what about the famous peroration? The version most historians cite is, "To His care commending you, as I hope in your prayers you will commend me, I bid you an affectionate farewell." But the on-the-scene reporter heard the same expression and transcribed it as, "To Him I commend you all—permit me to ask that with equal security and faith, you will all invoke His wisdom and guidance for me. With these few words I must leave you—for how long I know not. Friends, one and all, I must now bid you an affectionate farewell." [16]

There is nothing wrong with the more prosaic version. But it is hardly the heartfelt elegy most of us have been led to recall. And it is not the speech Lincoln would have delivered had he taken the time to write it beforehand. So he did the next best thing. He wrote it afterward. This superlative writer, whose words Harriet Beecher Stowe thought "worthy to be inscribed in letters of gold," wisely occupied the first few minutes aboard his inaugural train obliging those reporters traveling with him who had failed to record the speech as it poured forth from him: he rewrote it as he perhaps wished he had delivered it. The text of the revised

The Gift of Language and the Language of Gifts

version survives, and from it we can deduce precisely how Lincoln prepared it. The manuscript begins in his hand, and after a few lines that famous, clear penmanship begins to sway and jolt with the jostling of the speeding train. Then Lincoln's handwriting is replaced by that of his secretary, John G. Nicolay. The president-elect evidently found that writing speeches on moving trains was unpleasant (and so much for another indelible legend, that Lincoln wrote his Gettysburg Address on board a train a few years later). So he handed his paper to his secretary and dictated. The result was beautiful words—but not the words he had delivered spontaneously.[17] Harriet Beecher Stowe could hardly have known the genesis of this particular speech, but she did know enough to realize of Lincoln's speeches that they evidenced "a greater power in writing than the most artful devices of rhetoric." For Lincoln, the most artful rhetoric was always written. It could not be spoken nearly as well, not without preparation.[18]

No event of Lincoln's lifetime ever inspired him more unforgettably than the sacrifice and victory at Gettysburg. We all know what that battle moved him to say—or we think we know. To serenaders who gathered outside the White House on July 7, 1863, to celebrate that victory, Lincoln responded with a tribute to the living and dead who gave their lives that the nation might live. In effect, this was Lincoln's first Gettysburg Address, the one he gave spontaneously and fumblingly. He said, "How long ago is it?—eighty odd years—since on the Fourth of July for the first time in the history of the world a nation by its representatives, assembled and declared as a self-evident truth that 'all men are created equal.' That was the birthday of the United States of America." Not for another four months were these stumbling thoughts refined into what may be the most famous opening line of any speech ever delivered in America: "Fourscore and seven years ago our fathers brought forth on this continent a new nation conceived in liberty and dedicated to the proposition that all men are created equal"—words delivered, marveled John Hay, who heard both versions, "with more grace than is his wont." Translation: Lincoln seldom orated so gracefully, especially extemporaneously.[19]

Gettysburg also proved an exception to Lincoln's rule of silence. By then, he had made it his practice to reject even the most compelling speaking opportunities and to remain close to Washington, a seclusion that in today's presidents would undoubtedly arouse suspicions of some devious "rose garden strategy" or worse. But the political culture required fewer appearances of nineteenth-century presidents, and Lincoln seemed genuinely to believe that a president belonged at his White House desk where the voters or, more to the point, the elite and remote electoral college, had sent him. As he well knew, his most famous and successful extemporaneous effort, the Lincoln-Douglas debates, had been rewarded by a popular-vote majority but an electoral defeat. His silence as presidential candidate may have generated less than 40 percent of the popular vote, but it also produced an electoral majority.

Silence, he may well have concluded, was more rewarding than stump speaking. Others agreed. Stephen A. Douglas, who shattered tradition by speaking on his own behalf in 1860, was vilified simply for refusing, as he put it (with a sly shot at his opponent), "to put a padlock on my lips or to appoint a committee to . . . explain that I did not think it proper to express any opinion." "No other candidate for the presidency ever degraded himself by . . . delivering partisan harangues," the Republican press jeered in response, "Mr. Douglas is doing what Mr. Lincoln would scorn to do. . . . May he be the last as he is the first." In truth, Douglas was neither. Winfield Scott had been attacked eight years earlier for taking the stump in the 1852 presidential campaign "contrary to the taste of all good men." Henry Clay had been castigated for similar transgressions. Thus one paper could declare itself "disgusted" by the mere "spectacle" of President Buchanan speaking openly in the 1860 campaign. As Lincoln's hometown, pro-Republican newspaper, the *Illinois State Journal,* insisted, "The American people have always believed it would be in exceedingly bad taste and censurable in a candidate for the high office of President to . . . electioneer by making political speeches." Lincoln the celebrated political orator agreed that the presidency was beyond both politics and oratory—"an office no man should seek by direct means," in the words of the *State Journal.* His tongue silenced by what he called "the lessons of the past," Lincoln's career as a stump speaker came to an end.[20]

Surely his subsequent, stubborn determination to refuse presidential speaking opportunities cannot fully be explained, as some historians have maintained, merely as evidence of his desire to remain close to the White House to ensure uninterrupted communication with his generals in the field. Even though Lincoln's White House, astonishingly, was not equipped with its own telegraph, there were enough lines in the large cities of the East and at railroad stations along the way to provide a traveling president, out on the hustings to inspire his people, all the assurances he needed that he would remain in close contact with his government and military.

Lincoln ignored this possibility. The historian Waldo Braden has calculated that he made ninety-five speeches in four years as president. That may sound like a large number, but seventy-eight were delivered in or from the White House. Most were not really speeches at all but formal remarks to visiting delegations

The Gift of Language and the Language of Gifts

or brief responses to serenaders. Another seven talks were delivered elsewhere in the city of Washington. Of course, during this era even the president's annual messages to Congress — the nineteenth-century equivalents of today's State of the Union messages — were by tradition written by the president but then delivered to Capitol Hill to be read by a clerk. But as president, Lincoln was more wary of making impromptu speeches than even tradition required. When, for example, a delegation of Missouri Radicals arrived at the White House and demanded a response to their disgust with military affairs in their home state, Lincoln told them that they would have to wait for his official answer. He was not willing to extemporize on so sensitive an issue as relations with the crucial border states. Not until several days later did Lincoln have his reply ready. He had carefully written it out and then sent it to his visitors.[21]

As for his remaining ten presidential addresses, just one, the Gettysburg Address, can truly be called a formal presidential speech, and perhaps Lincoln accepted the summons to Gettysburg precisely because it asked that he deliver not the main oration but merely "a few appropriate remarks." Even then he couched his effort with a caveat: "The world will little remember what we say here." Of the other Lincoln speeches, two impromptu talks were given the day he visited Frederick; two more were delivered bumblingly en route to and at Gettysburg before he appeared at the Soldiers' Cemetery; another five were given at two Sanitary Fairs in 1864; and another was delivered unexpectedly in Jersey City as Lincoln was returning to Washington from a brief conference with Winfield Scott at West Point. As Lincoln said in this typical impromptu effort, "When birds and animals are looked at through a fog they are seen to disadvantage, and so it might be with you if I were to attempt to tell you why I went to see Gen. Scott." He ended with a less-than-sublime coda: "The Secretary of War, you know, holds a pretty tight rein on the press, so that they shall not tell more than they ought to, and I'm afraid that if I blab too much he might draw a tight rein on me."[22]

Uninspiring as it was, the talk revealed the extemporaneous Lincoln at his best — "talking amusing to you," as he had put it, but without so rising to the occasion, earlier in Frederick. Lincoln generally felt that such "amusing" bursts of wit were inappropriate to his station, especially once his demeanor and dignity had become subjects of campaign mockery in 1860. So he would hold a "tight rein" on himself. He would not, if he could help it, "blab too much." Like Clay, he would never speak, as Lincoln had recalled admiringly, "merely to be heard."[23]

Sometimes Lincoln could not help it. At a banquet at the Philadelphia Sanitary Fair in June 1864, the man who had already achieved sublime greatness at

Gettysburg was called upon to address attendees. He said, "I do not really think it is proper in my position for me to make a political speech . . . and being more of a politician than anything else, and having exhausted that branch of the subject at the fair, and not being prepared to speak on the other, I am without anything to say. . . . I must beg of you to excuse me from saying anything further." This was the impromptu Lincoln at his most honest. He believed that it was inherently improper for him to deliver speeches, and he was "not prepared" to deliver a formal one. And being unable to avoid making an impromptu speech, he could do no better than produce a disjointed one. It is hardly surprising that a reporter for the anti-Lincoln *New York World* reported with mock seriousness on Lincoln's remarks in Philadelphia: "The second Washington did not, on this occasion . . . crack many jokes—smutty or otherwise. Whether the solemnity of the occasion overpowered him, or whether he felt bilious, I am uninformed."[24]

The double irony was that the roster of impromptu opportunities maimed was dwarfed by the list of opportunities for formal oratory Lincoln rejected in advance. During the war he turned down enticing invitations to speak at events honoring war heroes David G. Farragut and Ulysses S. Grant. He declined an invitation to return to New York's Cooper Union to rally Northerners to enlist, despite its organizers' promise that he might thus "encourage, by [his] voice, the active efforts of the loyal men . . . in support of the Union Cause." And even when James Conkling invited Lincoln home to Springfield to address what promised to be "a Grand Mass Meeting" of "unconditional union men . . . the most imposing demonstration that has ever been held in the Northwest," Lincoln could summon enough enthusiasm only to reply cautiously, "I think I will go or send a letter—probably the latter." In the end, he chose the latter course. He constructed a majestic letter to be read aloud there: "You say you will not fight to free negroes. Some of them seem willing to fight for you. . . . Among free men, there can be no successful appeal from the ballot to the bullet." Had Lincoln chosen to deliver these carefully written remarks in person, the result might well be counted today as one of his great presidential orations.[25]

Lincoln surely knew how successful he could be when he could read his prewritten speeches rather than invent them on the scene. Writing home after his triumph at Cooper Union, he boasted that it "gave me no trouble whatever, being within my calculation before I started"—meaning that he had written the speech in advance and researched it exhaustively. His law partner, William H. Herndon, remembered that Lincoln worked on it for weeks: "He searched through the dusty volumes of Congressional proceedings in the state library, and dug deeply into political history. He was painstaking and thorough in the study of his subject." It was a thoroughness in speech preparation he no longer had the liberty—or desire—to practice as president.[26]

Still, even if Lincoln chose to follow a tradition of silence he thought appropriate, it is worth recalling that, in stark contrast, his Confederate counterpart, who unlike Lincoln is seldom remembered today as a great orator, undertook several morale-building speaking tours during the war. His biographer William C. Davis calls them evidence of "how conscious he had become of the need to reach out." Jefferson Davis even used a speech dramatically to quell the Richmond bread riot. Lincoln, by comparison, hardly rushed north to use personal persuasion to quiet a far more dangerous situation—the worst urban disturbance in American history—the New York draft riots. So by 1865, when the vice president recalled that the president's speeches had become "bold and undaunted," filled with "loftiness of sentiment and . . . magnetic . . . delivery," it comes as little surprise that it was Confederate Vice President Alexander H. Stephens speaking, and about Jefferson Davis, not Abraham Lincoln.[27]

Although there can be little dispute about the hollow legacy of Lincoln's lackluster impromptu oratory, there remains a lingering mystery. How did a politician who earned fame as an orator and a debater regress so dramatically as president? Was it a matter of declining skill, the pressures of running a government and a war, a stubborn belief in the impropriety of presidential oratory, a combination of these elements, or something more?

To understand the evolution of Lincoln's rhetorical skills, it is useful to begin virtually at the beginning, with his education as a public speaker.[28] One of the first primers Lincoln acquired in New Salem was *A Guide to the English Tongue* by a schoolmaster, Thomas Dilworth. Here Lincoln found instruction on syntax, analogy, and comparison; lessons in effectively using monosyllables (perhaps the original inspiration for his subsequent and effective use of one-syllable words in such masterpieces as the Gettysburg Address); a guide to pronunciation, perhaps the first he ever read; advice on debating ("upbraid no man's weakness to discomfit"); and stories in verse with which to practice oration ("On the Diligent Ants" was one; "Life is Short and Miserable" was another).

Or Lincoln could try reciting and gaining insight from an instructive verse:

> Henceforth our Youth, who tread thy flow'ry way,
> Shall ne'er from the roles of proper *Diction* stray!
> No more their speech with Barb'rous terms be fill'd;
> No more their pens a crop of nonsense yield;

> But chosen words in due arrangement stand,
> And *Sense* and *Eloquence* go hand in hand.

"Vain-glory destroys all the fruits of good action," warned Dilworth in another passage, adding in a fatuous rhyme, "On Ambition" (which Lincoln clearly ignored, perhaps to his own subsequent psychological detriment):

> When wild Ambition in the Heart we find,
> Farewell Content, and quiet of the mind:
> For glitt'ring Clouds, we leave the solid shore,
> And wonted Happiness returns no more.[29]

Lincoln also read William Scott's *Lessons in Elocution*. Perhaps no book more informed or influenced his early development as a public speaker. From its pages came specific instruction from which the roots of Lincoln's oratorical style can be glimpsed: "Let your articulation be Distinct and Deliberate. . . . Let your Pronunciation be Bold and Forcible. . . . Pitch your voice in Different Keys. . . . Acquire a just variety of Pause and Cadence. . . . Pronounce your words with propriety and elegance." Readers were given practice passages from Hume, Sterne, and others; a series of famous sermons; and crowd-pleasing soliloquies from Shakespeare, some of the political kind, like the St. Crispin's Day call to arms from *Henry V* and Antony's funeral oration from *Julius Caesar*. There was even practical advice to debaters: "A wise man endeavors to shine in himself; a fool to outshine others."[30]

Here, too, was one lesson Lincoln never learned: "It were much to be wished, that all public speakers would deliver their thoughts and sentiments, either from memory or immediate conception: For, besides that there is an artificial uniformity which almost always distinguishes reading from speaking, the fixed posture, and the bowing of the head, which reading requires, are inconsistent with the freedom, ease, and variety of just elocution."[31]

Scott's *Lessons* even offered specific instructions on how to accomplish that spontaneous-looking "ease" the author recommended so strongly. The book provided specific lessons on the art of gesture (Fig. 8.1), complete with woodcut illustrations in which ludicrously portrayed long-haired boys in dandified, not to mention outmoded, eighteenth-century costume were shown raising their arm loftily or shifting daintily from hip to hip. Through these words and pictures, Lincoln learned, for example, that "a boy should . . . rest the whole weight of his body on his right leg . . . the knees should be straight . . . the right arm must be held out, with the palm open, and the fingers straight and close, the thumb almost distant from them as it will go . . . [and] the very moment the last accented word is

Fig. 8.1 Illustration from *Lessons in Elocution* by William Scott
(Boston, 1811), which Lincoln read as a youth.
   *(Rare Books and Manuscripts Division, the New York Public Library,
   Astor, Lenox, and Tilden Foundations)*

pronounced . . . the hand, as if lifeless, must drop down to the side . . . as if dead." Then, the lesson continued, the "left hand raises itself, into exactly the same position as the right was before . . . and so on, from right to left, alternatively, till the speech is ended." Scott advised further that a bent arm could be employed for emphasis; an arm brought down suddenly could highlight a crucial word or expression. But at all costs, the book cautioned, "Great care must be taken . . . not to bend [one's arm] at the wrist." Proper gesture, Scott preached, was essential "to keep the audience awake." It was important not to put one's hands in one's pockets, or stare at one's hat, or play with a spool of thread or other prop. "Avoid ridiculous gestures," the author warned, but don't be a "speaking statue," either.[32] "The arms are sometimes both thrown out . . . sometimes they are lifted up as high as the face. . . . With the hand we solicit, we refuse, we promise, we threaten, we dismiss, we invite, we entreat, we express aversion, fear, doubting, denial, asking, affirmation, negation, joy, grief, confusion, penitence. . . . The hands serve us instead of many sorts of words, and where the language of the tongue is unknown, that of the hands is understood, being universal." It was expected that the face also be used to express gravity, fear, remorse, denial, exhortation ("a kind, compliant look"), judgment, pardon, veneration, and other emotions, including mirth, raillery, even flashing hatred, but never sloth, which yawning would inevitably suggest. Lincoln learned these lessons well. Years later a contemporary marveled that when Lincoln moved his head with "a quick jerk" for emphasis, it was like "throwing off electric sparks into combustible material."[33]

Scott granted, in a cautionary note to teachers using his volume as a textbook, "The master will be a little discouraged, at the awkward figure his pupil makes, in his first attempts. . . . But this is no more than what happens in dancing, fencing, or any other exercise that depends on practice." And Lincoln surely practiced. By the time he was a matured stump speaker, engaging Stephen A. Douglas in head-to-head debate, observers were taking appreciative note of individualistic habits of gesture and expression that surely originated in Scott's primitive lessons. And these gestures came in large part to make Lincoln a unique orator — even if he never totally outgrew the awkwardness his old primer promised would eventually vanish.[34]

One observer remembered that Lincoln often "pointed his theories into his hearers' head with a long, bony forefinger." He could "fling both hands upward" or "clench his fists in silent condemnation." Still another recalled that every so often, to emphasize a point, Lincoln would suddenly "bend his knees so they would almost touch the platform, and then . . . shoot himself to his full height, emphasizing his utterances in a very forcible manner." And still, as one eyewitness to the debates concluded, the overall result was that Lincoln remained strikingly "ungraceful in his gestures."[35]

Lincoln's law partner and biographer William H. Herndon concurred that "on the stump" Lincoln was "at first . . . very awkward, and it seemed a real labor to adjust himself to his surroundings. He struggled for a time under a feeling of apparent diffidence and sensitiveness, and these only added to his awkwardness." Herndon insisted that Lincoln "never sawed the air nor rent space into tatters and rags as some orators do. He never acted for stage effect." Yet he conceded that "to express joy or pleasure, he would raise both hands at an angle of about fifty degrees, the palms upwards, as if desirous of embracing the spirit of that which he loved. If the sentiment was one of detestation — denunciation of slavery, for example — both arms, thrown upward and fists clenched, swept through the air. . . . This was one of his most effective gestures."[36]

Thus Herndon and other onlookers recorded one explanation for Lincoln's early success as a stump speaker, even when he lacked the written text that so often elevated his performances into the realm of poetry. That quality was gesture — the unrecordable element of Lincoln's speaking style, now and forever lost, except through generic period descriptions. Lincoln's style of gesture, weaned from Scott's primer, developed on the stump, and refined in the Great Debates of 1858, set him apart from other speakers as much as his direct, forthright approach and his "illustrations," as one admirer called them, which boasted "romance and pathos and fun and logic all welded together." Here was an extremely tall man with a homely face whose expression could change with the toss of a head — whose eyes could flash, Herndon recalled, "in a face aglow with the fire of his profound thoughts"; whose long arms could sweep dramatically through the air; and who sometimes bent at the knee and shot upward, looking heaven only knows how tall on the platform. He could be earnest and impassioned at one moment, scathingly sarcastic at another. His voice, even if high-pitched, as some contemporaries recalled, could be heard to the farthest reaches of large outdoor crowds. A worried Stephen A. Douglas conceded on the eve of their debates that his rival's "droll ways and dry jokes" made him nothing less than "the best stump speaker . . . in the West." Even so, unless they were edited by partisan reporters, Lincoln's riveting stump performances — characterized by explosions of humor and outlandish gestures — seldom scanned in newspaper reprints. However considerable his reputation as a stump speaker, the evidence suggests that his extemporaneous performances were, in terms of syntax and substance, far less effective than the orations he wrote in advance.[37]

And herein may very well lie the elusive explanation for Lincoln's diminishing skill as an impromptu speaker. There are no period descriptions of President-elect Lincoln or President Lincoln ever gesturing awkwardly, gesturing dramatically, or gesturing at all. Photographs show him clutching his manuscript as he reads his great Second Inaugural. Eyewitnesses recalled that he held either his manuscript or his lapels at Gettysburg. Hard experience had taught Lincoln to rethink the advice of Scott's *Lessons in Elocution.* Although he surely never lost his ability to engage his audiences with the twinkle of his eye or the tilt of his head, Lincoln volitionally abandoned the great prop he had learned in Scott and honed to perfection on the prairie: the dramatic use of gesture to engage the emotions as the book *Elocution* had taught.

On the eve of his greatest speech, Lincoln responded to calls for a greeting by a crowd gathered outside the David Wills house in Gettysburg and appeared at the door to offer, as John Hay bluntly confided in his diary, "half a dozen words meaning nothing." "The inference is a very fair one," Lincoln said that evening, "that you would hear me for a little while, at least, were I to commence to make a speech. I do not appear before you for the purpose of doing so, and for several substantial reasons. The most substantial of these is that I have no speech to make. In my position, it is somewhat important that I should not say any foolish things." Just then a voice in the audience shot back, "*If* you can help it." Replied Lincoln, "It very often happens that the only way to help it is to say nothing at all."[38] And perhaps that is why, as president, Lincoln said nothing at all whenever he could and said as little as possible when he was unable to keep silent. More often than history has recalled, when he could not avoid speaking extemporaneously he could not avoid saying foolish things.

Tellingly, Lincoln's last response to a crowd of well-wishers gathered outside the White House, delivered a few days before his assassination, was anything but spontaneous. "The President had written out his speech," recalled the journalist Noah Brooks, "being well aware that the importance of the occasion would give it significance, and he was not willing to run the risk of being betrayed by the excitement of the occasion in saying anything which would make him sorry when he saw it in print." Lincoln had had much reason to be sorry in the past. His impromptu speeches probably read far worse than they sounded.[39]

He might have refined his skills at impromptu oratory, but he did not. He might have continued using gestures to entertain his audiences but apparently did not. He might have filled the void between expectation and performance by delivering more formal speeches, but he did not even do this. And he remained perpetually ambivalent about which forms of expression were most proper. As he said in his second lecture on discoveries and inventions in 1859, "Speech alone, valuable as it ever has been, and is, has not advanced the condition of the world much. . . . *Writing* . . . is the great invention of the world." Yet in that very same lecture he contradicted himself. "*Writing*," he said, "although a wonderful auxiliary for speech, is no substitute for it. . . . One always has one's tongue with him, and the breath of life is the ever-ready material with which it works." [40]

Lincoln once declared, "I shall never be old enough to speak without embarrassment when I have nothing to talk about." [41] He lived to be fifty-six. And the man acknowledged as one of the greatest public speakers ever to occupy the White House must have been embarrassed many times. The leader often remembered as the first modern president may have failed fully to comprehend the power of public oratory in molding public opinion and maintaining public support during a crisis. Instead, as he admitted in Chicago on November 21, 1860, and continued to believe for the next four-and-a-half years, "I am not in the habit of making speeches now."

Perhaps he hinted at his rhetorical doubts most revealingly when he declared in his 1862 message to Congress: "Men should utter nothing for which they would not be responsible through time and in eternity." The man who knew, as he put it in the same message, that he could not "escape history" found it prudent to escape the dangers of extemporaneous public speaking as often as possible. Had Lincoln been a better impromptu speaker, or had he taken advantage of the frequent opportunities offered him to make formal presidential speeches in public, he might well be remembered not only as the Great Emancipator but also as the Great Communicator. [42]

The Poetry and Prose of
the Emancipation Proclamation

"THE SCENE was wild and grand," Frederick Douglass remembered of the day when the words of the final Emancipation Proclamation first came over the telegraph wires on January 1, 1863. "Joy and gladness exhausted all forms of expression, from shouts of praise to joys and tears."[1]

Yet eighty-five years later, looking back at those same words, Richard Hofstadter declared that they boasted "all the moral grandeur of a bill of lading"—a cargo receipt. Mark E. Neely Jr. echoed that view in 1993: he condemned the text of the Emancipation Proclamation as "leaden legalese." And those modern assessments were not unlike the view that had been advanced a century earlier by an ardent Lincoln admirer named Karl Marx, who complained that the style of the proclamation called to mind the "mean pettifogging conditions which one lawyer puts to his opposing lawyer." Even Frederick Douglass conceded at the time, "It was not a proclamation of 'liberty throughout the land, unto all the inhabitants thereof,' such as we had hoped it would be, but was one marked by discriminations and reservations."[2]

Such comments, from the recent and distant past alike, have understandably served to nourish a growing sense among modern Americans that Abraham Lincoln was at best a reluctant and uninspiring Emancipator—and, as others have added, a superfluous one as well. It is difficult to deny that the reputation of the Emancipation Proclamation has fallen into historical decline.

Unenlightened on issues of race, the fashionable arguments go, Lincoln used emancipation as a desperate weapon of war only when it became clear that the Union could not be preserved without depriving the South of the "slave power" and without arming blacks in the North to put down the rebellion. Furthermore, critics suggest, Lincoln's document really had little effect: it freed slaves only where Lincoln had no power to free them and left them enslaved where he exercised the authority to break their chains. And finally, detractors assert, so many slaves

The Gift of Language and the Language of Gifts

were in the process of liberating *themselves* by the time it was written, fleeing into Union lines throughout the South, that even if Lincoln had not proclaimed it, black freedom was inevitable anyway. As Barbara Fields has argued, "No human being alive could have held back the tide that swept toward freedom."[3]

But is it fair to imply that Lincoln simply did *not hold* back the tide of freedom? Exactly how and why has the Emancipation Proclamation faded from its original reputation as a revolutionary act? And, most important, does it deserve revisionist dismissal or renewed appreciation?

As to why the proclamation has declined in prestige, five likely reasons may help explain the downward spiral. The first has to be the shocking absence of scholarship on the subject. Great acts call for great books, yet the Emancipation Proclamation has inspired a total of one: John Hope Franklin's slim, 130-page volume, issued for the centennial of the proclamation in 1963 and now more than thirty-five years old.[4] Meanwhile, some 10,000 books on Lincoln have been published since emancipation took effect. As readers become more and more familiar with every other detail of Lincoln's personal and political life, the act he himself believed his greatest fades into memory—so seldom analyzed for so many generations that students and specialists alike reasonably infer from the scholarly vacuum that it did not deserve the attention it generated when it was first issued.

Second, what little has been published in recent years about the proclamation has been largely critical, cynical, or fictional. In his best-selling novel, *Lincoln,* Gore Vidal maintains that Lincoln issued his proclamation merely to one-up his newspaper critics; Vidal's Lincoln was more a schemer than a dreamer. As for Lincoln's reputation among African Americans, much time has passed since Frederick Douglass called Lincoln "the first American President who . . . rose above the prejudice of his times." Martin Luther King did call emancipation "a joyous daybreak to end the long night of captivity." But more frequently quoted is Lerone Bennett Jr.'s seminal article in *Ebony Magazine* declaring Lincoln "the embodiment . . . of a racist tradition" whose proclamation was designed to *delay,* not *advance,* the cause of liberation.[5]

Problem number three: the proclamation's limited reach. It exempted loyal slaveholding states from its mandate, forever encouraging charges that it was a toothless, unenforceable document. At the time, even a common soldier like Sgt. Cyrenus G. Tyler of New York recognized that the proclamation seemed "rather lame in some points. I do believe in the theory of the thing," he wrote, "but the practical working as devised by President Lincoln I cannot see. The idea of giving liberty to bondsmen that are not within reach of his benificencies [*sic*], and in the same article withholding the same from those that are within reach seems to me rather mixed." But Tyler was writing only a month after the proclamation took effect. He could not yet know the impact it would have subsequently, giving the war new purpose and actually liberating hundreds of thousands of slaves as Union armies marched into the South, enforcing the proclamation in their wake.[6]

But Lincoln enjoyed the constitutional authority to abolish slavery only in those areas in active rebellion against the federal government. He surely knew from the start of his deliberations about emancipation that a presidential proclamation would be a paper tiger unless and until Union armies overran the Confederacy and liberated the slave population, in much the same way the Declaration of Independence did not establish freedom for white Americans a century earlier, until the Continental army won the Revolutionary War. And to provide a "king's cure for all the evils" of slavery, as he put it, Lincoln made certain that the 1864 Republican (or National Union) party platform called for a constitutional amendment abolishing slavery *everywhere,* thus giving to emancipation "legal form, and practical effect . . . in the joint names of Liberty and Union."[7]

Problem number four was the way the proclamation was announced—or, to be more precise, the way it was *not* announced. The first draft was read in private and kept secret for two months. The preliminary proclamation was published, but unaccompanied by the kind of public event that might have enshrined it in visual memory. And when he signed the final proclamation on January 1, 1863, Lincoln missed the chance for what surely would have been the greatest photo opportunity of the century. Unaware of the power of image-making, Lincoln made the proclamation official in his private office, before just a few witnesses. He made no speech that day, met no delegation of African Americans, visited no slave families, saw no abolitionists, presided over no ceremony. The "Emancipation Moment," as one historian has called such milestones, reached its climax without Abraham Lincoln to consecrate it—a truly lost opportunity.

The president had his own way of conducting public relations, and in that convoluted approach lies the root of problem number five. No leader ever cloaked a great act in more intentionally deceptive public relations and in more intensely stultifying prose. Lincoln overexplained it and underwrote it. To understand why is to suggest a new historiographical assessment of Lincoln's most important presidential act.

Why did the man capable of writing so dazzlingly, who counted Harriet

The Gift of Language and the Language of Gifts

Beecher Stowe, Leo Tolstoy, and Walt Whitman among his admirers, hold in check the power of his pen in writing the document he called, with rare bravado, "the great event of the nineteenth century"?[8]

There can be little justification for arguing that Abraham Lincoln failed to craft an undistinguished, uninspiring document, as some historians now maintain, because he was a reluctant Emancipator. "I am naturally anti-slavery," he reminded a Kentucky editor in April 1864. "If slavery is not wrong, nothing is wrong. I can not remember when I did not so think and feel." More likely, Lincoln wrote an undistinguished document because he was a deliberate, perhaps even a fearful Emancipator. A modern political leader once declared that political leadership requires 10 percent poetry and 90 percent prose — the poetry being the inspiration and the prose the perspiration. Lincoln had to choose between inspiration and perspiration for his most momentous state paper, and he intentionally chose function over form. Only when Lincoln's initial qualms evaporated did he temper the prosaic writing style of his document with some of the most masterful poetry he ever crafted — the kind of sublime rhetoric that should really be considered side by side with the document as part of his overall message of liberty. But at the time, as Gabor S. Boritt has noted, Lincoln's "largely nonmoral language protected the Constitutional basis of the act" and "also reduced the hostility of Northern and border state conservatives."[9]

To understand Lincoln's stubborn hesitation, and his subsequent use of confusing public statements and rigidly stilted prose, one must consider the hotly charged race issue in terms of his time, not ours — an age of rampant racism in which only a small percentage of white America supported emancipation and but a fraction of that minority would have tolerated, much less supported, the then-radical notion of racial equality.

It is true that many leaders of the day urged prompter action on slavery, but many others cautioned against it, leaving Lincoln whipsawed by the conflicting demands from within the disparate elements of his fragile Union coalition. Abolitionists prodded him. Two generals — John C. Frémont and David Hunter — issued orders confiscating slave property in their respective military departments, and Lincoln promptly revoked them. Congress passed a confiscation act, and Lincoln questioned how Congress could act against an institution existing in the individual states and protected in the Constitution. Looking at the record from the vantage point of the new millennium, Lincoln seems to have *impeded* liberty. But judged by public sentiment of his own time, he was merely postponing it. As Frederick Douglass understood, "While he hated slavery, and really desired its destruction, he always proceeded against it in a manner the least likely to shock or drive from him any who were truly in sympathy with the preservation of the Union." If the Union died, Lincoln knew, so did any chance for democratic government or equal opportunity, here or throughout the world, then or in the future.[10]

Lincoln had ample reason for concern. On the opposite end of the political spectrum were generals and politicians as committed to preventing emancipation as the progressives were committed to hastening it. With crucial, slaveholding border states teetering on the verge of secession or conquest, Lincoln worried that if an emancipation proclamation propelled them into the Confederacy, the city of Washington would be isolated, the balance of power roiled, and the Union lost irrevocably. He nervously joked that he hoped to keep God on his side. But he simply had to keep Kentucky.

And so he took small steps. He signed one law abolishing slavery in the federal territories and another liberating slaves still held in the nation's capital. He implored the border states to accept gradual, compensated emancipation, although without success. But for a time, he felt he could not risk further action that might propel them into the Confederate orbit.

Nor had any war ever been reconsecrated while it was being fought, and Lincoln worried that the Union cause could not survive redefinition into an abolitionist crusade. As late as March 1862, the commanding general of the Army of the Potomac, George B. McClellan, warned him that "neither confiscation of property . . . or forcible abolition of slavery should be contemplated for a moment." McClellan could not easily be ignored; he perhaps had lost a few battles, but he might yet win the war. In Washington, one Democrat took to the floor of Congress to thunder, "If emancipation means taxation on the free States, now lavishing their all for the Union and the Constitution . . . I am opposed to that cause . . . and here take my stand . . . against it."[11]

Ultimately, the time did come: a confluence of moral belief, political opportunity, and "indispensable" military necessity. "Things had gone on from bad to worse," Lincoln admitted, "until I felt that we had reached the end of our rope . . . that we had about played our last card, and must change our tactics or lose the game!" As he put it: "We must free the slaves or ourselves be subdued."[12]

In late spring or early summer 1862, Lincoln began writing, and there is some evidence that he found it an agonizing process from the very beginning. One witness remembered him composing no more than a few words each day, "studying carefully each sentence," revising and re-revising each line, each word.[13]

The Gift of Language and the Language of Gifts

On July 17, he assembled his cabinet to read them the rather tepid result: a brief executive order that called emancipation "a fit and necessary war measure" to restore federal authority. Cabinet ministers were accustomed to being asked to vote on major policy initiatives, but this time Lincoln told them he had "resolved upon this step." He sought neither advice nor consent.

Yet no proclamation was issued that day, because Secretary of State Seward counseled delay. The war was going poorly, and the country would most likely view a proclamation aimed at slavery as "the last measure of an exhausted government — a cry for help . . . our last *shriek,* on the retreat." Lincoln saw the wisdom in this objection. He put aside his draft and waited for military victory.[14]

Meanwhile, his cabinet actually kept the plan secret. Imagine such a thing happening in today's world of daily White House press briefings, all news all the time on CNN and MSNBC, and TV-camera stakeouts at the slightest hint of breaking stories. Lincoln enjoyed time to reflect — to rewrite — but also, most harmfully in terms of his reputation, to calculate and implement a public relations strategy designed to convince America that he was not prepared to do precisely what he had decided irrevocably to do as soon as his armies won a victory. It was a brilliant manipulation of popular sentiment at the time, but it left a paper trail of half-hearted pronouncements that have dogged Lincoln's future reputation as a liberator.

One such opportunity arose in August when Horace Greeley, editor of the *New York Tribune,* published an editorial, "The Prayer of Twenty Millions," condemning Lincoln as "strangely and disastrously remiss" for not acting to end slavery.[15] Of course, Lincoln was prepared to act — just not prepared to say so. Instead, he seized on Greeley's attack as an opportunity to present a tenable rationale for emancipation to the public in advance.

His reply has often been cited as evidence of Lincoln's belief that emancipation was for him a secondary concern. But since he already knew that his course was leading irrevocably to emancipation, the letter should really be viewed as a shrewd, advance public relations effort to set the stage for the new initiative — to rally public support for the measure as a military, not a moral, imperative — so more people would accept it. Lincoln still worried that the white majority would not welcome the proclamation unless he couched it carefully.

"My paramount object in this struggle *is* to save the Union, and is not either to save or destroy slavery," Lincoln wrote in his widely published letter to the editor. "If I could save the Union without freeing any slave, I would do it; and if I could save it by freeing all the slaves, I would do it; and if I could save it by freeing some and leaving others alone, I would also do that." That, of course, is precisely what he had decided to do.[16]

Was Lincoln lying to the American people? Certainly he was guilty of a sin of omission. But he was struggling with what LaWanda Cox has called the simultaneous tug of "sweeping principle" and "limited authority." To succeed, Lincoln felt he must sometimes "conceal his hand or [even] dissemble."[17]

Lincoln would not admit that emancipation was certain even to a delegation of free black citizens visiting the White House on August 24. Instead, he virtually told them to move to Haiti or the Caribbean. "It is better for us both ... to be separated," he said. "There is an unwillingness on the part of our people, harsh as it may be, for you free colored people to remain with us."[18] These were harsh words, to be sure. But Lincoln knew that African Americans would cheer emancipation; this performance was again designed specifically for white audiences who might have been willing to accept a militarily necessary emancipation, he reasoned, but not an integrated society.

Just as Lincoln hoped, the speech was quickly published verbatim in newspapers across the North. To the detriment of his future reputation, Lincoln had set the stage for releasing his proclamation beyond the controversial realm of humanitarianism, by advocating colonization — a flirtation he soon abandoned. It was a risky strategy, if Lincoln was worried about his legacy. He might have contributed more by beginning to educate Americans about the inevitability of a biracial society. But this he calculated he could not do without losing the border states, the military, the Congress, and, as he put it, proclamation or no, "the whole game." Ultimately, he left a record of cautionary and intentionally misleading caveats; and some observers seem to take them far more seriously today than his reminder to Horace Greeley that he still wished privately that "all men every where could be free." Gabor S. Boritt has called this and other examples of Lincoln's "avoidance" — especially of the colonization issue he professed to embrace at the time, most likely to placate conservatives fearful that emancipation would lead to equality and integration — his "detour from reality."[19]

The dissembling continued a bit longer. As late as September 13, Lincoln asked a group of religious leaders visiting the White House, "What good would a proclamation of emancipation from me do? ... Would my word free the slaves when I cannot even enforce the Constitution in the rebel states?" Once again he was skillfully provoking false expectations of government inertia on slavery, ending the meeting by admitting, "I have not decided *against* a proclamation of liberty to the slaves, but hold the matter under advisement." Here was yet another untruth, this time illuminated by a faint ray of hope. If he took any action at all, he cautioned, it would come "as a practical war measure, to be decided upon according to the advantages and disadvantages it may offer to the suppression of the rebellion." [20]

The military success that Lincoln needed as a prerequisite for emancipation finally came on September 17 at the Battle of Antietam. Five days later, he assembled his cabinet again, read aloud his new preliminary proclamation, and issued it publicly, though without fanfare, that very day. "It is now for the country and the world to pass judgment on it," Lincoln told a small crowd of serenaders a few days after its release. He could not have been pleased with the first of those judgments. They more than justified his worst fears about public reaction. For example, although there are scholars who believe that Lincoln issued the proclamation solely to prevent Europe from joining the war on the Confederate side, the evidence suggests otherwise. Workingmen's groups applauded, but the British prime minister, Lord Palmerston, denounced the proclamation as "trash," declaring the government that issued it "utterly . . . contemptible." The *London Times* blasted it as incendiary. And William Gladstone predicted it would result in "certain Confederate independence." From a French newspaper came the charge of "barbarity. . . . God Grant that this error not produce new convulsion more terrible than those which already rend the country." [21]

At home, reaction was equally troubling, just as Lincoln had predicted. One soldier wrote home, "I sware I wish that all the abolissions sons of bitches had to come downe here and take the front . . . and all Git blowd to hell." A regiment from the president's own home state of Illinois promptly deserted, defiantly vowing to "lie in the woods until moss grew on their backs rather than help free slaves." Illinois political leaders added fuel to the fire by declaring, "We will not render support to the present administration in carrying on its wicked abolition crusade against the south." [22]

There was praise, to be sure — but mostly from the abolitionists, and most of them were angry that the document offered an escape clause — 100 days notice for the Confederate states to end the rebellion, in return for which they could keep their slaves after all.[23]

Approbation appeared in the Northern press, of course, which was no more surprising than the denunciation Lincoln received from newspapers in the South. But plenty of Northern journals assailed the proclamation as well. Reaction ultimately split along predictable party lines. Lincoln, the Democratic papers charged, was "adrift on the current of radical fanaticism." To the *Chicago Times,* the proclamation was a "monstrous usurpation, a criminal wrong, and an act of national suicide."[24]

In issuing the proclamation, Lincoln had admitted, "I hope for greater gain than loss; but of this, I was not entirely confident. By the time his vice president wrote to him to praise the proclamation as "the great act of the age," Lincoln's lack of confidence seemed entirely justified. "Stocks have declined, and troops come forward more slowly than ever," he wrote confidentially. "This, looked soberly in the face, is not very satisfactory." The worst political aftershock was yet to come: the fall 1862 congressional elections. Lincoln's Republicans took a severe beating.[25]

Lincoln had been proven politically correct in his decision to couch the proclamation as a military necessity and to lay a groundwork that sidestepped the moral imperative for liberty. The result of his strategy, however, was a document that does little retrospectively to inspire historical acknowledgment of his considerable, and probably essential, cunning. For the greatest writer among American presidents constructed his grandest document with the literary flair of a subpoena. He intentionally chose the format of the rigid presidential proclamation — and he had written many of them, on subjects ranging from Thanksgiving holidays to military conscription to suspension of the writ of habeas corpus — most of them deadly dull.

For emancipation, he created a legally sound document that African Americans could later use, "if necessary, to establish judicially their title of freedom," as LaWanda Cox has argued. Ralph Waldo Emerson, noting that the document was a "dazzling success," conceded that it was an act "without inflation or surplusage," that demonstrated that "Liberty is a slow fruit." He was not certain, not in September 1862, that the courts would even uphold the proclamation and keep slaves, in the words of the most quotable line of the document, "thenceforward and forever free." Lincoln had carefully rejected the impulse to place the proclamation on "high moral grounds," as the *New York Times* insightfully detected, and framed it instead "as a war measure from the Commander-in-Chief of the Army, but not . . . one issuing from the bosom of philanthropy."[26] That was the only way he could defend it to border states, Democrats, even Northern racists vital to the Union coalition. The poetry could wait.

So while our historic literature boasts a Declaration of Independence that ringingly begins, "When in the course of human events," and a Constitution starting memorably with "We the people, in order to form a more perfect Union," the first sentence of the preliminary Emancipation Proclamation began, "I, Abraham Lincoln, President of the United States and commander-in-chief of the Army and

The Gift of Language and the Language of Gifts

Navy thereof." The rest of the text features such words as "hereafter" and "heretofore" and "aforesaid" and offers such prosaic phrases as "attention is hereby called," "I do hereby enjoin," and "in witness whereof, I have hereunto set my hand," writing that not only does not inspire but practically paralyzes.

The final Emancipation Proclamation, issued on January 1, 1863, did not add much to the vocabulary of freedom. Its first word was "whereas." "Thereof," "hereby," "hereafter," and "heretofore" clutter the document. Space is devoted to a list of the states and counties exempted from the order. The most inspiring sentence—"I invoke the considerable judgment of mankind, and the gracious favor of Almighty God"—was suggested by someone else. At least Lincoln did insert his belief that it was "sincerely believed to be an act of justice," hastily adding, "warranted by the Constitution, based upon military necessity." "Old Abe," an abolitionist critic complained, "seems utterly incapable of a really grand action." [27]

But eventually, Lincoln did provide the poetic accompaniment he initially resisted. In his annual message to Congress that December one finally hears the voice of a genuine liberator declaring, "We cannot escape history. . . . The fiery trial through which we pass, will light us down, in honor or dishonor, to the latest generation. . . . In giving freedom to the slave, we assure freedom to the free, honorable alike in what we give and what we preserve. We shall nobly save, or meanly lose the last, best hope of earth." [28]

There were more ringing statements to come. By the time Lincoln rose at Gettysburg to consecrate the soldiers' cemetery that November, pettifogging legalities had yielded to great literature. "The great task remaining before us," he declared, now promised nothing less than a "new birth of freedom." [29]

Yet another moment of high drama and glorious prose came with Lincoln's magnificent apology for the sin of slavery, at his Second Inaugural Address on March 4, 1865. More than a century and a quarter later, in 1998, President Clinton issued his own formal statement of regret for slavery in Africa, noticeably stopping short of a full apology. "Going back to the time before we were even a nation, European-Americans received the fruits of the slave trade," Mr. Clinton stated. "And we were wrong in that."

This was not exactly poetry either, yet the criticism it ignited was swift and severe. Republican Congressman Tom DeLay of Texas promptly railed, "Here's a flower child with gray hairs doing exactly what he did in the sixties: he's apologizing for the actions of the United States. . . . It just offends me." And Pat Buchanan, calling Clinton "America's sorry apologist," devoted a column to defending America's innocence in the African slave trade. But criticism was heard from the left as well; Clinton had not gone far enough. Apparently not much has changed; race can still be a blazing issue. The wisest comment may have come from a "senior White House aide," who insisted, "Lincoln already apologized in his second inaugural. Why duplicate what Lincoln said? It's as definitive and eloquent an apology for slavery as you can get." [30]

Indeed it was. Best remembered today for its conciliatory ending, urging "malice toward none" and "charity for all," the second inaugural also boasts a thunderbolt invocation of a vengeful God who "gives to North and South, this terrible war, as the woe due those by whom the offence came" — the "offence" being slavery. Lincoln showed — in perhaps the most epic of all the poetry he produced to accompany his prose proclamation — exactly what kind of national apology the sin of slavery required:

> Fondly do we hope — fervently do we pray — that this mighty scourge of war may speedily pass away. Yet, if God wills that it continue, until all the wealth piled up by the bond-man's two hundred and fifty years of unrequited toil shall be sunk, and until every drop of blood drawn with the lash, shall be paid by another drawn with the sword, as was said three thousand years ago, so still it must be said "the judgments of the Lord, are true and righteous altogether." [31]

Our judgment of history must be true as well. And though it is true that the words of the Emancipation Proclamation itself do not resonate with the passion and beauty of Abraham Lincoln's greatest public statements, sometimes, even with the greatest writer of all presidents, actions do speak louder than words.

Frederick Douglass, who more than any leader of the day understood the restraints on Lincoln and his heroic response in spite of them, knew the document would never stand the test of time as literature, line by line. But Douglass read between the lines. Even though the proclamation had been inspired, Douglass said, by "the low motive of military necessity," he realized at once that it was "a little more than it purported." As he put it, "I saw that its moral power would extend much further." In that dry document Frederick Douglass sensed a "spirit and power far beyond its letter." [32]

Beyond its letter is clearly where modern readers must look for the true meaning of this second Declaration of Independence: beyond the conflicting public relations statements that preceded it, past the lifeless prose that characterized it, and on to the grand oratory that defended it.

The Gift of Language and the Language of Gifts

The day he signed the final emancipation, Lincoln took up his pen, then stopped abruptly and put it down, fingers quivering from hours of handshaking that New Year's morning. "My hand is almost paralyzed," he told the few on-lookers gathered in his office. "If my name ever goes down in history, it will be for this act, and my whole soul is in it. If my hand trembles when I sign the Proclama-tion, all who examine the document will say, 'He hesitated.'" When it counted, he did not. After a few moments, the president took up the pen again, and as one witness remembered, "slowly, firmly wrote that 'Abraham Lincoln' with which the whole world is now familiar. He looked up, smiled, and said: 'That will do.'"[33]

Perhaps it should do for us as well. Lincoln may have used too much per-spiration and too little inspiration to guarantee that America's slaves would be "thenceforward and forever free." But that should not fool all of the people all of the time. The Emancipation Proclamation surely was the greatest act of Lincoln's age. And its legally necessary, politically expedient prose was, after all, garnished soon enough by unforgettable poetry.

Lincoln's "Flat Failure":
The Gettysburg Myth Revisited

SOME SIX SCORE and thirteen years ago, Abraham Lincoln brought forth at Gettysburg a speech universally remembered as one of the greatest ever written, a gem not only of American political oratory but also of American literature. Tributes have been devoted to it, re-creations staged of it, and books written about it. It is surely fair to say that no other American speech has ever inspired so much writing and so many more speeches. This chapter may be the latest, but it certainly will not be the last.

Perhaps the speech remains especially appealing to modern Americans because of the handicaps Lincoln faced in delivering it: a late invitation to appear, a rude reminder that he should deliver no more than "a few appropriate remarks," the distraction of a sick child at home, an unenviable spot on the program that day—following a stem-winder by the greatest orator of the era—and Lincoln's deep aversion to public speechmaking of any kind once he became president. We have come to love the Gettysburg Address, in part, because, in spite of these obstacles, Lincoln somehow composed a masterpiece.[1]

We also love it because, as Lincoln described it, it was "short, short, short"— decidedly not in the tradition of our current chief executive, whose famously interminable 1996 speech at the Democratic National Convention and 1997 State of the Union address, to name two examples, have tested the endurance of increasingly impatient American audiences.[2]

But we love the Gettysburg Address, too, because we sense that Lincoln wrote it in a burst of passion and genius. And perhaps some Americans learned to love it because they still believe that Lincoln summoned the divine inspiration to write it on a railroad train en route to Gettysburg, at the last possible minute.

We love it because we have heard that the press hated it, and everybody in late-twentieth-century America seems to have hated the press. And maybe, most of all, we love it because we have learned that Lincoln himself thought it was a failure. In fact, we have been taught that most of Lincoln's contemporaries failed to appreciate it, too, just as they failed to appreciate Lincoln himself until he was gone. It only makes us love the Gettysburg Address more.

If it is true that all or any of these myths have inspired our affection for Abraham Lincoln's greatest speech, then we may well love the Gettysburg Address for the wrong reasons.

The fact is, the reputation of no other speech in American history has ever been so warped by misconception and myth. True enough, Lincoln was invited late, he was told to keep it brief, he did have a challenging spot on the program that day, and he did have a sick child at home whose suffering surely reminded his worried parents of the illness that had taken the life of another son only a year and a half before. But much of the rest of the legend that makes the Gettysburg Address so appealing was conceived in liberties with the truth and dedicated to the proposition that you can fool most of the people most of the time.[3]

Take the myth of its creation on board the train from Washington. The legend originated with newspaperman Ben Perley Poore, who contended that the address was "written in the car on the way from Washington to the battlefield, upon a piece of pasteboard held on his knee." [4]

Another passenger contended that Lincoln finished the entire manuscript by the time he reached Baltimore. Even more impressive was the claim by a corporal traveling with the president that not until their train reached Hanover—just twelve miles from Gettysburg—did Lincoln stand up after hours of storytelling and declare, "Gentlemen, this is all very pleasant, but the people will expect me to say something to them tomorrow, and I must give the matter some thought." But the most absurd recollection came from Andrew Carnegie, of all people, then a young executive with the B & O Railroad, who claimed that not only did Lincoln write the Gettysburg Address on the train but that Carnegie himself had personally handed Lincoln the pencil he used to do the writing.[5]

The fact is, Lincoln had been "giving the matter some thought" since at least November 8, 1863, eleven days before dedication day at Gettysburg. On that day, newspaperman Noah Brooks asked the president if he had written his remarks. "Not yet," Lincoln replied, quickly adding, "not finished anyway." This means that he had already started writing. According to Brooks, Lincoln further explained, "I have written it over, two or three times, and I shall have to give it another lick before I am satisfied." [6]

In the week and a half that followed, Lincoln anguished over Tad Lincoln's precarious health, worked on his correspondence, held a cabinet meeting, watched a parade, met with Italian sea captains, and took time to see a play starring — of all people — John Wilkes Booth. Yet by November 17 he was able to tell his attorney general that fully half his address was in final form. Not long afterward, former Secretary of War Simon Cameron got to see a copy, written, he remembered, "with a lead pencil on commercial notepaper." Ward Hill Lamon, the marshal of the District of Columbia who traveled to the event with the president, claimed that Lincoln read him the entire speech before they left together for Gettysburg on November 18. But the notoriously self-serving Lamon could not help adding froth to the legend by claiming that the president confided, "It does not suit me, but I have not time for any more." By then, of course, he had devoted a good deal of time — as well as thought — to his Gettysburg Address.[7]

The idea that Lincoln did not take his Gettysburg opportunity seriously is preposterous. He did not even want to travel to the village on the same day as the ceremony, as originally planned by the War Department, for fear of missing the event, as he put it, "by the slightest accident." It was Lincoln who insisted on starting out for Gettysburg the day before, to make certain that he was rested and prepared for the ceremonies. This was not a man who left things to the last minute.[8]

Besides, anyone who has seen the autograph copy of his February 11, 1861 Farewell Address to Springfield, truly written on a train, knows how difficult Lincoln found it to write on the rocking, rolling railroad cars of the 1860s. He had agreed to write out the farewell remarks he had just given extemporaneously for reporters traveling with him to his inauguration. But midway through the effort, he gave up. The jostling of the cars was transforming his usually precise penmanship into an indecipherable scrawl. Perhaps the effort was making him queasy. So he asked his secretary, John G. Nicolay, to take over the task. The rest of the surviving document is in Nicolay's handwriting. If Lincoln did write anything en route to Gettysburg it has not survived. But chances are he recalled his Springfield experience and did not even try. Lincoln was too careful when it came to writing speeches in advance, too poor an impromptu speaker — and well aware of his shortcomings in that department — to make plausible the idea that he waited until the last minute to write his Gettysburg Address.[9]

The most stubborn of the Gettysburg myths is the resilient legend that holds that the speech was poorly received when Lincoln delivered it, that at best, only a few enthusiasts appreciated it while most eyewitnesses did not. Such conclusions are inherently suspicious. In truth, eyewitnesses disagreed about almost everything to do with Lincoln's appearance there, even the weather.

The Gift of Language and the Language of Gifts

One spectator remembered November 19, 1863, as "bright and clear." Yet the *Washington Chronicle* reported rain showers. Some said 15,000 people crowded the town for the event. Others counted 100,000. Some went to their deaths insisting that Lincoln took a tour of the battlefield in the early morning hours on dedication day. Others swore that he stayed inside the Wills House until it was time to mount up for the procession to the ceremony.[10]

People even disagreed about the president's horse. One visitor proclaimed that Lincoln looked "like Saul of old" that day as he sat astride "the largest . . . Chestnut horse" in the county. Another testified that he rode "a diminutive pony." And yet another thought the horse was so small that Lincoln's long legs almost dragged along the ground, inspiring one old local farmer to exclaim at the sight of him, "Say Father Abraham, if she goes to run away with yer . . . just stand up and let her go!" People on the scene did not even agree on the color of the horse. Surviving recollections state with equal certainty that it was "a white horse," a "chestnut bay," a "brown charger," and a "black steed."[11]

When such wildly diverse recollection becomes the rule, not the exception, how seriously should we take the claims of those observers who asserted that Lincoln's speech fell on deaf ears at Gettysburg? This is especially so when it comes to the crucial question: Did the listeners appreciate the address? True, they had just heard a two-hour-long speech from the principal orator of the day, Edward Everett. Drained and most likely exhausted, they may not have been ready to focus on another major speech. Then again, they were about to see and hear the president of the United States, some for the first and only time.

Did Lincoln's speaking style prevent the audience from appreciating the novelty of his appearance and the beauty of his words? Presidential assistant secretary John Hay remembered that Lincoln spoke "in a firm free way." But a journalist from Cincinnati complained about his "sharp, unmusical, treble voice."[12]

Then there is the issue of whether Lincoln read from a text or spoke from memory. Private secretary Nicolay maintained he "did not read from a manuscript." A student in the audience, on the other hand, remembered that Lincoln kept a "hand on each side of the manuscript" while he spoke, though he "looked at it seldom." And yet another eyewitness recalled that Lincoln "barely took his eyes" off the speech while he read it.[13]

There is the testimony from the Associated Press reporter, Joseph L. Gilbert, who said he was so transfixed by Lincoln's "intense earnestness and depth of feeling" as he spoke that he stopped taking notes just to gaze "up at him." He had to borrow Lincoln's manuscript afterward to fill in the gaps, inserting several interruptions for "applause," plus "long continued applause" at the conclusion. Did he really remember such outbursts of enthusiasm? Or did he add them charitably to an address that otherwise elicited no reaction at all? Whom do we believe?[14]

Stenographer-correspondents were both imprecise and partisan in the Civil War era. The real Lincoln-Douglas debates, to cite the most famous casualty of their work, are irrevocably lost to us, since we have left only the Republican-commissioned transcripts that make Lincoln sound perfect and Douglas bombastic, and the Democratic-commissioned transcripts that make Lincoln sound hesitant and Douglas eloquent.

Political stenography had not advanced much toward nonpartisanship by 1863. One Chicago shorthand reporter at Gettysburg, for example, heard Lincoln say "our poor *attempts* to add or detract," not "our poor *power*" (emphasis added). And three New York papers heard Lincoln dedicate Americans not to "the unfinished work that they have thus far so nobly advanced" but the "*re*finished work" (emphasis added), as if he were a home-remodeling contractor. Another stenographer recorded not "we here highly resolve," but "we here highly imbibe." And one Democratic paper claimed that Lincoln could not even count; he had started his speech referring not to the events of "four score and seven years ago" but to "four score and *ten* years ago" (emphasis added).[15]

There was more than sloppy stenography at work here. There was highly partisan stenography as well, just as in the days of the Lincoln-Douglas debates. Thus, to no one's surprise, the *Illinois State Journal,* the old pro-Lincoln paper from Springfield, reported that "immense applause" had greeted the president at Gettysburg. But a far less sympathetic observer reported "not a word, not a cheer, not a shout."[16]

Which version of the audience reaction was correct? We may never know for sure. The truth is buried within the nineteenth-century tradition of partisan journalism. The question boils down to the credibility of the Republican versus the Democratic party press.

Thus it seems foolish that biographers have made so much of the fact that many of the newspapers commenting immediately on the Gettysburg Address failed to realize its greatness. Indeed, it was Lamon who fueled this most stubborn of legends by insisting "without fear of contradiction that this famous Gettysburg speech was not regarded by . . . the press . . . as a production of extraordinary merit, nor was it commented on as such until after the death of its author."[17]

Perhaps Lamon was thinking of one of the most frequently quoted criticisms — from the *Chicago Times:* "The cheek of every American must tinge with shame as he reads the silly flat and dishwatery utterances of the man who has to be pointed out to intelligent foreigners as the President of the United States." On the other hand, the rival Chicago newspaper, the *Tribune,* quickly appreciated, and announced, the importance of the speech, countering: "The dedicatory remarks by President Lincoln will live among the annals of the war." [18]

As genuine evidence of Lincoln's performance at Gettysburg, however, both appraisals were in a sense totally insignificant. Of course, the *Tribune* predicted great things for the Gettysburg Address. It had been a pro-Lincoln paper since at least 1858, when it hired the stenographer who recorded the Republican version of the Lincoln-Douglas debates and filled the paper's pages daily with attacks on Douglas and praise of Lincoln. Why would the *Tribune* not cheer the speech at Gettysburg? It had cheered nearly every speech Lincoln ever made.

And of course the *Chicago Times* hated it. It hated Lincoln! It hated him when he ran against Douglas, charging that "the Republicans have a candidate for the Senate of whose bad rhetoric and horrible jargon they are ashamed." And surely the *Times* had not grown fonder of Lincoln after his army closed the newspaper down in 1863, the same year as the Gettysburg Address, even if it was Lincoln who later countermanded the order. "Is Mr. Lincoln less refined than a savage?" the *Times* thundered in its predictable attack on the address.[19]

Nor is it surprising that the Democratic party newspaper in Harrisburg declared, "We pass over the silly remarks of the President; for the credit of the nation, we are willing that the veil of oblivion shall be dropped over them and that they shall be no more repeated or thought of." Those lines are probably the most frequently quoted by historians seeking to prove that the press, in general, did not appreciate the Gettysburg Address. Seldom is the paper's political affiliation mentioned, only its ambiguous name: the *Patriot and Union.* And almost never are the first few lines of its review quoted, which seem far more revealing of its motives than a disdain for Lincoln's literary style. "The President," it began, "acted without sense and without constraint in a panorama that was gotten up more for the benefit of his party than for the glory of the nation and the honor of the dead." *For the benefit of his party!* There, in a nutshell, is the Harrisburg Democratic party newspaper's grievance with the Gettysburg Address: to the *Patriot and Union* it represented Republican party propaganda.[20]

In fact, the address elicited a number of prompt, rave reviews at the time it was delivered. They came from Republican papers like the *Providence Journal,* which pointed out, "The hardest thing in the world is to make a five minute's speech. . . .

Could the most elaborate, splendid oration be more beautiful, more touching, more inspiring, than those thrilling words?"[21]

It is true that the *London Times* did complain that the ceremony at Gettysburg was "rendered ludicrous by some of the luckless sallies of that poor President Lincoln." But the *London Times* seldom praised Abraham Lincoln. Interestingly, a quote from the same review that several historians have used to illustrate the period press's foolhardy dismissal of the Gettysburg Address — that it was "dull and commonplace" — has long been quoted inaccurately. The paper actually used those words to criticize not Abraham Lincoln's Gettysburg Address, but Edward Everett's.[22]

As for Everett, his own assessment, sent to Lincoln the day after the ceremonies, conceded, "I should be glad if I could flatter myself that I came as near to the central idea of the occasion in two hours, as you did in two minutes." Thus, even if we cling to the ultimate Gettysburg legend — that Lincoln himself thought he missed a golden opportunity on November 19 — we can at least be satisfied that he knew better by November 20, the day he received Everett's letter of praise and replied modestly that he was "pleased to know" that what he said "was not entirely a failure."[23]

We probably owe the legend of Lincoln's lack of enthusiasm for his own performance at Gettysburg to Ward Hill Lamon, one of the most consistently undependable sources in the annals of Lincoln biography. It was Lamon who claimed that when Lincoln took his seat after the address, he confided sadly, "That speech won't scour! It is a flat failure, and the people are disappointed." And it was Lamon who added that when they returned to Washington, Lincoln repeated, "I tell you, Hill, that speech fell on the audience like a wet blanket. I am distressed about it. I ought to have prepared it with more care."[24]

As historians Don E. Fehrenbacher and Virginia Fehrenbacher recently pointed out, however, the original personal notes from which Lamon adapted this recollection show that it was he who claimed the speech fell on the audience like a "wet blanket." Lincoln himself never uttered the statement. Later, Lamon simply put his own words in Lincoln's mouth. In short, we have no authentic, reliable reason to believe that Lincoln ever felt that he failed at Gettysburg.[25]

Of nearly equal importance, even if audience reaction was as disappointing as Lamon claimed, Lincoln knew that he was delivering the Gettysburg Address that day to two audiences: the relatively small crowd at the cemetery, whether it was 15,000 or 100,000, and the millions who would read the text in the press.

The Gift of Language and the Language of Gifts

For several years Lincoln had perfected the art of delivering state papers and political messages through the newspapers. He made few formal speeches as president. But he made sure that when he greeted special visitors with important remarks, they were quickly printed in the newspapers. If he wrote an important letter — such as the one to Erastus Corning defending his suspension of the writ of habeas corpus — they too were published for the benefit of other readers.[26]

The Gettysburg Address lived because Lincoln made certain that it lived: by giving his transcript to the Associated Press, by writing additional copies for souvenir albums and charity auctions, by basking in the knowledge that it would be reprinted worldwide and praised at least in the Republican journals. From the beginning, then, the Gettysburg Address was recognized — and applauded — because the brilliant public relations strategist who made certain his remarks were widely read was also a consummate literary craftsman who enjoyed his finest hour during his two minutes at Gettysburg.

It is therefore fitting and proper to here highly resolve that Lincoln did indeed triumph at Gettysburg, not just in history but on the very spot where he summoned all his great powers to reconsecrate a scene of death into an unforgettable metaphor for birth: a new birth of freedom.

Notes

Chapter 1. "Prized in Every Liberty-Loving Household"

1. Francis Bicknell Carpenter, *Six Months at the White House with Abraham Lincoln: The Story of a Picture* (New York: Hurd and Houghton, 1866), 350.

2. Harold Holzer, Gabor S. Boritt, and Mark E. Neely Jr., "Francis B. Carpenter: Painter of Abraham Lincoln and His Circle," *American Art Journal* 16 (spring 1984): 75; Carpenter, *Six Months at the White House,* 28, 353–54.

3. Francis B. Carpenter, "Anecdotes and Reminiscences," in Henry J. Raymond, *Life, Public Services, and State Papers of Abraham Lincoln* (New York: Derby and Miller, 1865), 763–64.

4. P. J. Staudenraus, ed., *Mr. Lincoln's Washington: The Civil War Diaries of Noah Brooks* (New York: Thomas J. Yoseloff, 1967), 361.

5. Ibid., 362.

6. Ibid., 363.

7. See Harold Holzer, Gabor S. Boritt, and Mark E. Neely Jr., *The Lincoln Image: Abraham Lincoln and the Popular Print* (New York: Scribner's, 1984).

8. Herbert Mitgang, ed., *Lincoln as They Saw Him* (New York: Rinehart, 1956), 304; Roy P. Basler et al., eds., *The Collected Works of Abraham Lincoln,* 9 vols. (New Brunswick, NJ: Rutgers University Press, 1953–1955), 5:444 (hereafter cited as *Collected Works*).

9. Carpenter, *Six Months at the White House,* 22.

10. LaWanda Cox, *Lincoln and Black Freedom: A Study in Presidential Leadership* (Columbia: University of South Carolina Press, 1981), 13.

11. Charles Eberstadt, *Lincoln's Emancipation Proclamation* (New York: Duschnes Crawford, 1950), 23.

12. J. W. Forney to Abraham Lincoln, December 30, 1862, Abraham Lincoln Papers, Library of Congress, Washington, DC (hereafter cited as Lincoln Papers).

13. Holzer, Boritt, and Neely, *The Lincoln Image,* 109–10.

14. Richard L. Pease, "Edward Dalton Marchant," *Vineyard Gazette,* August 26, 1887.

15. For the photograph, see Charles Hamilton and Lloyd Ostendorf, *Lincoln in Photographs: An Album of Every Known Pose,* rev. ed. (Dayton, OH: Morningside Books, 1985), 88–89.

16. Edward Dalton Marchant to Richard L. Pease, May 24, 1863, *Vineyard Gazette,* August 26, 1887, in Andrew Thomas, "Portraiture, Politics, and Patronage: Edward Dalton Marchant's *Abraham Lincoln* (1863) and the Union League of Philadelphia," lecture.

17. Marchant quoted in Thomas, "Portraiture, Politics, and Patronage." The best study of racial politics in the 1864 campaign is David L. Long, *The Jewel of Liberty: Abraham Lin-*

coln's *Re-election and the End of Slavery* (Mechanicsburg, PA: Stackpole Books, 1994), esp. 153–77.

18. See Mark E. Neely Jr., *The Last Best Hope of Earth: Abraham Lincoln and the Promise of America* (Cambridge: Harvard University Press, 1993), opp. 118.

19. Carpenter, *Six Months at the White House,* 157–58.

20. Ibid., 25.

21. Carpenter's sketchbook was examined by the author in the home of his descendants near Syracuse, New York.

22. Carpenter, "Anecdotes and Reminiscences," 763; advertisement for "Carpenter's Great National Picture" in Raymond, ed., *The Life and Public Services of Abraham Lincoln,* endpapers.

23. Trumbull's *Declaration of Independence,* to which period critics often compared the Carpenter painting, was 12 by 18 feet in size; *First Reading* was 9 by 14 feet, 6 inches. See *Art in the United States Capitol* (Washington, DC: U.S. Government Printing Office, 1976), 132, 152.

24. See pamphlet for an exhibition of the Carpenter original, published by Williams and Everett Gallery, Boston, Massachusetts, n.d., in the Illinois State Historical Library, Springfield.

25. *New York Times,* May 1, 1866.

26. Inscription on an advance woodcut copy of the Ritchie print in the collection of the Prints Division of the New York Public Library.

27. Carpenter, *Six Months at the White House,* 20.

28. David Brion Davis, *The Emancipation Moment* (Twenty-second Annual Robert Fortenbaugh Memorial Lecture, Gettysburg College, Gettysburg, PA., 1983), 10.

29. Katherine Morrison McClinton, *The Chromolithographs of Louis Prang* (New York: Clarkson N. Potter, 1973), 37.

30. *Collected Works,* 5:537.

31. L. Franklin Smith, *Proclamation of Emancipation. The Second Declaration of Independence! By President Lincoln, January 1st 1863* (advertising sheet in the Stern Collection, Library of Congress). For a reproduction, see Harold Holzer, Gabor S. Boritt, and Mark E. Neely Jr., *Changing the Lincoln Image* (Fort Wayne, IN: Louis A. Warren Lincoln Library and Museum, 1985), 71.

32. Ibid.

Chapter 2. "That Attractive Rainbow"

1. *London Punch,* March 25, 1865.

2. Herbert Mitgang, ed., *Lincoln as They Saw Him* (New York: Rinehart, 1956), 343–44.

3. Ibid., 371, 379.

4. *Collected Works,* 4:64.

5. Ibid., 1:509–10; Gabor S. Boritt, ed., *Lincoln the War President: The Gettysburg Lectures* (New York: Oxford University Press, 1992), xxvii.

6. Harold Holzer, ed., *The Lincoln-Douglas Debates: The First Complete, Unexpurgated Text* (New York: HarperCollins, 1993), 51.

7. See, for example, the following prints by lithographers Currier & Ives of New York: *The National Game. Three "Outs" and One "Run"/Abraham Lincoln Winning the Ball; The Political Gymnasium;* and *Political "Blondins" Crossing Salt River,* in Rufus Rockwell Wilson, *Lincoln in Caricature: A Historical Collection with Descriptive and Biographical Commentary* (New York: Horizon Press, 1953), 27, 35, 37.

8. Portrait of *President-Elect Abraham Lincoln* in *Frank Leslie's Illustrated Newspaper,* November 21, 1860; for Charles Alfred Barry's controversial, Jacksonian portrait of Lincoln, see Harold Holzer, Gabor S. Boritt, and Mark E. Neely Jr., *The Lincoln Image: Abraham Lincoln and the Popular Print* (New York: Scribner's, 1984), 51–55.

9. *Harper's Weekly,* March 9, 1861.

10. Don E. Fehrenbacher and Virginia Fehrenbacher, eds., *Recollected Words of Lincoln* (Stanford, CA: Stanford University Press, 1996), 306.

11. See *The Abe-Iad,* illustrated sheet-music cover published by John H. Parrott, Richmond, in Weldon Petz, *In the Presence of Abraham Lincoln* (Harrogate, TN: Lincoln Memorial University, 1973), 44.

12. T. Harry Williams, *Lincoln and His Generals* (New York: Alfred A. Knopf, 1952), vii; David Herbert Donald, *Lincoln* (New York: Simon and Schuster, 1996), 285, 329; Howard K. Beale, ed., *The Diary of Edward Bates . . .* (Washington, DC: U.S. Government Printing Office, 1933), 220; Stephen Sears, ed., *The Civil War Papers of George B. McClellan: Selected Correspondence, 1860–1865* (New York: Ticknor and Fields, 1989), 85, 106.

13. Mark E. Neely Jr., Harold Holzer, and Gabor S. Boritt, *The Confederate Image: Prints of the Lost Cause* (Chapel Hill: University of North Carolina Press, 1987), 15–19.

14. Fehrenbacher and Fehrenbacher, eds., *Recollected Words of Lincoln,* 126.

15. For Blythe, see Harold Holzer and Mark E. Neely Jr., *Mine Eyes Have Seen the Glory: The Civil War in Art* (New York: Orion Books, 1993), 82–83; for Kimmel and Forster's print, *The Outbreak of the Rebellion,* see Holzer, Boritt, and Neely, *The Lincoln Image,* 85.

16. See Harold Holzer, "Lincoln at the Front: Abraham Lincoln Visits the Battlefields of the Civil War," *Blue and Gray Magazine* 1 (February–March 1984); 50.

17. Robert Colby to Abraham Lincoln, May 18, 1861, Lincoln Papers.

18. Original drawings in the Prints and Photographs Division, Library of Congress.

19. Charles Hamilton and Lloyd Ostendorf, *Lincoln in Photographs: An Album of Every Known Pose,* rev. ed. (Dayton, OH: Morningside Books, 1985), 107.

20. David Donald, ed., *Inside Lincoln's Cabinet: The Civil War Diaries of Salmon P. Chase* (New York: Longmans, Green and Company, 1954), 85; for Reinhart, see William O. Stoddard, *Abraham Lincoln: The True Story of a Great Life,* rev. ed., (New York: Fords, Howard and Hulbert, 1896), opp. 210.

21. Fehrenbacher and Fehrenbacher, eds., *Recollected Words of Lincoln,* 113, 200; Mark E. Neely Jr., "Wilderness and the Cult of Manliness: Hooker, Lincoln, and Defeat," in *Lincoln's Generals,* ed. Gabor S. Boritt (New York: Oxford University Press, 1994), 65.

22. *Collected Works,* 6:78; Donald, *Lincoln,* 429; James M. McPherson, "Lincoln and

the Strategy of Unconditional Surrender," in Boritt, ed., *Lincoln the War President,* 46; Fehrenbacher and Fehrenbacher, eds., *Recollected Words of Lincoln,* 331.

23. Earl Schenck Miers, ed., *Lincoln Day by Day: A Chronology, 1809–1865,* 3 vols. (Washington, DC: Lincoln Sesquicentennial Commission, 1960), 3:271–72; Jay Monaghan, *Diplomat in Carpet Slippers: Abraham Lincoln Deals with Foreign Affairs* (Indianapolis: Bobbs-Merrill, 1945), 378.

24. Allen Thorndike Rice, ed., *Reminiscences of Lincoln by Distinguished Men of His Time* (New York: Century Company, 1888), 147.

25. See Currier and Ives, *The Great Exhibition of 1860,* in Wilson, *Lincoln in Caricature,* 51; for Volck, see Neely, Holzer, and Boritt, *The Confederate Image,* 44–54.

26. LaWanda Cox, *Lincoln and Black Freedom* (Columbia: University of South Carolina Press, 1981), 13.

27. See Currier and Ives's *Freedom to the Slaves . . . ,* in Holzer, Boritt, and Neely, *The Lincoln Image,* 102.

28. See, for example, Currier and Ives, *The Old Bull Dog on the Right Track,* original lithograph cartoon in the Lincoln Museum, Fort Wayne, Indiana, and Currier and Ives, *The Gunboat Candidate at the Battle of Malvern Hill,* in Bernard F. Reilly Jr., *American Political Prints, 1766–1876: A Catalog of the Collections in the Library of Congress* (Boston: G. K. Hall, 1991), 526.

29. See, for example, M. W. Siebert, *Union and Liberty! Union and Slavery!* in Reilly, *American Political Prints,* 534; and M. Martinet, *Le plus rude projectile qu'ait encore recu le sud!* original print from *Actualités,* in the Lincoln Museum, Fort Wayne, Indiana.

30. Holzer, Boritt, and Neely, *The Lincoln Image,* 193, 195.

31. See Thomas Kelly's 1866 lithograph, *President Lincoln and His Cabinet. With General Grant in the Council Chamber of the Whitehouse* [sic], in Harold Holzer, Gabor S. Boritt, and Mark E. Neely Jr., *Changing the Lincoln Image* (Fort Wayne, IN: Louis A. Warren Lincoln Library and Museum, 1985), 19.

32. Ibid., 65–67.

33. Miers, ed., *Lincoln Day by Day,* 3:321–27; *Collected Works,* 4:439.

34. Holzer and Neely, *Mine Eyes Have Seen the Glory,* 156.

35. Harold Holzer, *The Mirror Image of Civil War Memory: Abraham Lincoln and Jefferson Davis in Popular Prints,* Seventeenth Annual R. Gerald McMurtry Lecture (Fort Wayne, IN: Lincoln Museum, 1997), 32–34.

36. John S. Barnes, "With Lincoln from Washington to Richmond in 1865," *Appleton's Magazine* 11 (June 1907); 515–24, 742–51; Harold Holzer, "I Myself Was at the Front," *Civil War Times Illustrated* 29 (January/February 1991); 34–35.

37. Holzer, "Lincoln at the Front," 54.

38. Ibid.

Chapter 3. Dying to Be Seen

1. Waldo W. Braden, ed., *Building the Myth: Selected Speeches Memorializing Abraham Lincoln* (Urbana: University of Illinois Press, 1990), 66.

2. U.S. Copyright Records for the Southern District of New York for 1865, Library of Congress.

3. See Richard P. McCormick, *Party Formation in the Jacksonian Era* (Chapel Hill: University of North Carolina Press, 1966), 349–50.

4. Over the years, the author consulted print collections in the Lincoln Museum, Fort Wayne; the Library of Congress, Washington, DC; the Chicago Historical Society; the Museum of the City of New York; the Abraham Lincoln Museum at Lincoln Memorial University, Harrogate, Tennessee; and in the bins and catalogs of private dealers such as the Abraham Lincoln Book Shop in Chicago, the Old Print Shop in New York, the Old Print Gallery in Washington, DC, and the Philadelphia Print Shop.

5. See the issues of April 29, 1865. The illustrated weeklies bore dates three days *later* than the Currier & Ives separate-sheet print, but, like publications of today, the weeklies may have been postdated by a week, indicating the last, not the first, date they could be sold by news dealers.

6. "Nothing equals Macbeth," Lincoln wrote to actor James Hackett on August 17, 1863. See *Collected Works,* 6:392.

7. The Lincoln family's photograph of Booth is now in the Lincoln Museum. See Mark E. Neely Jr. and Harold Holzer, *The Lincoln Family Album* (New York: Doubleday, 1990), 108–9.

8. Sales brochure, *Ritchie's Picture Death of Lincoln* (New York: A. H. Ritchie, 1868), 5.

9. Ibid., 7–8.

10. The original photograph is in the Chicago Historical Society, as is Chappel's canvas. See Harold Holzer and Frank J. Williams, *Lincoln's Deathbed in Art and Memory: The "Rubber Room" Phenomenon* (Gettysburg, PA: Thomas Publications, 1998), 29–34.

11. Original in the Chicago Historical Society.

12. *Prospectus of Works Published by John B. Bachelder* (New York: John B. Bachelder, 1866).

13. Printmaker M. David finally issued a lithograph copy of the Chappel canvas in 1908. A copy is in the Lincoln Museum.

14. *Cincinnati Daily Gazette,* April 22, 1865, copy in the author's collection; for the story of Middleton's print portrait of Lincoln, see Harold Holzer, Gabor S. Boritt, and Mark E. Neely Jr., *The Lincoln Image: Abraham Lincoln and the Popular Print* (New York: Charles Scribner's Sons, 1984), 136–40, and Lincoln to Middleton, December 30, 1864, *Collected Works,* 8:191–92.

15. *Ritchie's Death of Lincoln,* 5.

Chapter 4. The Mirror Image of Civil War Memory

1. Avraham Yarmolinsky, quoted in Noble E. Cunningham Jr., *Popular Images of the Presidency from Washington to Lincoln* (Columbia: University of Missouri Press, 1991), 19.

2. Harry Twyford Peters, *Currier & Ives: Printmakers to the American People* (New York: Doubleday, Doran and Company, 1942), 12. The sales letter quoted is dated 187–.

3. Clement Eaton, *Jefferson Davis* (New York: Free Press, 1977), 89.

4. Ibid., 90–98.

5. Ibid., 92; Jefferson Davis, *The Rise and Fall of the Confederate Government,* 2 vols. (1881; rpt., New York: DaCapo Press, 1990), 1:176–77 (hereafter cited as *Rise and Fall*).

6. Charles Hamilton and Lloyd Ostendorf, *Lincoln in Photographs: An Album of Every Known Pose,* rev. ed. (Dayton, OH: Morningside Books, 1985), 30; Lincoln to Edward Mendel, June 8, 1860, in *The Collected Works of Abraham Lincoln, Supplement 1832–1865,* ed. Roy P. Basler, (Westport, CT: Greenwood Press, 1974), 55 (the original letter is in a secretary's hand, signed by Lincoln); Cunningham, *Popular Images of the Presidency,* 17.

7. Harold G. and Oswald Garrison Villard, eds., *Lincoln on the Eve of '61: A Journalist's Story by Henry Villard* (New York: Alfred A. Knopf, 1941), 93.

8. Davis, *Rise and Fall,* 1:198.

9. *Collected Works,* 4:192–93, 204; Victor Searcher, *Lincoln's Journey to Greatness* (Philadelphia: John C. Winston, 1960), 134.

10. Benson J. Lossing, *Pictorial History of the Civil War in the United States of America,* 16 vols. (Philadelphia: George W. Childs, 1866), 1:279–80; Don E. Fehrenbacher and Virginia Fehrenbacher, eds., *Recollected Words of Abraham Lincoln* (Stanford, CA: Stanford University Press, 1996), 314, 394; Alan Pinkerton, *History and Evidence of the Passage of Abraham Lincoln from Harrisburg, Pa., to Washington, D.C.* (privately printed, 1868), 22.

11. Herbert Mitgang, ed., *Abraham Lincoln: A Press Portrait* (Chicago: Quadrangle Books, 1971), 234.

12. Cunningham, *Popular Images of the Presidency,* 283.

13. Steven E. Woodworth, *Davis and Lee at War* (Lawrence: University Press of Kansas, 1995), 9.

14. William C. Davis, *Jefferson Davis: The Man and His Hour—A Biography* (New York: HarperCollins, 1991), 55; Davis, *Rise and Fall,* 1:176, 198, 297; Katharine Clinton, *Heroines of Dixie: Confederate Women Tell Their Story of the War* (Indianapolis: Bobbs-Merrill, 1955), 148.

15. John B. Jones, *A Rebel War Clerk's Diary at the Confederate States Capital,* 2 vols. (Philadelphia, 1866), 1:64.

16. C. Vann Woodward and Elisabeth Muhlenfield, eds., *The Private Mary Chesnut: The Unpublished Civil War Diaries* (New York: Oxford University Press, 1984), 105; Davis, *Jefferson Davis,* 553.

17. Jones, *A Rebel War Clerk's Diary,* 1:65.

18. Ibid.; Eaton, *Jefferson Davis,* 243.

19. C. Vann Woodward, ed., *Mary Chesnut's Civil War* (New Haven: Yale University Press, 1981), 84; R. Colby to Abraham Lincoln, March 18, 1861, Lincoln Papers.

20. *London Punch,* May 9, 1863.

21. *Southern Illustrated News,* July 25, 1863.

22. See Mark E. Neely Jr., Harold Holzer, and Gabor S. Boritt, *The Confederate Image: Prints of the Lost Cause* (Chapel Hill: University of North Carolina Press, 1987), esp. 44–54.

23. Harold Holzer, Mark E. Neely, and Gabor S. Boritt, *The Lincoln Image: Abraham Lincoln and the Popular Print* (New York: Scribner's, 1984), 102–10.

24. See especially David E. Long, *The Jewel of Liberty: Abraham Lincoln's Re-election and the End of Slavery* (Mechanicsburg, PA: Stackpole Books, 1994).

25. Fehrenbacher and Fehrenbacher, eds., *Recollected Works of Abraham Lincoln,* 143; Theodore C. Blegen, ed., *Abraham Lincoln and His Mailbag: Two Documents by Edward D. Neill, One of Lincoln's Secretaries* (St. Paul: Minnesota Historical Society, 1964), 40; Neely, Holzer, and Boritt, *The Confederate Image,* 79.

26. Davis, *Rise and Fall,* 2:701–2; *New York Herald,* May 15, 1865.

27. Allan Nevins and Milton Halsey Thomas, eds., *The Diary of George Templeton Strong,* 3 vols. (New York: Macmillan, 1952), 3:598.

28. David B. Cheesebrough, *No Sorrow Like Our Sorrow: Northern Protestant Ministers and the Assassination of Abraham Lincoln* (Kent, OH: Kent State University Press, 1994), 57–59.

29. Davis, *Rise and Fall,* 2:595; Neely, Holzer, and Boritt, *The Confederate Image,* 95; Woodward, ed., *Mary Chesnut's Civil War,* 819.

30. Barry Schwartz, *George Washington: The Making of an American Symbol* (New York: Free Press, 1987), 154.

31. J. C. Derby, *Fifty Years Among Authors, Books, and Publishers* (New York: G. W. Carleton, 1884), 489; Harold Holzer, Mark E. Neely, and Gabor S. Boritt, *Changing the Lincoln Image* (Ft. Wayne, IN: Louis A. Warren Lincoln Library and Museum, 1985), 20.

32. Roger Fischer, *Them Damned Pictures: Explorations in American Political Cartoon Art* (North Haven, CT: Archon Books, 1996), esp. 175–201; see also Fischer's review of this chapter in its original form, as the published R. Gerald McMurtry Lecture, in *Lincoln Herald* 100 (spring 1988); 114.

33. Horace Greeley, *Recollections of a Busy Life* (New York: J. B. Ford and Company, 1868), 410–11.

34. Davis, *Rise and Fall,* 1:177.

Chapter 5. "Ridicule Without Much Malice"

1. George G. Bryan letter, ca. 1845, quoted from Historic Furnishings Report, Martin Van Buren National Historic Site, 248.

2. Colta Ives, Margaret Stuffmann, and Martin Sonnabend, *Daumier Drawings* (New York: Metropolitan Museum of Art, 1992), 174, 253.

3. Harold G. Villard and Oswald Garrison Villard, eds., *Lincoln on the Eve of '61: A Journalist's Story by Henry Villard* (New York: Alfred A. Knopf, 1941), 28.

4. Rufus Rockwell Wilson, *Lincoln in Caricature* (privately printed, 1903), 1.

5. Rufus Rockwell Wilson, *Lincoln in Caricature* (Elmira, NY: Primavera Press, 1953); Albert Shaw, *Abraham Lincoln: His Path to the Presidency: A Cartoon History,* and *Abraham Lincoln: The Year of His Election: A Cartoon History* (New York: Review of Reviews, 1929).

6. Wilson, *Lincoln in Caricature,* 1903 ed., 1; Stefan Lorant, *Lincoln: A Picture Story of His Life* (New York: W. W. Norton, 1969), 182.

7. See Harold Holzer, Gabor S. Boritt, and Mark E. Neely Jr., *The Lincoln Image: Abra-*

Lincoln Seen and Heard

ham *Lincoln and the Popular Print* (New York: Scribner's, 1984); Gabor S. Boritt, " '*Punch*' Lincoln: Some Thoughts on Cartoons in the British Magazine," *Journal of the Abraham Lincoln Association* 15 (winter 1994): 1–22; Roger A. Fischer, *Them Damned Pictures: Explorations in American Political Cartoon Art* (North Haven, CT: Archon Books, 1996), 175–200.

8. Bernard F. Reilly Jr., *American Political Prints, 1766–1876: A Catalog of the Collections in the Library of Congress* (Boston: G. K. Hall, 1991), 10, 84, 355.

9. Ibid., 49–120.

10. *Only Authentic Life of Abraham Lincoln, Alias "Old Abe"* (copy in the Illinois State Historical Library, bound with *The Life of Gen. George B. McClellan* [New York: J. C. Haney, 1864]).

11. The reference to the tradition of "gravity" is from Herbert J. Muller, *Adlai Stevenson: A Study in Values* (New York: Harper and Row), 9; see also Charles E. Schultz, *Political Humor: From Aristophanes to Sam Ervin* (London: Associated University Presses, 1977), 190. For an example of a Lincoln jokester, see Robert M. DeWitt, *Old Abe's Joker or, Wit at the White House* (New York: Henry J. Wehman, 1863), and *Old Abe's Jokes, Fresh from Abraham's Bosom Containing all His Issues* (New York: T. R. Dawley, 1864).

12. The cartoon is one of the first listed for the 1860 campaign in Reilly, *American Political Prints,* 437.

13. See, for example, Cecil K. Byrd and Ward W. Moore, eds., *Abraham Lincoln in Print and Photograph: A Picture History from the Lilly Library* (Mineola, NY: Dover Publishing, 1997), 46–48.

14. State-by-state results from 1860 can be found in Stefan Lorant, *The Glorious Burden* (Lenox, MA: Author's Edition, 1976), 1066.

15. Original in the collection of the Lincoln Museum, Fort Wayne, Indiana.

16. Original lithographs in the collection of the Museum of the City of New York.

17. Original in the Library of Congress.

18. *All the Year Round,* April 13, 1861, quoted in Matthew Noah Vosmeier, " 'Election-Time in America': An Englishman's View of Popular Politics During the 1860 Campaign," *Lincoln Lore* 1832 (October 1991); 2. For analysis of the prints of Douglas in search of, and finding, his mother, see Mark E. Neely Jr., "Lincoln, Douglas, and the 'Maine Law,' " *Lincoln Lore* 1622 (April 1973); 2.

19. Stephen Hess and Milton Kaplan, *The Ungentlemanly Art: A History of American Political Cartoons* (New York: Macmillan, 1968), 74–75; *Collected Works,* 4:38–39.

20. Reilly, *American Political Prints,* 143–88, 275–325, 418–54.

21. Original in the author's collection.

22. See Mark E. Neely Jr., Harold Holzer, and Gabor S. Boritt, *The Confederate Image: Prints of the Lost Cause* (Chapel Hill: University of North Carolina Press, 1987), 44–54.

23. *Southern Illustrated News,* November 8, 1862; January 31, 1863; February 28, 1863; November 14, 1863; February 27, 1864. Original run in the New York Public Library.

24. For examples, see Howard Lesoff, *The Civil War with "Punch"* (Wendell, NC: Broadfoot Publishing, 1984); the book's pages are unnumbered.

25. Diana Donald, *The Age of Caricature: Satirical Prints in the Reign of George III* (New Haven: Yale University Press, 1996), 2, 4.

26. A good beginning was made in David E. Long, *The Jewel of Liberty: Abraham Lincoln's Re-election and the End of Slavery* (Mechanicsburg, PA: Stackpole Books, 1994).

27. Reilly, *American Political Prints*, 518–47.

28. Inscription on the Library of Congress' copy of the lithograph, in the Prints and Photographs Division.

29. Reilly, *American Political Prints*, 46.

30. For examples of these Napoleon caricatures, see Robert Philippe, *Political Graphics: Art as a Weapon* (New York: Abbeville Press, 1980), 21.

31. Reilly, *American Political Prints*, 539.

32. Michael Burlingame and John R. Turner Ettlinger, eds., *Inside Lincoln's White House: The Complete Civil War Diary of John Hay* (Carbondale: Southern Illinois University Press, 1997), 243.

33. *London Punch*, December 3, 1864.

34. Ibid., May 6, 1865.

35. Original prints in the Library of Congress: *"Uncle Sam" Making New Arrangements* and *Uncle Sam Protecting His Property Against the Encroachments of His Cousin John*.

36. *Collected Works*, 6:558–59.

Chapter 6. Lincoln in Confederate Cartoons

1. Seth Stimmel, *Personal Reminiscences of Abraham Lincoln* (Minneapolis: William H. M. Adams, 1928), 5.

2. Robert Philippe, *Political Graphics: Art as a Weapon* (New York: Abbeville Press, 1982), 9, 14.

3. Martin Abbott, "President Lincoln in Confederate Caricature," *Journal of the Illinois State Historical Society* (fall 1958): 306–19.

4. Ron Tyler, *The Image of America in Caricature and Cartoon* (Fort Worth: Amon Carter Museum, 1975), 2.

5. For examples of early caricatures, see Bernard Reilly, *American Political Prints: 1866–1876—A Catalog of the Collections in the Library of Congress* (Boston: G. K. Hall, 1991), 9–11.

6. *Houston Telegraph* quoted in Wayne C. Williams, *A Rail Splitter for President* (Denver: University of Denver Press, 1951), 145; *Richmond Examiner* quoted in Robert S. Harper, *Lincoln and the Press* (New York: McGraw-Hill, 1951), 92; *Southern Confederacy* for September 27, 1861, quoted in Abbott, "President Lincoln in Confederate Caricature," 313; *Charleston Mercury* quoted in Williams, *A Rail Splitter for President*, 144.

7. See Mark E. Neely Jr., Harold Holzer, and Gabor S. Boritt, *The Confederate Image: Prints of the Lost Cause* (Chapel Hill: University of North Carolina Press, 1987), esp. 3–9.

8. The New York Public Library's rare books and manuscript collection contains what appears to be a complete set of the *Southern Illustrated News*, with no issue published after October 29, 1864. For *Leslie's* comment, see *Southern Illustrated News*, October 11, 1863.

9. T. Michael Parrish and Robert M. Willingham Jr., *Confederate Imprints: A Bibli-*

ography of Southern Publications from Secession to Surrender (Austin: Jenkins Publishing Company, n.d.), 12–13.

10. Ibid., 17; Richard Harwell, "A Confederate Hell-Box," *Civil War Quarterly* 8 (March 1987): 44.

11. C. Vann Woodward, ed., *Mary Chesnut's Civil War* (New Haven: Yale University Press, 1981), 626; the attack on "Porte Crayon" was voiced by a Confederate colonel, Angus McDonald, a prisoner of war who reportedly captured and imprisoned Strother's own father. See Cornelia McDonald, *Diary and Reminiscences of the War and Refugee Life in the Shenandoah Valley*, quoted in Cecil D. Eby Jr., *Porte Crayon: The Life of David Hunter Strother* (Chapel Hill: University of North Carolina Press, 1960), 148. One loyal Confederate artist, L. M. D. Guillaume, had much trouble getting Southern printmakers to adapt his equestrian portraits of Davis, Lee, Jackson, and others; see Annabel Shanklin Perlik, "Signed L. M. D. Guillaume: Louis Mathieu Didier Guillaume, 1816–1892" (master's thesis, George Washington University, 1979), 6, 15–16, 35–36, 44, 60, 70–71.

12. The sole known copy is in the Abraham Lincoln Museum, Lincoln Memorial University, Harrogate, Tennessee. See Weldon Petz, "The Musical Note in Lincoln's Life," *Lincoln Herald* 100 (fall 1998): 120–21.

13. Original issues of the *Southern Illustrated News* were consulted at the New York Public Library.

14. The principal reference is George McCullogh Anderson, *The Work of Adalbert Johann Volck, 1828–1912* (Baltimore: Anderson Publishing, 1970). Original copies of Volck's portfolios of etchings may be found in the Maryland Historical Society, Baltimore. For later celebration of his work, see Stefan Lorant, *Lincoln: A Picture Story of His Life* (New York: W. W. Norton, 1969), 168–69. A reassessment can be found in Neely, Holzer, and Boritt, *The Confederate Image*, 44–54.

15. Neely, Holzer, and Boritt, *The Confederate Image*, 51, 53.

16. Anderson, *The Work of Adalbert Johann Volck*, x.

Chapter 7. "Tokens of Respect" and "Heartfelt Thanks"

1. *New York Times*, May 18, A–15 and May 27, B–15, 1982. The stories also pointed out that the president had acted in the absence of regulations governing the acceptance of gifts from domestic sources but had turned over to the State Department all gifts from foreigners valued at $100 or more. The president's office also issued a warning to donors not to use official acknowledgments for business purposes.

2. Lincoln to Lulu Waldron, April 27, 1862, *Collected Works*, 5:200.

3. Ward Hill Lamon, *The Life of Abraham Lincoln* (Boston: James R. Osgood and Company, 1872), 480; William O. Stoddard, in Rufus Rockwell Wilson, *Intimate Memories of Lincoln* (Elmira, NY: Primavera Press, 1945), 232–33.

4. Lamon, *Life of Lincoln*, 482; Lincoln's reply to New York Workingmen's Democratic-Republican Association, March 21, 1864, *Collected Works*, 7:259–60.

5. Lincoln to Robert Allen, June 21, 1836, *Collected Works*, 1:49. In fairness, Lincoln

made this particular statement in the course of *refusing* a favor, noting, "In this case, favour to me, would be injustice to the public."

6. Ibid., 4:137; John Comstock to Lincoln, November 2, 1860, Lincoln Papers.

7. Lincoln to Daniel P. Gardner, September 28, 1860, *Collected Works,* 4:122–23.

8. Harold G. Villard and Oswald Garrison Villard, eds., *Lincoln on the Eve of '61: A Journalist's Story by Henry Villard* (New York: Alfred A. Knopf, 1941), 28; Lincoln to James F. Babcock, September 13, 1860, and Lincoln to Doney, July 30, 1860, *Collected Works,* 4:114 and 89; Lincoln to Mendel, June 8, 1860, in *The Collected Works of Abraham Lincoln: Supplement, 1832–1865,* ed. Roy P. Basler (Westport, CT: Greenwood Press, 1974), 55; *Tazewell Republican* (Pekin, IL), July 13, 1860, p. 2, col. 1; Lincoln to John M. Read, October 13, 1860, *Collected Works,* 4:127; Harold Holzer, Gabor S. Boritt, and Mark E. Neely Jr., *The Lincoln Image: Abraham Lincoln and the Popular Print* (New York: Scribner's, 1984), 23, 32–34, 57–66.

9. Lincoln to Harriet Snedeker, August 13, 1860, Basler, ed., *Collected Works, Supplement,* 59 (peaches); Lincoln to Francis E. Spinner, September 24, 1860, *Collected Works,* 4:120–21 (books); Samuel Greer to Lincoln, September 28, 1860, Lincoln Papers (nail).

10. Helen Nicolay, *Lincoln's Secretary: A Biography of John G. Nicolay* (New York: Longmans, Green, 1949), 37, 38; *New York Daily Tribune,* November 14, 1860.

11. Digby V. Bell to Lincoln, June 4, 1860, Lincoln Papers; Lincoln to Bell, June 5, 1860, *Collected Works,* 4:71.

12. R. S. Bassett to Lincoln, October 17, 1860, and Samuel Artus to Lincoln, October 17, 1860, both in Lincoln Papers.

13. Villard and Villard, eds., *Lincoln,* 27, 28, 15.

14. Louisa Livingston Siemon to Lincoln, December 10, 1860, Lincoln Papers.

15. E. P. Oliphant to Lincoln, December 186[0], Lincoln Papers.

16. Thomas D. Jones, *Memories of Lincoln* (New York: Press of the Pioneers, 1934), 8; S. M. Orr to Lincoln, January 7, 1861, Lincoln Papers.

17. Victor Searcher, *Lincoln's Journey to Greatness* (Philadelphia: John C. Winston Company, 1960), 152.

18. Daniel Ullmann to Lincoln, January 25, 1861, Lincoln Papers; Lincoln to Ullmann, February 1, 1861, *Collected Works,* 4:183–84.

19. Lincoln to Isaac Fenno, January 22, 1861, *Collected Works,* 4:179 (overcoat); Donald McClennan to Lincoln, January 31, 1861, Lincoln Papers, and Lincoln to McClellan, March 20, 1861, *Collected Works,* 4:296 (shawl); Louis A. Warren, "Gifts for the President," *Lincoln Lore* 401 (December 14, 1936).

20. Francis Bicknell Carpenter, *Six Months at the White House with Abraham Lincoln* (New York: Hurd and Houghton, 1866), 113; Villard and Villard, eds., *Lincoln,* 69.

21. Jones, *Memories,* 8; Villard and Villard, eds., *Lincoln,* 69–70.

22. A. W. Flanders, quoted in Nicolay, *Lincoln's Secretary,* 59–60; Earl Schenck Meirs, ed., *Lincoln Day by Day: A Chronology, 1809–1865,* 3 vols. (Washington, DC: Lincoln Sesquicentennial Commission, 1960), 3:17, 18 (flowers and hats); Searcher, *Journey,* 152 (flowers and fruits).

23. Meirs, ed., *Day by Day,* 3:23 (carriage); Basler, ed., *Collected Works, Supplement,* 73n (carriage horses). According to Basler, a mare that Lincoln wanted sold in June 1861 may have been one of the pair of carriage horses originally given to Mary Lincoln.

24. John B. Bradt to Lincoln, March 25, 1861, Lincoln Papers.

25. Diary of Frances Seward, entry of August 31, 1861, quoted in Meirs, ed., *Day by Day,* 3:63.

26. Mary Hancock Colyer to Lincoln, March 22, 186[1], Lincoln Papers; Lincoln to Colyer, April 2, 1861, *Collected Works,* 4:319.

27. S. Shreckengaus to Lincoln, April 2, 1861 (slippers), and Joseph Kinsey to Lincoln, April 9, 1861 (wine), both in Lincoln Papers.

28. Ibid., Robert G. Thursby to Lincoln, May 9, 1861, and Eugene Frean to Lincoln, May 18, 1861.

29. Ibid., J. C. Lewis to Lincoln, June 4, 1861 (tolls), and P. Miller Jr. to Lincoln, June 27, 1861 (medicine); Lincoln to Susannah Weathers, December 4, 1861, *Collected Works,* 5:57 (socks).

30. Lincoln to King of Siam, February 3, 1862, and Lincoln to Senate and House of Representatives, February 26, 1862, *Collected Works,* 5:125–26 and 137.

31. Ibid., Lincoln to Michael Crock, April 2, 1862, 177 (rabbits), and Lincoln to John M. Clay, August 4, 1862, 363–64 (Clay relic). The younger Clay hoped, he wrote to Lincoln, that his father's "noblest sentiment 'that he would rather be right than be President' . . . may even be yours" (Clay to Lincoln, August 4, 1862, Lincoln Papers).

32. Nathaniel Hawthorne, "Chiefly About War-Matters," *Atlantic Monthly,* July 1862, 47, quoted in Wilson, *Intimate Memories,* 466; Lincoln speech to a Massachusetts delegation, March 13, 1861, *Collected Works,* 5:158.

33. Carpenter, *Six Months,* 93 (books); Lincoln to Hackett, August 17, 1863, *Collected Works,* 6:392–93, 558–59; William O. Snider, quotation from *Collected Works,* 7:457n (*Merrimac* cane); Lincoln to John Birley, May 12, 1864, *Collected Works,* 7:337 (*Alliance* cane); Weldon Petz, *In the Presence of Abraham Lincoln* (Harrogate, TN: Lincoln Memorial University Press, 1973), 73 (eaglehead cane); Lincoln speech at Philadelphia Sanitary Fair, June 16, 1864, *Collected Works,* 7:396n–97n (Washington arch relic). George C. Miller sent "a Cane in some Measure Emblematic of What I hope Our Nation will be. . . . Composed of as Maney Sections and Pieces as there Ware States. And of a verry Beautifull Curled White Oak Not of the kind that Could be Split into Railes" (Miller to Lincoln, December 30, 1864, Lincoln Papers, and Lincoln to Miller, January 18, 1865, *Collected Works,* 8:222).

34. Meirs, ed., *Day by Day,* 3:202 (Spencer rifles); Stoddard quotation from Wilson, *Intimate Memories,* 231.

35. Jay Monaghan, *Diplomat in Carpet Slippers: Abraham Lincoln Deals with Foreign Affairs* (Indianapolis: Bobbs-Merrill, 1945), 242 (moccasins); Carl Sandburg, *Lincoln Collector: The Story of Oliver R. Barrett's Great Private Collection* (New York: Harcourt, Brace, 1950), 15, 207, and *Lincolniana Collected by the Late Oliver R. Barrett,* auction catalog (New York: Parke-Bernet Galleries, 1952), 182–83 (watch chain). The chain sold at the Barrett auction for $1,300.

36. Lincoln to James H. Hoes, December 17, 1863, *Collected Works,* 7:75.

37. Meirs, ed., *Day by Day,* 3:297–98. Kinman presented the chair on November 26, 1863; for the family photo, see Mark E. Neely and Harold Holzer, *The Lincoln Family Album* (New York: Doubleday, 1990), 88–89.

38. Lincoln to Clara and Julia Brown, March 21, 1864, *Collected Works,* 7:258 (afghan); Lincoln to Solomon Foot, January 18, 1862, Basler, ed., *Collected Works, Supplement,* 120–21 (cheese); Lincoln to Stephen C. Massett, December 4, 1863, *Collected Works,* 7:34, and Carpenter, *Six Months,* 160–61 (book; the author was known as "Jeems Pipes of Pipesville," and he had performed for Lincoln at the White House); Lincoln to Mrs. Abner Bartlett, May 5, 1864, *Collected Works,* 7:331 (socks).

39. Lincoln to the Shakers, August 8, 1864, *Collected Works,* 7:485–86 (chair); Lincoln to L. J. Leberman, July 15, 1864, ibid., 442 (clothes from Rockhill and Wilson, New York clothiers); Lincoln to Anne Williamson, July 29, 1864, ibid., 471 (Scotch plaid); Lincoln to Alfred B. Justice, September 1864 and October 17, 1864, ibid., 529, and 8:51 (knife); Lincoln to Frederick A. Farley, April 1, 1864, ibid., 8:278 (bedspread); Meirs, ed., *Day by Day,* 3:290 (gold box, presented October 20, 1864).

40. Lincoln to Rogers, June 13, 1864, *Collected Works,* 8:389 (statuary group); Lincoln to Edward and Henry T. Anthony, January 13, 1864, ibid., 123 (Central Park scenes); Lincoln to Gardner, August 18, 1863, and Basler, ed., *Collected Works, Supplement,* 199 (photographs); Lincoln to Richardson, May 21, 1864, Basler, ed., *Collected Works, Supplement,* 244 ("Anteitam Gem"); Carpenter, *Six Months,* 157–58 (emancipation tribute). Lincoln also received engravings of McClellan; see Lincoln to Henry A. Brown, March 13, 1862, *Collected Works,* 5:157, in which he declares one "very beautifully executed . . . the likeness . . . perfect."

41. Carpenter, *Six Months,* 197–99.

42. Reply to Philadelphia delegation, January 24, 1865, *Collected Works,* 8:236.

43. Carpenter, *Six Months,* 199–201.

44. Lincoln to Alexander H. Rice, November 8, 1864, *Collected Works,* 8:96–97 (the ox, "General Grant"); for Thanksgiving gifts, see Meirs, ed., *Day by Day,* 3:298.

45. Garrison to Lincoln, January 21, 1865, Lincoln Papers; Lincoln to Garrison, February 7, 1865, *Collected Works,* 8:265–66.

46. William H. Crook with Margarita Spalding Gerry, "Lincoln's Last Day: new facts now told for the first time," *Harper's Monthly Magazine,* September 1907, 528–30.

Chapter 8. "Avoid Saying Foolish Things"

1. *Washington Star,* October 6, 1962.

2. *Collected Works,* 5:450.

3. Ibid.

4. Ibid., 4:209; Barry Schwartz, *George Washington: The Making of an American Symbol* (New York: Free Press, 1987), 49.

5. See Garry Wills, *Lincoln at Gettysburg: The Words That Remade America* (New York: Simon and Schuster, 1992).

6. Harold Holzer, ed., *The Lincoln-Douglas Debates: The First Complete, Unexpurgated Text* (New York: HarperCollins, 1993), 13; Emanuel Hertz, ed., *The Hidden Lincoln: From the Letters and Papers of William H. Herndon* (New York: Viking Press, 1938), 271.

7. *New York Tribune,* February 28, 1860; *Lowell [MA] Journal* (1848), and *Cincinnati Enquirer,* September 18, 1859, quoted in Robert S. Harper, *Lincoln and the Press* (New York: McGraw-Hill, 1951), 11, 37, 46: Elwell Crissey, *Lincoln's Lost Speech: The Pivot of His Career* (New York: Hawthorn Books, 1967), 241; *Collected Works,* 2:126.

8. *Collected Works,* 4:193, 204; Harold G. Villard and Oswald Garrison Villard, eds., *Lincoln on the Eve of '61: A Journalist's Story by Henry Villard* (New York: Alfred A. Knopf, 1941), 41, 48–49.

9. *Collected Works,* 4:198.

10. Ibid., 207.

11. Ibid., 204; Victor Searcher, *Lincoln's Journey to Greatness* (Philadelphia: John C. Winston, 1960), 134; Mark E. Neely Jr., *The Abraham Lincoln Encyclopedia* (New York: McGraw-Hill, 1982), 159; Herbert Mitgang, ed., *Abraham Lincoln: A Press Portrait* (Chicago: Quadrangle Books, 1971), 229.

12. *Collected Works,* 4:230–31.

13. Ibid., 194.

14. See, for example, Lincoln's address before the New Jersey Senate at Trenton, February 21, 1861, and at Independence Hall, Philadelphia, February 22, 1862, *Collected Works,* 4:235–36, 240–41; Searcher, *Lincoln's Journey to Greatness,* 35, 134.

15. Newspaper clipping, "Mr. Lincoln's Speeches at Indianapolis, as Revised by Himself," from John Hay's scrapbook, private collection.

16. For different versions of the Farewell Address, see *Collected Works,* 4:190–91.

17. Harriet Beecher Stowe's article about Lincoln appeared in *Littell's Living Age* on February 6, 1864. See Mitgang, ed., *Abraham Lincoln,* 377; see also Villard and Villard, eds., *Lincoln on the Eve of '61,* 73; for a reproduction of the post facto manuscript of Lincoln's Farewell Address, see Stefan Lorant, *Lincoln: A Picture History of His Life* (New York: W. W. Norton, 1969), 119.

18. Mitgang, ed., *Abraham Lincoln,* 377; Tyler Dennett, ed., *Lincoln and the Civil War in the Diaries and Letters of John Hay* (New York: Dodd, Mead, 1939), 120.

19. *Collected Works,* 6:319.

20. *Illinois State Journal,* June 19, July 24, and August 29, 1860; *Illinois State Register,* October 7, 1860; Wayne C. Williams, *A Rail Splitter for President* (Denver: University of Denver Press, 1951), 24, 30.

21. Waldo C. Braden, *Abraham Lincoln: Public Speaker* (Baton Rouge: Louisiana State University Press, 1988), 95; Dennett, ed., *Diaries of John Hay,* 101; *Collected Works,* 6:499–504. Lincoln's letter to Charles D. Drake and others was written on October 5, 1863, in response to a meeting held September 30.

22. Braden, *Lincoln;* David Wills to Abraham Lincoln, November 2, 1863, Lincoln Papers; *Collected Works,* 5:284.

23. *Collected Works,* 2:126.

24. Ibid., 7:398; *New York World,* June 18, 1864, in Mitgang, ed., *Abraham Lincoln,* 405.

25. See Harold Holzer, ed., *Dear Mr. Lincoln: Letters to the President* (New York: Addison-Wesley, 1993), 280–81, 288–89, 292–93; *Collected Works,* 6:399, 406–10.

26. *Collected Works,* 3:555; William H. Herndon and Jesse Weik, *Abraham Lincoln: The True Story of a Great Life,* 3 vols. (Springfield, IL: Herndon's Lincoln Publishing Company, n.d.) 3:454, 478.

27. William C. Davis, *Jefferson Davis: The Man and His Hour* (New York: HarperCollins, 1991), 466–69; Clement Eaton, *Jefferson Davis* (New York: Free Press, 1977), 27, 233.

28. See, for example, M. L. Houser, *Lincoln's Education* (New York: Bookman, 1957), 117; David C. Mearns, "Mr. Lincoln and the Books He Read," in *Three Presidents and What They Read,* ed. Arthur E. Bestor, David C. Mearns, and Jonathan Daniels (Urbana: University of Illinois Press, 1963), 54–57.

29. Thomas Dilworth, *A Guide to the English Tongue in Five Parts* (Philadelphia: John Bioren, 1809), i, 74, 78, 97, 102–4; for confirmation that Lincoln read Scott, see Ward Hill Lamon, *The Life of Abraham Lincoln, from His Birth to His Inauguration as President* (Boston: Jas. R. Osgood, 1872), 37.

30. William Scott, *Lessons in Elocution; or, A Selection of Pieces in Prose and Verse for the Improvement of Youth in Reading and Speaking . . . to which are prefixed Elements of Gesture* (Boston: Isaiah Thomas Jun[.], 1811), 33–36, 40, 46, 48, 49, 381–82, 385–86, 393.

31. Scott, *Lessons,* 56.

32. Ibid., 12, 15–16, 19, 135–36.

33. Ibid., 28, 33–36; Herndon and Weik, *Abraham Lincoln,* 2:407.

34. Scott, *Lessons,* 19.

35. Rufus Rockwell Wilson, *Intimate Memories of Lincoln* (Elmira: Primavera Press, 1945), 173–74, 184–85.

36. Herndon and Weik, *Abraham Lincoln,* 2:405–7.

37. Ibid., 408; Robert W. Johannsen, *Stephen A. Douglas* (New York: Oxford University Press, 1973), 640–41.

38. *Collected Works,* 7:16–17.

39. P. J. Staudenraus, ed., *Mr. Lincoln's Washington: Selections from the Writings of Noah Brooks, Civil War Correspondent* (New York: Thomas Yoseloff, 1967), 388.

40. *Collected Works,* 3:359–60.

41. Lois J. Einhorn, *Abraham Lincoln the Orator: Penetrating the Lincoln Legend* (Westport, CT: Greenwood Press, 1992), 17.

42. *Collected Works,* 4:143, 5:535, 537.

Chapter 9. Poetry and Prose of the Emancipation Proclamation

1. Frederick Douglass, *Life and Times of Frederick Douglass Written by Himself* (orig. pub. 1893), in *Frederick Douglass: Autobiographies,* ed. Henry Louis Gates Jr. (New York: Library of America, 1993), 792.

2. Mark E. Neely Jr., *The Last Best Hope of Earth: Abraham Lincoln and the Promise of America* (Cambridge: Harvard University Press, 1933), 113.

Lincoln Seen and Heard

3. Barbara J. Fields, "Who Freed the Slaves?" in Geoffrey C. Ward, Ric Burns, and Ken Burns, *The Civil War* (New York: Alfred A. Knopf, 1990), 181.

4. John Hope Franklin, *The Emancipation Proclamation* (1963; rpt., Wheeling, IL: Harlan Davidson, 1995).

5. Gore Vidal, *Lincoln: A Novel* (New York: Random House: 1984), 414–15; Lerone Bennet Jr., "Was Abraham Lincoln a White Supremacist?" *Ebony,* February 18, 1968, 35–43.

6. Cyrenus Tyler, 134th N.Y. Volunteers, to Peter Timkelpaugh, February 2, 1863, Manuscripts and Special Collections Unit, New York State Library, Albany.

7. *Collected Works,* 7:380, 8:254–55.

8. Mario M. Cuomo and Harold Holzer, eds., *Lincoln on Democracy* (New York: Harper and Row, 1990), xxxv.

9. *Collected Works,* 7:281; Gabor S. Boritt, *Lincoln and the Economics of the American Dream* (Memphis, TN: Memphis State University Press, 1978), 255–56.

10. Gates, *Frederick Douglass: Autobiographies,* 793.

11. Hans L. Trefousse, *Lincoln's Decision for Emancipation* (Philadelphia: J. B. Lippincott, 1975), 74, 76; Phillip Shaw Paludan, "Emancipating the Republic: Lincoln and the Means and Ends of Antislavery," in *"We Cannot Escape History": Lincoln and the Last Best Hope of Earth,* ed. James M. McPherson (Urbana: University of Illinois Press, 1995), 45.

12. Francis B. Carpenter, *Six Months at the White House with Abraham Lincoln: The Story of a Picture* (New York: Hurd and Houghton, 1866), 20–21.

13. David Homer Bates, *Lincoln in the Telegraph Office* (New York: Century Company, 1907), 138–41.

14. Carpenter, *Six Months at the White House,* 22.

15. *New York Tribune,* August 19, 1862.

16. *Collected Works,* 5:388–89.

17. LaWanda Cox, *Lincoln and Black Freedom: A Study in Presidential Leadership* (Columbia: University of South Carolina Press, 1981), 5, 7.

18. *Collected Works,* 5:372.

19. Ibid., 5:389; Gabor S. Boritt, "The Voyage to the Colony of Lincolnia: The Sixteenth President, Black Colonization, and the Defense Mechanism of Avoidance," *History* 37 (1975): 632. The article focuses principally on Lincoln's flirtation with the notion of colonizing freedmen.

20. *Collected Works,* 5:419–25.

21. Ibid., 438; Franklin, *The Emancipation Proclamation,* 58–59.

22. Lennox T. West, 16th New York Volunteers, N.Y. Artillery, to his wife, May 2, 1864, Manuscripts and Special Collections Unit, New York State Archives, Albany. See James McPherson, *Battle Cry of Freedom: The Civil War Era* (New York: Oxford University Press, 1988), 558–60.

23. John Hope Franklin, *From Slavery to Freedom* (1947; rpt., New York: Alfred A. Knopf, 1994), 207.

24. Franklin, *The Emancipation Proclamation,* 54–55.

25. *Collected Works,* 5:444; 7:49, 282.

26. Herbert Mitgang, ed., *Lincoln As They Saw Him* (New York: Rinehart and Company, 1956), 324–25; Cox, *Lincoln and Black Freedom,* 13. Cox cited an obscure item in the *New York Times* on December 31, 1862.

27. Mitgang, *Lincoln As They Saw Him,* 304.

28. *Collected Works,* 5:537.

29. Ibid., 7:23.

30. *New York Times,* March 25 and 28, 1998. See also, Patrick J. Buchanan, "America's Sorry Apologists," *New York Post,* March 28, 1998.

31. *Collected Works,* 8:332–33; see also Thomas Geoghegan, "Lincoln Apologizes," *New York Times,* April 5, 1998.

32. Gates, ed., *Frederick Douglass: Autobiographies,* 792.

33. Carpenter, *Six Months at the White House,* 269–70. The author cited the source for this story as the *Rochester (NY) Express.*

Chapter 10. Lincoln's "Flat Failure"

1. David Wills to Abraham Lincoln, November 2, 1863, Lincoln Papers; Harold Holzer, " 'Avoid Saying Foolish Things': The Legacy of Lincoln's Impromptu Oratory," in *"We Cannot Escape History": Lincoln and the Last Best Hope of Earth,* ed. James M. McPherson (Champaign: University of Illinois Press, 1995), 105–23.

2. Noah Brooks, "Personal Reminiscences of Lincoln," *Scribner's Monthly Magazine* 15 (February–March 1878): 565.

3. Garry Wills, *Lincoln at Gettysburg: The Words That Remade America* (New York: Simon and Schuster, 1992), 26.

4. William E. Barton, *Lincoln at Gettysburg* (New York: Peter Smith, 1950), 173.

5. Louis A. Warren, *Lincoln's Gettysburg Declaration: "A New Birth of Freedom"* (Fort Wayne, IN: Lincoln National Life Foundation, 1964), 61.

6. Brooks, "Personal Reminiscences of Lincoln," 565.

7. Earl Schenck Miers, ed., *Lincoln Day By Day: A Chronology, 1809–1865,* 3 vols. (Washington, DC: Lincoln Sesquicentennial Commission, 1960), 3:218–20; Philip N. Kunhardt Jr., *A New Birth of Freedom: Lincoln at Gettysburg* (Boston: Little, Brown, 1983), 65–66; Don E. Fehrenbacher and Virginia Fehrenbacher, eds., *Recollected Words of Abraham Lincoln* (Stanford, CA: Stanford University Press, 1996), 289.

8. *Collected Works,* 7:16.

9. Warren, *Lincoln's Gettysburg Declaration,* 61; for a reproduction of the autograph copy—in two hands—of Lincoln's Farewell Address to Springfield, see Stefan Lorant, *Lincoln: A Picture Story of His Life* (New York: W. W. Norton, 1969), 119.

10. Barton, *Lincoln at Gettysburg,* 71.

11. Ibid., 75; Warren, *Lincoln's Gettysburg Declaration,* 81–83; R. Gerald McMurtry, "Lincoln Rode Horseback in the Gettysburg Procession," *Lincoln Lore* 1425 (November 1956): 4.

12. Tyler Dennett, ed., *Lincoln and the Civil War in the Diaries and Letters of John Hay*

(New York: Dodd, Mead, 1939), 121; Warren, *Lincoln's Gettysburg Declaration*, 122; Harold Holzer, "A Few Appropriate Remarks," *American History Illustrated* (November 1988): 20–22.

13. Barton, *Lincoln at Gettysburg*, 78; Warren, *Lincoln's Gettysburg Declaration*, 122.

14. Kunhardt, *A New Birth of Freedom*, 215; the AP text is reprinted in Wills, *Lincoln at Gettysburg*, 261.

15. For a fully annotated version of the various, conflicting texts, see *Collected Works*, 7:19–21; see also *Chicago Times*, November 23, 1863.

16. Kunhardt, *A New Birth of Freedom*, 215–16; Benjamin Barondess, *Three Lincoln Masterpieces* (Charleston: Education Foundation of West Virginia, 1954), 43.

17. Barton, *Lincoln at Gettysburg*, 201.

18. Herbert Mitgang, ed., *Lincoln As They Saw Him* (New York: Rinehart and Company, 1956), 360; Warren, *Lincoln's Gettysburg Declaration*, 146.

19. Harold Holzer, ed., *The Lincoln-Douglas Debates: The First Complete, Unexpurgated Text* (New York: HarperCollins, 1993), 13; Mitgang, ed., *Lincoln as They Saw Him*, 360.

20. Barton, *Lincoln at Gettysburg*, 114–15.

21. Harold Holzer, " 'Thrilling Words' or 'Silly Remarks': What the Press Said About the Gettysburg Address," *Lincoln Herald* 90 (winter 1988): 144–45.

22. Mitgang, ed., *Lincoln As They Saw Him*, 362–63.

23. Edward Everett to Abraham Lincoln, November 20, 1863, Lincoln Papers; *Collected Works*, 7:24.

24. Dorothy Lamon Teillard, ed., *Recollections of Abraham Lincoln, 1847–1865*, 2d ed. (Washington, DC: n.p., 1911), 175.

25. Fehrenbacher and Fehrenbacher, eds., *Recollected Words of Abraham Lincoln*, 289.

26. The Corning letter was published in the *New York Tribune*, for example, on June 15, 1863, eight days before Corning acknowledged receipt of the original. *Collected Works* 6:260–61.

Index

Lincoln Seen and Heard

Lincoln Seen and Heard